NO LONGER PROPERTY OF
ANYTHINK LIBRARIES/
RANGEVIEW LIBRARY DISTRICT

D1015660

Live Work Work Work Die

Live Work Work Work Die

A JOURNEY INTO THE SAVAGE HEART OF SILICON VALLEY

COREY PEIN

METROPOLITAN BOOKS HENRY HOLT AND COMPANY
NEW YORK

Metropolitan Books
Henry Holt and Company
Publishers since 1866
175 Fifth Avenue
New York, New York 10010
www.henryholt.com

Metropolitan Books® and ® are registered trademarks
of Macmillan Publishing Group, LLC.

Copyright © 2017 by Corey Pein
All rights reserved.
Distributed in Canada by Raincoast Book Distribution Limited

Library of Congress Cataloging-in-Publication Data

Names: Pein, Corey, author.
Title: Live work work work die : a journey into the savage heart of
    Silicon Valley / Corey Pein.
Description: First edition. | New York : Metropolitan Books, 2017. |
    Includes bibliographical references and index.
Identifiers: LCCN 2017040258 | ISBN 9781627794855 (hardcover)
    ISBN 9781250198150 (international)
Subjects: LCSH: Internet industry—California. | High-technology
    industries—California. | Technological innovations—California. |
    New business enterprises—California. | Entrepreneurship—
    California.
Classification: LCC HD9696.8.U63 C374 2017 | DDC
    338.4/7004097947—dc23
LC record available at https://lccn.loc.gov/2017040258

Our books may be purchased in bulk for promotional, educational, or
business use. Please contact your local bookseller or the Macmillan Corporate and Premium Sales Department at (800) 221-7945, extension
5442, or by e-mail at MacmillanSpecialMarkets@macmillan.com.

First Edition 2018

Designed by Karen Minster

Printed in the United States of America

10 9 8 7 6 5 4 3 2 1

This is a work of nonfiction. However, the names of certain individuals
have been changed to protect their privacy, and dialogue has been
reconstructed to the best of the author's recollection.

Vom Affen zum Roboter

Modern man never asks himself what he will have to pay for his power. This is the question we ought to be asking.

—Jacques Ellul,
The Technological Society, 1954

CONTENTS

INTRODUCTION

Billionaire or Bust

Naïve believers make the loudest heretics. That's me. As a kid, I taught myself to code on a dusty old Commodore 64. By rights, I should have been a billionaire wunderkind before my sophomore year of college. But I screwed up. Instead of skipping class to build a world-changing website in a dorm room, I succumbed to the temptations of music, books, and girls. How shortsighted I was! How far astray I'd wandered! My earnings potential plummeted when I stopped writing software and started writing for news-papers. In the years to come, as my ill-chosen trade succumbed to digital disruption, I looked with envy at the techies, the winners, the pioneers. They had ideas. They had momentum. Most impor-tant, they had money. Why not me?

In 2010, my girlfriend and I quit our newspaper jobs and eloped to England, where I launched my first startup. It was a niche news website. Earnestly following the example of the gung-ho "journo-preneurs" who had preceded me, I powered my startup with cheap labor—my own. After two years working twelve-hour days as pub-lisher, developer, editor, and reporter, I hit a wall. I let the site go dormant and took another job. My first startup had failed. Thus I had failed. What other explanation could there be? As everyone knew, the internet was a level playing field, a free and frictionless medium for exchange, where the best ideas would inevitably rise to the top. Such was the foundational rhetoric of the internet, repeated like scripture, questioned only by cranks and cynics. It was also a load of crap, though I didn't yet recognize it as such.

Throughout my career change, I became a religious follower of tech blogs. At first I visited them for help solving esoteric coding problems. But they soon became a habit, and in a misguided effort to become more "productive," I devoured page after page of the self-help and motivational material these websites featured, most of it directed at startup wannabes like me. Lying awake in bed, arm stiff from holding my smartphone aloft, I sought solace in the sanguine stream of updates on Hacker News, a techie discussion forum run by a venture capital fund and startup "incubator" called Y Combinator. This outfit seemed vaguely prestigious, the commenters knowledgeable.

The titles of the inspirational homilies on Hacker News reassured me that I was not alone: "Fail Fast, Fail Often, and Fail by Design," "Failing Fast Means . . . Failing a Lot," and, most succinctly, "Success Through Failure." I took it all to heart. I reinterpreted my failure as a character-building experience. But something else was going on with this self-guided tutelage. I wasn't just changing careers and jumping on the "learn to code" bandwagon. I was being steadily indoctrinated in a specious ideology. As proud as I was of having learned "valuable" new skills—I could deploy a Ruby on Rails application! I could manage a virtual server!—I didn't understand that the only way to turn those skills into a livelihood was to embrace the economy of the digital world, where giant corporations wrote the rules. As an eager website proprietor and aspiring journopreneur, I was like a stockyard calf who thought he owned the farm.

In 2012, I went to work for an avant-garde online news service called Demotix, which sold the work of freelance photographers around the world to news outlets. When I joined as editor in chief, Demotix had already signed up thirty thousand photographers plus a small full-time staff. The open-plan office, furnished with beanbag chairs and an espresso machine, felt like a proper tech startup. It was tucked within the London branch of its largest investor, the Seattle-based Corbis Corporation that belonged to Bill Gates.

Just as I took the job, Corbis bought Demotix outright. The founders—who meant well, I think—"exited" permanently. Everyone was told this was great news. "The acquisition represents an enormous step towards our goal," the official announcement said. It went on to promise that Corbis would maintain our "values of supporting free speech and covering the under-reported." I wondered how big my editorial budget would be with the Gates windfall—five figures or six?

The horrible truth emerged when a Corbis manager from New York flew over for a visit. I called him the Drone. Although he bragged about not reading newspapers—our main clients—he had somehow wound up in charge of "news, sports and entertainment." The Drone greeted us with a PowerPoint presentation, which I supposed was how they said hello back at the mothership in Seattle. Then, turn by turn in small groups, we joined the Drone on the office's twin red loveseats. Grinning nefariously, he explained the new reality. "There are two things Corbis cares about," he said. "The first is making money. The second is innovation and disruption. I think Bill is especially interested in that second piece, innovation and disruption."

We stared at him, mute. I knew that my English colleagues would sit in awkward silence forever, but I also knew that the Drone expected a response. Since he had already raised the subject of money, I explained that many of our photographers were going into debt—not to mention risking arrest, abduction, and death—to go into war zones for the purpose of sending pictures to our little startup. With the vast resources of Corbis behind us, perhaps we could begin to pay these photographers a base rate— say, $100 per day? "That's never going to happen," the Drone said. Ditto health insurance.

That was just the beginning. Corbis, it turned out, seemed to have a radically different view of what constituted news, complaining that our coverage focused too much on street protests and factory fires in far-flung countries. Too difficult. Too obscure. Instead, management wanted our street photographers to chase reality TV stars around red-carpet events. Apparently there was no such thing as too much Kardashian. The Drone did make clear that Corbis was happy to keep receiving newsy images of combat in Syria or Mali or whatever sorry country was sinking into hell, so long as we didn't get too involved when our freelancers wound up in trouble.

Soon enough we lowly "acquihires" discovered that the Drone had a secret plan to ax half the staff. Incidentally, he would be assuming the key duties of my job as editor in chief, while I would be responsible for "community" or some such nonsense. I resigned.

Several years later, Gates sold Corbis to a Chinese distributor for its chief competitor, Getty Images. Demotix went dark without warning, leaving thousands of freelancers out of pocket on assignments—with many, again, in dangerous situations—and cutting off their access to images they'd uploaded to Corbis servers. Included in the sale was Corbis's vast archive of historical photos, such as the famous image of "Tank Man" from the Tiananmen Square protests. Gates sold this iconic portrait of courage and dissent to a company that would be obliged by the Chinese government to censor it.

For a few days after I quit working for the Man, I basked in the afterglow of my own righteousness. "I think I'll go back to writing for a while," I told friends. I spent the next year getting real comfortable in my pajamas. I knew the time had come to pick myself up and find something new to fail at—but what?

I considered my options. I could try my luck again with another short-fused tech startup. I could return once more to my dying profession, the print press. Or I could go back to mopping floors, as I had after college. Where had I gone wrong? What did Bill Gates have that I didn't have—apart from billions upon billions of dollars? This line of thinking eventually led me to the realization that the solution to all my problems was simple: I needed to become a billionaire, like my former employer.

Billionaireship is easily the most desirable career of the twenty-first century, with numerous advantages over fast-growing occupations like serfdom. And the perks are unbeatable! Prior to the incorporation of U.S. Steel in 1901, the world didn't have a single billion-dollar company, much less a billion-dollar individual. Today more people than ever are becoming billionaires—two thousand and counting have made the great leap upward, according to the "global wealth team" at *Forbes*. Virtually no aspect of the geopolitical arena, the natural environment, or the human experience escapes their influence. And America's hottest billionaire factory happens to be located in the most hyped yet least understood swath of suburban sprawl in the world: Silicon Valley.

Seat of disruptive innovation and home to the heroes of high tech, the Valley calls out like an alluring siren to ambitious, skilled, and forward-thinking people from all over. Its singular approach to wealth creation—let's call it "the Silicon Valley way"—was endorsed by former president Barack Obama himself. In a State of the Union address, he pledged to support "every risk-taker and entrepreneur who aspires to become the next Steve Jobs."

Really, shouldn't we all be in the top one percent?

Despite what you may have heard, hard work in your chosen trade is absolutely the stupidest way to join the billionaires club. In Silicon Valley—that warm, inviting cradle of cutthroat entrepreneurship—the world's most brilliant MBAs and IT professionals discovered a shortcut to fabulous riches. By harnessing the miraculous powers of the internet, it seemed, any indigent fool could transform him- or herself into the contemporary manifestation of a feudal lord. The annual *Silicon Valley Index*, an economic survey produced by a regional think tank and the local Community Foundation, shows precisely how well the Valley has done relative to the rest of the country. The report notes that

Silicon Valley has enjoyed marked increases in overall job numbers since 2007, the prelude to the economic crash, while the United States remained, at best, stagnant. The Valley's ownership class—startup founders, investors, equity-holding executives, and fee-taking middlemen—have thrived above all. The aspirations of these companies were once confined to computer hardware and software but are rapidly expanding into areas including governance, finance, and biology. Ambitious Ivy Leaguers who once flocked to Wall Street are now packing up and moving westward. CNBC reported that "an increasing number of finance professionals and business school students are flocking to tech jobs, leaving their banking careers behind." Forget Goldman Sachs. Think Google.

Make no mistake: The only way to guarantee your long-term survival through the difficult days ahead is to possess fantastic material wealth. No one will care how you got the money. With inequality rising to historic levels, there is no choice at all—it's either billionaire or bust. You may scoff now, but you'll definitely wish you'd taken the time to become a billionaire when the robots have taken over your profession and you can't afford financing for the new fuel-efficient car you need to make your tiresome hours driving for Uber pencil out. Besides, do you really want to work for the rest of your life? Of course not. No one does. Not me, that's for sure.

When I started writing this book, it was provisionally titled "How to Make $30 Billion the Silicon Valley Way." My idea was to pitch a tech startup and get obscenely rich while writing a book about how to pitch a tech startup and get obscenely rich—the Silicon

Valley way! I had already failed twice in this same basic effort, but I had not yet tried to fail in the hottest startup market in the world, the Bay Area. I left home with some homemade business cards and a bunch of half-baked ideas. Probably the stupidest idea I had was that I could somehow safely execute a swan dive into the fast-draining kiddie pool that was the San Francisco startup scene without doing permanent damage to myself. I didn't strike gold, obviously—I didn't even strike pyrite—just hard cold cement.

The real problem wasn't bad timing or slapdash execution, though I had both. The problem was that I was tragically confused. Was I going as a journalist or a businessman? I had fooled myself into believing that I could carry out both roles without creating irreconcilable conflicts. Not so. My journalistic mission was inspired by an overwhelming sense of hostility toward the tech industry. After all, it had stolen my livelihood and left me with nothing but memes to eat. It had kidnapped my friends and sent me a daily ransom note called Facebook, where everyone insisted that everything was going great, that they were being treated well, that the food was always excellent—but I knew better. Big Tech trampled over every enjoyable experience in the world. It wouldn't stop until everything felt like the same damn thing: staring at a screen. My entrepreneurial mission, meanwhile, required me to outwardly embrace what I privately abhorred. It was an impossible situation of my own design. Over time, the contradictions wore me down until I lay broken in a fetal ball on a sagging mattress in a decrepit Airbnb, surrounded by empty beer bottles and small, sad keepsakes of the life I'd left behind.

My double role as journalist and businessman also created

sundry ethical dilemmas and conflicts of interest. I exploited the ambiguity to my advantage time and again. For instance, the tech conference racket charges hundreds or thousands of dollars to each of the poor suckers who line up to hear the equivalent of a live infomercial from a nerd of slightly higher status. I simply did not have the money to pay for all those conferences, but I knew that as a reporter and author, I could finagle VIP access for free, with the implicit promise of publicity. And that's what I did, every chance I got. There were other occasions on which it did not behoove me to dwell upon my background as a journalist. I almost always told people I was working on a book about tech. But I rarely asked anyone for an interview. I simply assumed that everything was on the record all the time. And almost nobody asked me not to quote them. Granted, I never said precisely what sort of book I was writing. And I was discreet. My notebook was in my back pocket more often than in my hand. However, I am no terrorist. I believe special consideration should be given to civilians. So where it seemed unfair to use someone's real name—with roommates, for instance— I made up a name for them. There are no "composite" characters. Everything I have written in this book actually happened, sometimes out of order. The quotes are accurate to the best of my recollection and the sources verifiable. It is not straitlaced journalism, but it is truthful. My hope was to have as authentic an entrepreneurial experience as possible without the phony pretense of going "under cover." In retrospect, it would've been a lot simpler to make up a name, fake a résumé, and go straight for the kill. But I am not a great liar, and I suppose there was some self-destructive impulse behind my mad scheme.

The most amazing thing about Silicon Valley in the heady days of 2015 was that most people did not laugh in my face when I told them I planned to make billions of dollars in short order with a startup literally no one had ever heard of. In that particular time and place, such miracles were commonplace, at least if you believed the press. Look at Uber! It came from nowhere. Snapchat! Instagram! Facebook! Every story seemed to confirm our national mythos that pluck and progress deliver milk and honey. But that's bullshit. The only way 99.99999 percent of us are going to become billionaires is through some Weimaresque economic cataclysm that leaves us pushing wheelbarrows full of high-denomination bills to barren grocery stores, where we can wait in long lines to buy stale bread and muesli cut with sawdust. Another thing I didn't know when I packed up and flew to San Francisco in 2015, but which appears evident today, was that those days might come faster than most "reasonable" people thought.

I

Poor Winners

Within hours of my arrival in the gleaming consumer paradise of boom-time San Francisco, people started giving me free things. Free snacks, free liquor, free T-shirts, free tchotchkes, free personal brand-building buzz, free advice—it was all there for the taking, emblazoned with corporate logos and gifted, ultimately, by benefactors who rarely showed their faces. Not to us mortals, anyway. The quasimythical tech industry elite would never be expected to mingle with the rest of us; they inhabited a higher plane, one with robot servants and Bay views. I recognized the freebies for what they were—not simple acts of personal generosity, but manna from above, bestowed by the invisible hand of venture capital.

The first free thing I got was a bright pink coupon that I fished out of a basket next to a cash register. The coupon bestowed a free introductory taxi ride from the city's second-largest "app-based pickup service," Lyft. I found the corporate vowel swapping obnoxious. (Couldn't it just be Lift?) Ditto the twee mustache logo. But I was much too "frugal," as my wife put it, to refuse a $25 value on aesthetic grounds. So I installed the Lyft app on my phone, allowed the company to track my geospatial location and who knows what

else, and then summoned a car to carry me and my luggage to my
new digs across town.

When I looked up, there was a car puttering away by the curb.
I'd never used an app like Lyft before, and it didn't seem possible
that my ride had shown up so fast. I stood around futilely scanning
the horizon for a few minutes. The driver didn't seem annoyed.
She seemed happy for the break.

Simone was bone-tired. I didn't blame her. She was the model
of a twenty-first-century microentrepreneur, which is to say she
was a grossly exploited worker. She lived in Oakland but woke up
early to drive to central San Francisco, where she picked up two
shifts as a public school bus driver. She drove for Lyft on her lunch
break and again after work until bedtime. Both employers classified Simone as a part-time independent contractor, and neither
seemed at all concerned about her level of fatigue behind the
wheel. She wasn't expecting a raise. "I want to wean away from
Lyft," she told me. "I'm just making someone else rich. I know I
could be putting that time into my own company."

In Hollywood, everybody has an unfinished script. In the Bay
Area, everybody has a "pre–Series A" tech company running in
"stealth mode" (meaning they have an idea without any money
behind it that's ostensibly secret but in fact hungry for publicity).
"What's your startup?" I asked.

She hesitated. Then she asked if I was religious or easily offended.
"Not really," I said.

As the car rolled slowly through the Tenderloin—under freeways,
past bustling homeless camps and twilight trash fires—Simone
told me all about her company. It was called Racy Laydeez. She'd

hired someone out of pocket to build the website. Racy Laydeez was a catalog of sex toys, featuring detailed instructions for newbies and . . . "demonstrations." Naturally, I was intrigued. Yet I wasn't totally clear on what twist Simone brought to the saturated market for sexual accoutrements, except perhaps that working-class black women like her might be more comfortable ordering dildos from an online outfit than browsing the aisles at a downtown sex shop full of white yuppies. While there may have been holes in Simone's business plan, that hadn't stopped a thousand much stupider startups from attracting large investments. And I certainly couldn't fault her enthusiasm. "I know I can be a million-dollar baby!" she said as we pulled up to the curb. I wished her luck, waved goodbye, and took in my surroundings.

Amid the concrete spider's web of elevated highways and dingy warehouses stood a shining new multistory condo tower. Somewhere inside it was my new home. I carried my bags to the front door, which bore a curious inscription. LIVE/WORK, it said. Presumably this was an indication of progressive mixed-use urban zoning practices, or something, but it read more like a commandment. Live, work. What else can we do until death but work? Or perhaps the inscription offered a choice. You can live or you can work.

This place, which I called Hacker Condo, was the best deal I could find on short notice. Like most Bay Area newcomers, I was relying on the short-term apartment rental app Airbnb. At $85 per night, the place cost less than the market average, but still more

than I could afford. On the upside, it was in what the real estate
hucksters called SoMa—a trendy neighborhood well suited to my
journalistic and entrepreneurial purposes. Once a low-rent manufacturing district, the South of Market Street area had become
the go-to place for startups seeking industrial-chic open-plan
offices, though the poor and homeless had not yet been fully purged.
The ad for Hacker Condo stated an express preference for techies:
"We would like to welcome motivated and serious entrepreneurs
who are looking to expand their network," it said. Perfect. The
best part: "No bunk beds." I told the hosts, Brody and Mike, that I
was an "embryo-stage" startup founder and author. That, along
with my smiling profile photograph and full upfront payment, was
enough to sail me through the interview. Brody and Mike didn't
own the place. I looked it up. The mortgage was held by some European guy who seemed to spend most of his time surfing at a resort
and dabbled in the tech business as a hobby, as bored blue bloods
were wont to do. The legal status of this rental arrangement was,
let's say, unclear.

I rang the buzzer for a unit labeled TENANT. A man answered
right away. He'd been waiting. After a moment, the door opened,
and I met my new roommate, a gangly Kiwi named Liam. We took
the elevator three floors up and entered a silent, beige-carpeted
hallway. "Have you met the neighbors?" I asked. "I've never seen
anyone else," he said. "There was a party the other night in no. 14.
We knocked, but no one opened the door." Our unit was no. 16. The
first thing I noticed inside was a small mountain of men's shoes.
The view got better from there. Hacker Condo was modern and
more spacious than seemed possible from the outside. The unit

was spread out over three floors—a humdrum lower level that might've been intended as a den or exercise room, a main-floor studio comprising a kitchen, living room, and dining area, and a master bedroom hanging over everything, designed as a sort of interior balcony. The ceilings rose twenty feet or more over dark hardwood floors, with spectacular paned windows soaring all the way up. The furniture consisted of a picnic bench and a sectional couch spanning the width of the living room. Not bad! "What's the key situation?" I asked.

"There's one key," Liam said.

"One key?" I said. "For everybody?"

A voice called out from across the room: "You have twenty-four hours to tell Airbnb the place isn't as advertised." Uh-oh. What else was wrong with it?

Liam showed me the wall-mounted light in the hallway where they stashed the interior door key. To reach it required long arms or a leap. There were more tricks to learn, as a consequence of the possibly illicit nature of this type of rental arrangement and the evident stinginess of our Airbnb hosts. The Condo Hackers never came in through the front door, Liam explained. It was too conspicuous. I followed Liam down to the ground-floor garage, then outside to the rear of the building. He showed me how to slide my hand along a grate to locate the tiny combination safe that contained the exterior door key. It was best to do this when no one was looking.

We returned upstairs to meet the roomies. I knew not to spend too much time getting to know them, for we were all rootless high-tech transients, our relationships temporary, our status revocable.

The room I'd booked was available for only two weeks. As soon as I connected to the WiFi network, I would need to start looking for another place with new furnishings, new cupboard layouts to learn, new passwords to memorize, and new roommates to meet and forget.

By the window, at the only proper desk: Raj, a brawny coder who affected a halfhearted machismo. He was the one who had shouted across the room. He was helpful like that.

On the middle of the couch, hunched over his laptop and radiating nervousness: Arun, a waifish intern, born in Bangalore and enrolled as an undergrad at Dartmouth.

At the far end of the couch, with tiny headphones in his ears: Yuri, from Norway. "Yuri is half Russian and half Arab. He drinks every day," Raj said. Yuri nodded austerely.

Alone at the kitchen table: Diego. He, like the others, was a software guy, but his unique after-hours passion was "hardware hacking." In a less pretentious time he might've been described simply as an electronics enthusiast, or a humble Radio Shack customer. Diego was an oddity. I wondered if the fumes from his soldering iron hadn't somehow affected his mind. I was partly right.

I asked Liam to show me my room. A puzzled look crossed his face, then he motioned for me to follow him to the lower floor of the condo. I cursed when I reached the landing. "My" room had five beds in it. I thought I had paid for a private space. "I thought so, too," Liam said. "The ad was vague." I double-checked. The listing clearly stated "no bunk beds," but down in the fine print I finally found the words "shared room." "It's sneaky that way," Yuri concurred.

Dinnertime looming, I ascended to the kitchen on the main floor. "Is there anything to boil water in?" I asked.

"No. Welcome to the house," Diego said.

The Condo Hackers were all immigrants or the children of immigrants, and therefore accustomed to getting jerked around. They were also too busy to raise a fuss. They rarely stopped working, even when drinking. The office always followed them home. They fancied themselves budding entrepreneurs, but they were chiefly migrant laborers with MacBook Pros. Like thousands of other tech workers, the foreign-born among them had entered the country on H-1B "specialty occupation" work visas conditional upon their continued employment. Like me, they each had a startup idea. Unlike me, they had professional training, exceptional in-demand skills, and the potential to one day earn a living wage.

I plopped down on an empty couch cushion. Everyone typed silently for a while. Then Raj stood up and stared at me. "This is a frat house," he said. I had gathered as much. In two hours I'd heard two rape jokes. "You're going to be hazed," Raj went on. I stared back at him. He was bigger than me, but perhaps if I hit him first, hard, in the nose, I could save myself from whatever ritualized debasement he had in mind.

Liam emerged from downstairs and stood at Raj's shoulder. "Do you smoke?" Liam said.

"What?" I said.

"That's the right answer," Raj said.

As hazings went, a shared spliff on the rooftop wasn't terrible. We talked about computers and took in the view as the sun sank behind the Bay—not that we could see it. In one direction were the

Hall of Justice, the county jail, and a row of shingles for bail bonds-
men. In the other, a freeway overpass, under which tarpaulin blan-
kets and cardboard mattresses appeared nightly and vanished in
the daylight. "Don't walk that way," Liam said.

Someone proposed ordering a pizza. The nearby restaurants
catering to cops and lawyers were all closed for dinner. "No one
lives here," Yuri said. "Except us."

I was only beginning to get acquainted with the infinite solipsism
of my new milieu. This was a world where scoring points on social
media mattered more than getting to know the people you shared
a bathroom with, where fulfillment in life was seen as the culmina-
tion of a simple, replicable process, like the instructions on the back
of a box of macaroni and cheese. We were grown men who lived
like captive gerbils, pressing one lever to make food appear and
another for some fleeting entertainment—everything on demand.
Airbnb and Foodpanda served the flesh, Netflix and Lifehacker
nourished the soul.

This is not to say the techies lacked all personality. Yuri, for
instance, was clearly a jerk. I liked him anyway. I invited Yuri out
to join me at a party celebrating "girl developers." He assumed I
had some inside source, which made me feel pretty savvy, but like
most of the freebies around town, the party was openly advertised
online. I relied on sites like like Eventbrite and Meetup.com to keep
my social calendar full and my expenses down. Yuri was grateful
for the invitation. He offered to order an Uber for us, even though
the party was less than a mile away. I goaded him into walking.

Just as I predicted, we traversed the homeless encampments around Hacker Condo without incident. Contrary to local law and custom, they were poor people, not cannibals.

The venue was a forbidding Gothamesque Art Deco tower—the old PacBell building, constructed for the California branch of the national telephone monopoly in its heyday. Now the tower's largest tenant was Yelp, a website that allows anonymous semiliterates to post critiques of grocers, doctors, restaurants, bars, and other local establishments. The reviews aren't much to read, and the dominant tone is one of petty disgruntlement, but in a sense that's the point. Yelp makes money by calling the owners of businesses named in the reviews and selling advertising. Some of the businesses have claimed that salespeople, who are under immense quota pressure, have sometimes promised to make negative comments "go away," or to suppress listings for competing businesses, in exchange for a monthly ad buy amounting to several thousand dollars per year. Yelp, founded in 2004, began reporting $370 million in annual revenue within a decade. Yelp's practices sounded to some businesses like an "extortion" racket. But Yelp had prevailed in lawsuits attacking its practices. Per *Vanity Fair*, Yelp's leaders were accredited members of "the new establishment." Fortysomething CEO Jeremy Stoppelman had personally donated $125,000 to the Democratic Party and its candidates. So when Yelp moved into its new global headquarters in 2013, Congresswoman Nancy Pelosi of Pacific Heights, the most ostentatiously wealthy neighborhood in the city, cut the ribbon. Pelosi praised Yelp as "a model of good business" and an exemplar of the "social and economic engines that drive the American dream"—a dream "built on faith in the future, faith in the entrepreneurial spirit, faith in innovation, faith in technology, and really faith in community, because community is what Yelp is all about." Even better, unlike the local newspapers that Stoppelman and his fellow tech execs helped to drive out of business, Yelp didn't subsidize a small army of journalists to pester politicians like Pelosi with questions about her coziness with campaign donors, or to write honest, competent restaurant reviews.

Yuri and I stood outside the reinforced doors of the tower and peered into the imposing lobby with its black marble walls and an intricately painted ceiling in the style of a Chinese tapestry. We had a problem. The party was overbooked. Yuri offered the steely doorman an insouciant shrug and, to my surprise, we were waved on toward the golden elevator. I noticed it had no buttons. This was my first experience with a "smart elevator," a devious device that furnished an additional line of defense against external rabble, whether dodgy moochers like us or restaurateurs driven to violent extremism by moronic Yelp reviews.

The doors opened to a beer-soaked huddle of coeds in matching T-shirts standing rigidly around a deejay booth. Pandora, the online radio service that seems to have a passion for putting musicians out of business, had ironically sent a live human to supply muffled musical accompaniment to the pulsing backbeat of shop talk. Above the crowd, in lights, was the name of the great benefactor: Yelp.

As advertised, the party boasted more "girls" than the usual tech soiree, although they were mostly segregated in defensive circles. I spoke to the eminently well-intentioned organizer and heard about the abuse, derision, rejection, and condescension faced by women in the technical professions, which the party was part of a larger effort to remedy. I couldn't honestly say I was doing my best to help, as I'd brought along someone who was just cruising for a hookup. Over by the deejay booth, a big blond oafish boy on crutches stumbled through a circle of women in company T-shirts, seized the mic, and began rapping, horribly. Time to move on.

I zigzagged through the opulent throng, confronted at every turn with bizarre juxtapositions of pleasure and toil. What was the point of it all? Networking, of course. To get a better job, and then a better one, and so on until you earned your "fuck you" money—as in "Fuck you, boss, I quit." Everyone had a different idea what sort of sum qualified as "fuck you" money, but it was generally understood to mean enough money that you wouldn't need to work anymore and could skip these stupid fake parties. Most of the crowd seemed to work at Yelp, and being far from having earned their "fuck you" money, felt obliged to stick around for the event. But there was something else keeping these people here—an overriding anxiety toward unfamiliar spaces.

Life outside the startup bubble was frightening and unpredictable. Inside, it was safe. "Fun" was mandatory in the Bay Area tech world, and inebriation strongly encouraged. The bar at Yelp, for instance, featured three kegs of high-end craft beer and an array of wines and spirits. This was not a temporary selection for the benefit of us honored guests, but a permanent fixture of the commissary. Normally open only to employees, the Yelp Café had a perfect five-star rating . . . on Yelp. "Well, looks like I'm never leaving my office compound!" one reviewer wrote. Well, yeah—that's the idea.

"This is not that unusual around here, for the bigger companies," Yuri said. "At GitHub, they have a bar on every floor and a secret room with rare whiskies. It's crazy." (Our roommate Arun claimed to have been inside this room but was told that pictures were forbidden.) It did seem slightly crazy, giving away bottomless food and booze to whoever walked in off the street. I refilled my plastic cup with potent ale and fetched a plateful of peanutty spring rolls to share. Yuri and I looked at each other and then at the crowd. It was a cacophonous pageant of geeky profligacy, carrying on high above the city all through the night, or rather until nine o'clock at the latest, because everyone had to work in the morning.

"Do you think this will last? Or is it a bubble?" I asked Yuri. He swallowed his spring roll. "Maybe," he replied. This was an impolite subject, I would learn, but clearly I wasn't the only person preoccupied with the question of whether and when the easy money would come to an end, as it had suddenly in the dot-com bust a decade and a half before. "But it's a different kind of bubble than 2000," Yuri continued. "These companies have users and profits." Indeed, only a week before the party, Yelp had announced its first annual profit—after two years of losing money as a publicly traded stock, and eight years before that as a privately held startup that was, while large and fast-growing, nevertheless unprofitable. So Yuri had a point. But it was not a conclusive point. The profits were fragile, because users were fickle—especially the Yelping masses. Only a few months after this party Yelp's stock would take a 75 percent dive from its peak, with some investors even saying the company had entered a "death spiral." (Its stock price rebounded but thus far has not fully recovered.) Easy come, easy go.

"I guess we should go mingle," Yuri said. We parted. I chatted with a swarthy single dude over by the beer taps. "I don't know why I ever paid for alcohol!" he said. Indeed. I bade my fellow moocher goodbye, for someone caught my eye whom I knew I needed to meet. He looked and sounded like an undernourished Eurovision contestant who'd just wandered out of a rave that had started sometime in the late nineties. The centerpiece of his outfit was a headband adorned with a pair of fluffy white robotic rabbit ears that seemed to move of their own volition. He stood across the room braying madly at a circle of women. I joined them and tried to get his story, but try as I might, I couldn't understand his accent. The rabbit ears somehow sensed my bafflement, for they perked in my direction as we spoke. When I caught up with Yuri, he said he had met the rabbit-cyborg before at another party. "He has some startup to replace business cards with a personal onetime link. It's going to be the next LinkedIn," Yuri explained. Everyone I knew hated LinkedIn, the résumé sharing site, which had been likened to a computer virus for its practice of drawing from users' contact lists and sending spammy "reminder" emails to everyone on those lists. According to the crowd wisdom of capital, however, this plague on the internet was worth $25 billion. And here before us stood, supposedly, the founder of *the next LinkedIn*.

"Do you think so?" I asked. It was hard to imagine the guy in the bunny ears running a $25 billion company.

"No," Yuri said.

Our eyes fell across the room, where a fresh batch of curious partygoers had gathered around the flamboyant entrepreneur to inspect his headpiece and hear his pitch.

"But who knows?" Yuri said. "Sometimes it's the guy in the bunny ears."

Gimmickry was not so much a last resort for desperate startup founders as a necessary means of distinction. The techies all seemed to have come off an assembly line, and anyone who stood out just a little bit became instantly memorable. Programmers, designers, developers, and sundry internet Okies fled their own individual dust bowls by the thousands to settle in San Francisco, land of 13 percent postrecession job growth—and freebies! They looked alike, they talked alike, they ate alike, they thought alike. Before long, I had developed a private taxonomy of tech bros—and they were, mostly, guys. There were, I reasoned, three major categories: clowns, drones, and bullies.

Not all clowns were so obvious as Mr. Bunny Ears. In an environment suffused with social anxiety, it was enough to be merely outgoing. Another night, while wandering dissolutely through a tech conference pre-party, I found myself drawn to a table where a boisterous, chubby-cheeked young man was holding court. His name was Adrian. Adrian didn't stand out because of his ideas. Quite the opposite. He was cofounder of a startup that hawked coupons for local businesses. The businesses, in turn, paid a cut of every sale from the coupons back to Adrian's startup. It was a clever enough business model, but it had already been done—in this case by a famous startup called Groupon. One couldn't blame copycats like Adrian for trying, because Groupon made its founders very rich. In 2011, it was the biggest tech company IPO since Google. But within a year, Groupon was in the gutter, as investors wised up to the company's questionable accounting practices. Its ostentatious founder, Andrew Mason, along with early investors, unloaded shares and took big cash payouts prior to the IPO. With Groupon as his model, Adrian told me he had raised some $4 million over multiple investment rounds. Persistence was important, he said. But flair was irreplaceable. "So many people are doing the trendy thing," he said. "You've got to stand out!" Adrian stood out by wearing a bright blue shirt with a garish yellow holster clipped to his belt, which looked like it belonged on a Lego Man. The holster was more than big enough to accommodate Adrian's ginormous iPhone 6 Plus, which he eagerly demonstrated. His was the stereotypical showmanship of a used car salesman—and it worked!

The second category of tech bros genuinely believed that if they hit the big time, it would be on account of their hard work and dedication. These were the drones. Almost all the guys in Hacker Condo were drones. Each had a mysterious "side project"—a startup in the making—that was inevitably too ill-formed to talk about, or far too technically complicated to remember. The drones seemed doomed to be desk jockeys for life, forever dreaming of their star turn as Job Creators. At a tech party one night, I met an awkward postpubescent Estonian with severe halitosis. His startup was a mobile phone role-playing game that took players through the adventure of building a startup and raising venture capital. I reckoned this was the entrepreneurial equivalent of a debut novel about the insecurities of a group of young writers in Brooklyn. And no less thrilling!

What the drones lacked in creativity they made up for in elbow grease. During daylight hours, they flocked to unused power outlets like moths to a flame. One of my regular work spots featured a prize windowside table with a sturdy desk and a power supply. It was frequently claimed by an early-rising lad from Essex, that maligned land of mudflats and spray tans just northeast of London, England. I eavesdropped as he made one cold call after another, pitching his startup. His name was Toby and he told me he "absolutely" preferred San Francisco to Essex. "The first question there is, 'Where are you from and where did you go to school?' The first question here is, 'What's your idea and what are you doing?'" Toby said. So what was Toby doing? He tried to explain. I gathered his startup had something to do with signing up kids for summer camp. It was definitely the thing he was most passionate about, whatever it was.

All that aside, the drone thing seemed to be working for him. He had an enviable VC connection—another Brit who emigrated to work for Sequoia Capital, one of the biggest players in the industry. He also had a functioning product. He made me feel like a slacker. At the rate he was going, Toby would be the world's first online summer camp billionaire before I figured out where to catch the bus.

At least the drones were humble. The most unbearable tech scenesters were those who seemed most certain that they were destined to be the next Mark Zuckerberg. These fell into the final category—the bullies.

The bullies were binge-drinking gym rats who, regardless of age, seemed perpetually twenty-five years old. Most were white, but Raj, a Desi, was Hacker Condo's resident bully. By emulating the performative, coked-up machismo of their overlords in the finance sector, the bullies were determined to avoid the old stigma of the computer nerd as a simpering eunuch.

Being fundamentally insecure, bullies were rarely found alone. One day I was sipping tea on a bench near a huddle of corn-fed wannabe tech bros who sat spread-eagled and bragged about their recent job interviews. A beefy dude in a baseball hat said he had just received an offer from a cable TV network to work as a Web developer. But he planned to hold out as long as he could for a better offer from a more exciting company. Another guy had been making the rounds of startups. The beefy dude offered his unsolicited advice: Stay positive. Talk the talk. "Passion is every other word," he said. Good tip, thanks, bro.

Bullshitting skills mattered far more than a talent for coding, an eye for design, or a keen sense of market demand. Although compensating for an apparent lack of aptitude or charm, in a sense the bullies were cleverer than either the drones or the clowns, for their approach required little actual work, just bluster. This conferred a significant advantage upon the most ambitious bullies: free time.

Bullies were at their most entertaining when talking themselves into a corner, as I learned early on while conducting my nightly freebie foraging near the Marina, where I found myself talking to a stocky startup founder who liked to pose for pictures with a cigar in one hand and a glass of whiskey in the other. His startup was a photo service for media companies. As it happened, I'd worked for a similar company, and I asked him a few questions about what made some startups take off while others floundered. He sneered. "Boy, you really haven't been in the Valley very long," he said. "Otherwise you would be asking much more sophisticated questions." I said he was correct, I had been in town less than a week, and asked how long he had been there. "Six weeks," he said. A grizzled veteran, wouldn't you know it!

Every once in a while, someone hit the scene who defied all categories—who was neither clown nor drone nor bully, but a genuine, transcendent original. I met such a man one night when my on-demand social calendar led me to a large stone building on Market Street. On the ground floor, this building housed two high-end clothing retailers. Above them were several floors of premium office space, two of which had recently been leased by the host of that evening's party, NerdWallet. Neither I nor most of the other guests I met upstairs had ever heard of this operation. To us, it was just another oversized startup office with a great downtown view, a foosball table, and an open bar.

There was a price to pay, of course. Our presence was a validation of the existence of this enterprise, an implicit endorsement of NerdWallet's right to consume so many resources and to occupy so much space. To partake in the freebies on offer here was to consent for one's likeness to appear in online marketing. Guests were encouraged to post photos, quotations, and quips from the party to Twitter, Instagram, or wherever, along with a unique "hashtag."

This was standard startup practice: to ply party guests with drink and enlist them as agents of buzz. For some reason, Nerd-Wallet enlisted a cohost for its own get-to-know-us party—another obscure startup called Muck Rack, which sold profiles on journalists to marketing types. I never quite figured out why, but it was Muck Rack that wound up with top billing via the event's insufferable hashtag, #MuckedUp. The party planners took the extra step of setting up a projector that cast any and all Twitter posts marked #MuckedUp over the walls. Very few people were playing along as intended. However, some outside saboteur had hijacked the party hashtag by posting a link to a book called *Toxic Sludge Is Good for You: Lies, Damn Lies, and the Public Relations Industry*. Every few minutes, the cover of this heretical tome appeared on the walls, a censorious, five-foot-tall judgment upon all assembled. I contacted the culprit later, who explained that his intent was merely to harangue, in the time-honored tradition of Twitter. He had no idea that his fleeting keyboard jibe had become a constant scolding presence above the mass of media schmoozers, but he was delighted to learn about what had happened. Most people there pretended not to notice.

"I'm particularly excited that we have journalists and PR people here tonight," said one of the organizers, a twenty-year PR veteran, taking the mic to deliver a brief salute to the new spirit of conviviality between once hostile professions. "The best relationship is a symbiotic relationship. We like it when you like us. Enjoy your cocktails."

Unseemly? Certainly. But who was I, with my free booze and my plate of hors d'oeuvres, to judge? I bounced nimbly out of a

conversation with a bored Bloomberg News tech reporter only to
fall carelessly into the clutches of an agriculture industry spokes-
man who wanted to tell me all about plastics. Such were the tor-
tures of writers in the tech world. It was not possible to emerge
from this place as a whole, healthy person—not after one's brains
had been beaten to mush by buzzwords. I was quickly tiring of the
chintzy bribes and the phony passion. I longed for more cynical
company, but I would have settled for a few honest words.

I retreated to the windowsill, where a middle-aged man sat
alone, back turned on the streets below, shoulders drooped, eyes
down, fiddling with his phone. Although he was content to sip his
beer and silently observe the proceedings from a distance, his presence could not be ignored. He seemed above it all. I had heard it
said that in Silicon Valley, those most slovenly in appearance possessed the largest bank accounts. By that rule, this guy might've
been a Davos-class billionaire. A well-worn backpack lay between
his feet. His jeans were faded, his plaid shirt dull. Thick black
curls poured from beneath his baseball cap. I'd been in a grouchy
mood, but something about this man made me feel sociable. I took
a seat by his side. By way of making conversation, I asked about
his phone. I didn't recognize the model. "This? It's an Obamaphone," he said. He had the raspy voice of a longtime smoker.

"What's an Obamaphone?" I said.

"You can get this phone if you get government benefits," he
explained.

I knew there was something different about this man with the
curly hair. He shook my hand and smiled, regarding me benignly

with bloodshot eyes. "My name is Lawrence. I smoke a lot of weed," he said.

A fortuitous mixture of proximity and curiosity had lured him to the party that night. Like me, he had RSVP'd after coming across the online invitation. "A lot of the big players, they don't like to advertise their investments. I just wanted to see who these guys are," he said. "I don't need to tell you, this is prime real estate. I live five blocks from here."

Lawrence had lived in San Francisco for twenty years, he said, settling after a prolonged period of itinerancy that took him through New York and Texas—where, as a biracial African Jew, he was even more out of place than usual. Lawrence told me he had been born in the former British colony of Rhodesia and lived through its war of independence and the advent of modern Zimbabwe. "My dad is the guy who brought Bob Marley there for a concert. I met the dude when I was a little kid," he said. This proved difficult to verify. As did most of Lawrence's claims.

Lawrence had an app. This app was his ticket to free food and beer at all the tech parties around town. But it wasn't finished yet—not even close. It was in a predevelopment phase, and very much in stealth mode. When I asked what it did, this mystery app, Lawrence demurred. "Man," he said, "whatever happened to *trade secrets*?"

I cajoled. "Come on, tell me," I said. "I won't tell anyone. Who would I tell?"

"Okay, man. I'll tell you," he said, leaning in conspiratorially. "It's a game. You know Angry Birds?"

"Yeah," I said. "I know Angry Birds."

"It's like Angry Birds, except there are no birds, and nobody's angry."

Lawrence was my startup hero.

Here was a man who had devised the perfect startup pitch. Angry Birds had been downloaded, supposedly, three billion times, which implied that either one out of every two living humans was a player, or that most players deleted the game from their devices in frustration and then reinstalled it, over and over again. Whatever those numbers actually meant, analysts had valued the company that made Angry Birds at up to $9 billion. Therein lay the genius of Lawrence's delightfully coy elevator pitch: What investor could refuse the chance to back a game that was just like Angry Birds, but new and different?

Having pledged confidentiality, I can say little more regarding Lawrence's stealth app. However, I will disclose that it involved tapping on pot leaves that, for sundry reasons including Apple's App Store guidelines and impish stoner obscurantism, were not *obviously* pot leaves.

There were at least two solid reasons for Lawrence's paranoia. One was weed. The other was experience. People at startup events sometimes stole ideas, he said. And he had personally witnessed the secrecy with which the most prosperous tech companies treated their intellectual property. "I went on the Zynga tour. I had to sign a release form," he said. Zynga was the company behind Farm-Ville, a notoriously spammy Facebook game that catapulted the company to a $7 billion valuation at IPO, before allegations of insider fraud (later settled) and a fraying partnership with Facebook caused its stock value to collapse. A decade after its IPO, Zynga was trading at a meager $3 per share. Lawrence said Zynga had been most protective of its basement, which contained a massive data center. The sight of it blew his mind. "What are they storing? I don't know," he said. We could only speculate. A list of high scores? Secret cheat codes? Intricate consumer behavioral profiles revealing their private preferences for virtual livestock?

I sensed that Lawrence could become a kind of mentor to me. We had a couple more beers on the house and exchanged phone numbers.

As a consequence of the open bar, I got lost on my way to the bathroom. Wandering down a narrow hall, I spotted two touch-screen panels mounted on the wall beside a pair of sliding doors. Marked SLEEP POD NORTH and SLEEP POD SOUTH, the screens bore a welcoming green circle and the word OPEN. I slipped through the doors to peek inside one of the sleep pods. It was more spacious than many of the bedrooms I had seen advertised, and more private than my setup at Hacker Condo. Double-sized bunk beds, with finer sheets than those to which I was accustomed, were mounted on the wall. Would anyone notice if I moved in? The hard part would be getting past security every day without an employee badge. On the other hand, with cozy bunks and clean bathrooms, a shower, a yoga room, fast WiFi, vending machines that spat out computer peripherals, daily catered lunches and dinner, and liquor cabinets stocked with eighty labels of booze, why would I ever need to leave? Everything a human being needed to survive and efficiently output code was here inside NerdWallet HQ.

I wandered through an expansive unfurnished wing of the office. Who was paying for this? And why? What exactly was a NerdWallet? A woman at the party had tried to explain the company to me, but since she was a newish hire, she didn't seem quite sure, either.

I subsequently did some research. Longer-term NerdWalleteers who had posted anonymous accounts of their experiences on the website Glassdoor—like Yelp but for employers—described a culture of "fear, hypocrisy, and poor communication." One described its executive ranks as "treacherous, languishing souls who want to claw as much money as possible" from investors, employees, and clients. Said another, "It's unclear what the product is."

This company, an enigma even to its own staff, claimed to have thirty million users, although this was impossible to verify. More interesting, it had just secured "an outsized sum" from one of the Valley's top VC firms, Institutional Venture Partners. As Reuters reported, NerdWallet raised $64 million in its first fund-raising round—"far more cash than it needs"—with a valuation in the "mid-hundred millions." This was an indication that some big-time players in Silicon Valley hoped NerdWallet would be the next "unicorn"—a company valued at $1 billion or more. By proving its ambition with such a large investment, NerdWallet would be able to attract *even more* money later, which would further validate its future-unicorn status and hoover up still more money as, if all went according to plan, the company became a household name.

Thus were the unicorns of Silicon Valley literally wished into being. It was the most magical thing about them.

But unicorns, like many rare species, are at risk. By that time in 2015, there were murmurs of an impending unicorn die-off. Investors made do by fabricating long, swirling molluscan horns and fastening them like party hats around the heads of mules. Presto, NerdWallet! As evidenced by my luxurious surroundings, a lot of money was riding on this mule.

Large valuations were clearly critical to startup success. But what is a valuation, exactly? I spent a lot of time trying to figure that out. There's no rule, exactly. Valuations are the artful concoctions of founders and investors. After running a company's self-declared financial figures through various arbitrary formulae—factoring in *estimated* future revenue, *anticipated* growth rates, and *potential* overall market size—the interested parties settle upon a plausibly vainglorious figure that represents not how much their company is worth, but how much it hopes to raise. The larger the valuation, the more money a company's founders, and the early investors, stand to make.

This was no secret to Valley veterans. *Entrepreneur* magazine suggested that "pre-revenue" startups preparing their own valuations should demonstrate "sophistication" to investors by fudging the numbers. "Be creative," the magazine advised.

Despite the perception that we in the VC world employ armies of analysts working behind the scenes and prepping us to beat down the valuation expectations of poorly prepared entrepreneurs, nothing could be further from the truth.

As one lucky unicorn jockey told the tech-news site Pando: "It's arbitrary as fuck. There's no logic to what you get valued at."

Valuations are not the same as revenue, which refers to how much money a company makes from sales—or claims to make. Profit is whatever a company has left after paying its bills, like salaries, rent, catering, and the bar tab. In 2015, a startup "valued at" $1 billion was, more likely than not, losing money. These distinctions are not always clear to outsiders because few people in Silicon Valley—whether journalists, entrepreneurs, or tech employees—have the wherewithal to pursue such thorny questions, and the incentives all run against clarity. Besides, bigger numbers just sound better.

Appearance was everything. That's why NerdWallet—even before its big first round of funding—signed a seven-year lease on its lavish, two-story, forty-six-thousand-square-foot offices. It was, according to local press reports, "the last vacant contiguous block of space left" on Market Street. Custom renovations included a full broadcast studio and a fifth-floor "Fail Wall where employees affix Post-it notes describing a recent failure." On the sixth floor: a wall of Legos.

The spacious high-end real estate, like the valuation, indicated NerdWallet had "room to grow." Another floor in the same building rented for a reported $51 per square foot. Based on that, and median commercial rents in the area, NerdWallet was probably paying more than $2 million a year in rent to its landlord, a "vertically integrated" and publicly traded real estate company based in Los Angeles, Hudson Pacific Properties.

NerdWallet was unusual among unicorn-mules in that it

claimed to turn a profit. The company made money from advertising and referral fees earned whenever it steered users toward a certain credit card, mortgage, insurance policy, business investment, or student loan. "I want to cover every substantial financial decision that anyone can make in their life," CEO and cofounder Tim Chen, a former banker, told TechCrunch. "We're talking about a shitload of big decisions there." The NerdWallet homepage pronounced the company to be "your source of **truth** for all of life's financial decisions." A fine-print "advertiser disclosure" at the foot of the page revealed that the truth was proudly sponsored by Bank of America, Capital One, JPMorgan Chase, Citibank, Discover, and other financial institutions, noting that "compensation may impact which cards we review and write about and how and where products appear on this site."

No kidding! NerdWallet's reviews had titles like "The Best Bank of America Credit Cards 2015" and "CitiBusiness® / AAdvantage® Platinum Select® World MasterCard®: Your Company's Ticket to Perks." Because everyone loves perks. NerdWallet was credit card junk mail masquerading as "independent" financial journalism. Many stories had Apply Now buttons. I resisted that temptation, although a line of credit might have made my day-to-day existence in San Francisco a little less nerve-rending.

The tech boom, I had begun to see, was not a fount of opportunity, but an engine that transformed baby boomers' pension funds into canapés and booze for millennials through the marketing budgets of venture-backed startups. Which was all well and good, but I couldn't help feeling that there was something more unsettling going on. Were we young lambs being fattened only for the slaughter? Once we had grown dependent on artisanal bread-crumbs and tequila drippings from the table of our boomer masters, could there be any escape? Being educated through online pyramid schemes, and getting our news of the world filtered by Facebook, could we ever hope to apprehend the true nature of this mystifying apparatus that surrounded us from birth? Would we ride these unicorns over the rainbow to the land of plenty, or would we be gored to death by their sparkling horns?

Who really ran this place? And who kept buying my drinks? I wanted to know.

Luckily, I had a few friends in the city who were pretty plugged in. One old pal of mine had a good office job, a proper apartment, a medical marijuana card, and an impressive collection of pocket vaporizers. I asked him to give me a walking tour of the Pacific Heights subneighborhood called Billionaires' Row. And so we walked in the sunshine, vaping all the way, up the endless hills. Most of the mansions looked dead empty, with darkened windows and empty driveways. The streets, too, were conspicuously quiet, except for a few picturesque and well-trafficked routes.

We paused atop the Lyon Street staircase, where my friend pointed out U.S. senator Dianne Feinstein's red brick mansion, purchased with her third husband, the big-shot investor Richard C. "Dick" Blum, in 2006. Just a few years before that, Blum's company, Newbridge Capital, took a managing stake in a big bank in Shenzhen, the worldwide hub of electronics manufacturing, in time to cash in on the current tech boom.

Sundown from this vantage delivered a breathtaking medley of gold, green, and blue. It seemed like an okay neighborhood, albeit dull. Maybe some kindly billionaire would put me up in exchange for a little song and dance.

As we turned down Broadway, the mansions grew bigger and even more ostentatious. One house was adorned with a giant robot boasting an impressive mechanical dong. The silvery cock wagged in the direction of Oracle founder Larry Ellison's mansion across the street. Was this some decorative commentary on Ellison's reputation as a massive prick? The robot's owner happened to be married to the daughter of Ellison's late Oracle cofounder, Bob Miner, and the art installation was widely assumed to represent some filial beef, although the owners rejected that interpretation in a *Vanity Fair* dispatch from the neighborhood. One holiday season, the robot, named Goliath, was brutally beaten. According to the *San Francisco Chronicle*, police found "a trail of robot pieces— including a Santa hat—that led across the street, in the direction of the home of Oracle founder Larry Ellison."

Apparently, Ellison's college-age daughter Megan Ellison had thrown a party the night of the attack. Putting two and two together, it appears a couple of revelers may have been the attackers.

Mercifully, Goliath's appendage was left unharmed.

Not far from Ellison's place on Broadway was a seven-bedroom rental property valued at $8 million. The house was "a hive of startup activity," according to a news report, whose tenants were mostly strapping young go-getters like me and the Condo Hackers. It seemed that I would fit right in there, but unfortunately there was already a long waiting list of "entrepreneurs, robotics enthusiasts, and venture capitalists."

My friend and I paused for a vape break outside the boxy white facade of the most expensive home in San Francisco, which belonged to telecom tycoon, casino heir, and noted Deadhead Michael Klein, along with his wife, Roxanne, a "raw food" chef. The Kleins had the property on the market for $39 million. "Its interiors," I read,

are filled with white box-beam ceilings, marble fireplaces, and fancy light fixtures (even the kitchen lights look like mini-chandeliers). The house has multiples of nearly every room, with seven bedrooms, seven full bathrooms, four half-baths, two kitchens, two family rooms, two offices, and three rooftop terraces. There is, however, only one basketball court.

An architect who designed custom luxury homes featured in magazines like *Architectural Digest* told me that nobody lived in those houses anyway. "The people who own them," he said, "all have five others."

Some tech billionaires even owned five houses in the same place. Down in Palo Alto, Mark Zuckerberg purchased four properties adjacent to his $7 million five-bedroom home for a combined $39 million—more than ten times their assessed value. The purpose of the land grab was to maintain the seclusion of Zuckerberg's backyard and master bedroom. At around that time, the city of Palo Alto passed an ordinance restricting public records access in order to protect the privacy of certain "very high-profile tech-related residents."

Privacy was not, as the Big Data tycoons claimed, dead. Privacy was something that you paid for at a premium.

I, for one, was not on a five-house budget. I was on a five-guys-to-a-room budget. And it was remarkable how quickly living in such close quarters eroded my sanity. I couldn't sleep through the night for the snoring of my roommates. I couldn't talk to my wife on Skype without someone eavesdropping. It was as though I was being subjected to a cruel psychological experiment in which I was released each day to forage and prowl on the streets and then returned to the cage each night, only to discover that someone had moved my things while I was out. A few days on this zero-privacy regimen put me on a permanent hair trigger.

I returned to Hacker Condo to find a new guy on the couch. He was tall and blond and engrossed in his laptop. I said hello and asked where he was from. "I'm Norwegian. I'm in the middle of a Skype conversation," he said. "Uh, sorry," I said. I forgot his name immediately. Raj said New Norwegian Guy was the first in an impending wave of arrivals. Seven more Norwegian guys—a whole startup team—would be moving in. We calculated that Hacker Condo would soon have three more guests than it had beds.

The good news was that several people, including me, would soon be moving out. Raj was heading to the countryside, or maybe the beach—he hadn't decided. Diego was preparing for an eight-week road trip by blasting ABBA from his laptop speakers and blowing vapor rings from his handmade, industrial-strength pocket vaporizer. Yuri had scored a room in a Palo Alto mansion with a pool and a Jacuzzi.

While I had been out foraging, there had apparently been something of a revolt over the overcrowding, as well as the lack of house keys, kitchen implements, and so forth—which explained why so many people were eager to leave. Brody, our host, had taken Liam, the placid Kiwi, out for a beer to defuse the situation. "We're kind of like a startup, too," Brody had said, by way of an excuse.

II

Slums as a Service

Two weeks was not enough time to find an apartment in San Francisco. Not on my budget. Rents were higher than in New York or London. One-bedrooms were running around $3,000 a month; studios, around $2,500; shares, $1,500; and illegal crap shares, $1,000. It was the same deal across the Bay to the east in Oakland and Berkeley, as well as to the south in the Silicon suburbs of Redwood City, Palo Alto, and Mountain View. Whatever I might save in rent by living on the periphery I would lose in transportation costs and time.

In the mad scramble for shelter, people were resorting to live human sacrifice, public stoning, price gouging, and other barbaric practices. I met a humble salesman who lost an apartment to some high-flying "tech dudes" who snagged the rental before the open house by sending the landlord copies of their credit scores and a statement of their willingness to pay 30 percent above the asking price. Still the techies wondered, *Why do they hate us*?

My vaping buddy helpfully sent me an ad he found on Craigslist. It promised a "legit, but somewhat unique" living situation involving male prostitution. "No need to be weirded out," the ad began. Too late, alas. There were some clues that the ad was probably a joke, none more definitive than the price—only $500 per month for a room in Noe Valley, which was, at that time, the new "it" spot for up-and-coming techies. Geography connoted status and, despite the noisy meritocratic bent of the startup scene, telegraphing one's status was critical. "Mission: cool. Marina: not cool," as one entrepreneur broke it down for me.

However, there were other strange arrangements that I am positive were real, such as this listing from Airbnb:

STUDIO/NO WINDOW BEST PRICE!!! $39 PER NIGHT
Our home is what my kids call: "Safari"! I, the mom, am the one in charge of creating babies . . . I call myself "The Creature From The Forest" . . . that should tell you EVERYTHING about me!

No shoes, cooking or locks . . . We do not have locks in ANY rooms . . . Showers are one per day ONLY and as close as a maximum of 5 minutes as possible PLEASE!

Please, thank you, no. The reason I'm certain this ad was real: the long list of reviews, most vaguely creeped out, written by former guests.

Better deals could be found through word of mouth, but, as I was a newcomer, these eluded me. I found other opportunities, though, while making the rounds. I met a young woman at a hipster bar who offered me a room within ten minutes of our meeting. Her name was Magdalena and she was from Vladivostok. Thin and sandy-haired, she had a cast on her arm. Her "friend," a fat man from Alabama named Beau, had a menacing air. Beau's toy terrier wore a black jacket with rhinestone lettering that read MIMI. "Mimi, she doesn't know evil," Beau said wistfully.

"I have a place! I need to rent it because I'm living with him," Magdalena said, motioning to Beau. "I would like to stay with a good man like you. I know you are good." I asked how much she wanted in rent. She replied: $3,200. "Is that too much?" she said. "What can you pay?"

No landlord had ever asked me that. "I don't want to pay more than $1,200," I said, stunned. Magdalena and Beau conferred in whispers. Then she turned to me, beaming. "That's perfect!" she said. It was my most successful negotiation ever. I should have said $800. Unfortunately, subsequent discussions made clear that I had been haggling over the price of Magdalena for one night, not the price of her spare room for one month.

Lacking the financial stability required to secure a lease, much less a mortgage, my best hope upon leaving Hacker Condo was to find another "hacker house." These were the products of disruptive innovation in urban real estate. The city was once riddled with small apartments and single-family homes that sheltered trifling handfuls of obsolete laborers and their unproductive children, often for decades at a stretch. But the tech boom let such so-called family homes reach their full potential as investment properties. Unproductive residential zones now teemed with digital workhouses bursting with entrepreneurial brio and filled to capacity, or beyond, with techie forty-niners. Unlike a youth hostel or a skid row hotel, the hacker houses often required a minimum stay of one month or more. Some hacker houses were attached to startup investment incubators or shared workspaces. Others amounted to little more than flimsy bunks in a windowless room. A number of trend-savvy real estate investors purchased or leased dozens of residential properties around the Bay Area to rent out in this fashion.

I had my eye on one special property in the Mission District. It was called 20Mission, and it had been designated San Francisco's "best hacker hostel" in 2014 by a local alternative newspaper, *SF Weekly*. The paper said 20Mission was

a 41-room complex founded by Bitcoin trader and entrepreneur Jered Kenna, who recruited an international group of start-up founders and artists to coexist there. With a chicken coop, shared kitchen, and commanding view of the city's downtown, it has the feel of university student housing—the residents are young, the parties are crowded, the idealism is embedded in the architecture. And here's another perk: [the owner] accepts rent in Bitcoin.

It sounded ideal. I didn't have any Bitcoins, but they couldn't be harder to come by than real money.

As I researched further, it turned out 20Mission was so central to the San Francisco cryptocurrency scene that the Bitcoin Trader blog—an authoritative source on such matters—nicknamed it Bitcoin's Hogwarts. Keen to make a good impression, I looked up the owner, Jered Kenna.

A small-town Oregonian and U.S. Marine Corps veteran

turned Halliburton employee, Kenna found that the life of a mercenary in Afghanistan left him with "a palpable distaste for unethical and fraudulent business practices," he wrote. He moved to Chile and opened an online import-export business peddling Apple gadgets and alpaca socks. But then Kenna caught a lucky break by acting on his preoccupations—cryptography, "alternative finance," libertarian politics, and economic collapse. Kenna accumulated a small hoard of Bitcoin when it was virtually worthless. In 2011, he launched a Bitcoin exchange, Tradehill, from an office on the beach in Chile. His cofounders included New York bankers and a former senior engineer from Elon Musk's SpaceX. By 2013, when the goldbugs, money launderers, and Wall Street speculators joined the Bitcoin frenzy, Kenna had become a charter member of the "Bitcoin millionaires' club," and his distaste for "unethical" business practices had evolved. He now argued that the marketing of Ponzi schemes should be permitted so long as the terms were clearly stated. It was all in good fun, like a friendly game of poker. Of course, Bitcoin itself was a Ponzi scheme. As with so many other Bitcoin companies before it, Tradehill collapsed in a morass of litigation. Kenna was "pulling my hair out . . . not sleeping," and once more left holding the bag. "I was, like, completely broke and I needed somewhere to live in San Francisco, which is horrible," Kenna recalled in a video interview with a Bitcoin blogger. "I talked to a friend of mine and he said, 'Well there's this old crackhouse that you could get a good deal on, but it's terrible.' I said, 'OK that sounds perfect.'" Kenna took over the lease and persuaded friends to rent rooms there for $800 a month. Thus 20Mission was born. After a couple of years,

Kenna followed his girlfriend to Colombia, where he opened another hacker hostel and a brewery. He hadn't conquered the world, but neither had he gone to prison. For a Bitcoin trader, that wasn't bad.

In a promotional video for 20Mission targeting potential tenants and investors, the owner explained the building's phoenix-like transformation from "an old hotel for crackheads and homeless people" to "a live-space for tech people" and, ultimately, a self-sustaining locus of revolutionary innovation, running on untaxable digital drug dollars and laissez-faire spirit.

The 20Mission website featured an array of appealing photographs. There was a sun-bathed deck covered in bright green Astroturf and furnished with a large gas barbecue grill; a spotless, spacious lounge with an inviting plush leather couch; a hopping party in a high-ceilinged space; a rooftop yoga session; and a tidy, funkily furnished bedroom complete with a double-sized futon and a hammock. "With engineers, graphic designers, photographers, videographers, brand consultants, and well-connected Silicon Valley entrepreneurs among our permanent residents," the website said, "you have every resource at your fingertips." So it seemed! I composed a flattering self-introduction and announced my interest in joining the 20Mission community. Soon enough the manager, Steven Lombardi, replied with an invitation to "come by and chat." It felt like a job interview. I wrote back and set up a time. In the meantime, I read up on the history of the city's best hacker house. The neighbors, it seemed, were not thrilled with the arrival of such illustrious innovators. On the night before

Halloween—which happened to coincide with a World Series victory by the San Francisco Giants—riots had broken out around the city. In the Mission, windows were smashed and fires set inside an under-construction luxury condo. Someone spray-painted FUCK TECHIES on a bus shelter that carried an ad for the iPhone 6. A Google bus took a pelting. And 20Mission was besieged by an angry mob that threw garbage and bottles at the building and chanted "Techies! Techies!" The techies, for their part, seemed unperturbed. "We are the architects of the future!" one 20Mission resident proclaimed to a reporter.

When the day came for my appointment with the manager, Steven, I saw that the architecture of the future had its windows soaped over and its doors sealed shut. As it turned out, city code enforcers had shut down 20Mission's vaunted co-working space over a lack of proper permits. I found another entrance around the side. I rang the buzzer, and after a moment, a woman's voice came though the speaker. The lock clicked free and I opened the door into a dark, claustrophobic stairwell. There were tightly spaced rows of bike racks mounted to the ceiling, and as I climbed the stairs, I had to hug the far wall to avoid being whacked in the face by a handlebar or a tire. At the landing atop the stairs there was a sliding glass door leading to the deck. The place looked smaller than it had in the publicity photos—dumpier, too. The flooring wasn't Astroturf, as I thought, just a dirty length of wrinkled green carpet. There were pallets stacked against the walls and tarps thrown over benches. Wooden furniture and ceramic pots lay scattered around the deck. Farther inside, I found the tiny shared kitchen. So many pots, pans, and spatulas dangled overhead that in the event of an earthquake, whoever happened to be buttering their toast would certainly be crushed by falling cookware. The sink, too—filthy. Amid this mess stood a timid redhead with a bright red shirt and matching red-framed eyeglasses. I recognized her from a news story about the hacker house in which she had talked about her philosophy of "radical personal transparency"—she was a sometime camgirl, or online adult performer—as well as her day-to-day existence, which meant subsisting on whatever was marked "free" in the kitchen and paying her rent with laundry quarters. When I showed up, she was meeting another housemate, a quiet, scrawny guy, for the first time. "Are you going to be here long term?" she asked him. "In the city, yeah," he whispered. There was no room in the kitchen, so I stood outside in the hall and asked where I might find Steven. "Down the hall and all the way at the end," the redhead replied.

The hallways were dark, but I could see that the walls and doors were covered in posters and decals, like a student dorm. Bicycles were piled up everywhere. The smell of pot smoke, both stale and fresh, permeated every corner. The walls were thin enough that as I passed each door, I received an auditory tour of the private spaces inside—a little electronica in one room, a little orgasmic moaning in the next. At the end of the long hall, I found room no. 4—Steven's room. The door was decorated with a skull decal. I knocked and heard the muffled sound of a woman's voice. I thought she said "Come in," so I started to open the door. But I had misheard. "He's not here!" she screamed. I closed the door. I walked back outside to the deck and waited. Steven showed up maybe fifteen minutes later. Stocky, dome-headed, and brusque, Steven suffered from chronic administrative headaches, the latest of which involved the wall-mounted bike rack blocking the stairwell. A city code inspector wanted the bike racks gone. "It's gotta happen soon," Steven said. "I don't want him coming around and breaking my balls."

He led me on a perfunctory tour. The entire house, all forty-one units, shared two coed bathrooms. We popped inside the dark and dingy common room where two bong-baked residents halfheartedly acknowledged our presence without pausing their video game. Tour complete, Steven laid out the price structure. Small rooms—very small—cost $1,400 per month; mediums, $1,600; and the largest, $1,800—"just like McDonald's," he said. My face must have betrayed my honest reaction to the notion of paying so much money for the privilege of sleeping in a closet inside a painted-over onetime crack den while sharing a toilet with at least twenty other people. This was my undoing. Steven sensed my reticence. He said there were twelve or thirteen people ahead of me on the waiting list, all ready to make long-term commitments and put up cash (or Bitcoin) to move in at a moment's notice. "I'd prefer someone who stays at least six months. It makes my life easier. Nothing personal," Steven said. Then he said he had to go. Which meant I had to go, too. I begged off shaking his hand, explaining that I had a cold. "I don't care, man," he said, taking my hand anyway. "I ain't gonna die. I been shaking hands with dirty indigenous people half my life." Like his boss, Kenna, Steven was

an American war veteran. With that he was gone, along with my
hopes of moving in to the city's best Bitcoin playpen.

Although I envied them from my dark and squalid quarters, the
San Francisco longtimers who lived in rent-controlled apartments were in situations nearly as precarious—and certainly more
sympathetic—than my own. I met a musician, a young lesbian
bohemian who performed on streets and in clubs and organized a
backyard concert series called the Garden Sessions. Her name
was Julie Indelicato, and she lived in a $600 rent-controlled apart-
ment in the Mission. When I first met her, Julie was terrified that
her landlord would evict her and sell the building so that it could
be rented out at six times the price to white techie colonizers such
as myself. She was thinking of moving out to spare herself the pain
of an eviction proceeding. A year on, Julie, to her own surprise,
still occupied her apartment. "Were I to get an eviction notice
tomorrow, however, I would probably opt to leave the area, not
just the city. I would take it as a sign of the beginning of the end of
a bad relationship that has gone on for way too long," Julie told
me. She spoke of the city as if it were a person. "San Francisco used
to be cool. *Used to* like all the things I like, it *used to* not worry
about who I hung out with, or what clothes I wear, or how much
money I have," she said. "I don't get how this happened."

The great San Francisco gentrification quake sent tremors up
and down the West Coast. When we met, Julie asked me about
Portland, where she had heard that one could rent a decent place
for $300 a month. As a sometime Portlander, I knew that hadn't

been true for more than a decade, in part because so many Californians had moved north in search of cheaper rent. I later repeated Julie's misinformation to a bartender who had moved down from Portland seeking work. He said he actually knew of a $300 room in San Francisco. His ex-girlfriend lived there. It was literally a pantry. A growing subgenre of masochistic real estate blogs chronicled the conversion of storage space into illegal tenements. People were paying through the nose to live in concrete garages without bathrooms. In garden sheds. In tents. And in offices. A Yahoo employee who worked in the facilities department told me employees sometimes camped out for long periods in the company conference rooms while they searched for proper housing. She wouldn't let me bribe her to stay in one.

With landlords eager to cash in, formal evictions had increased 55 percent in five years. More often, though, landlords simply bullied their tenants into packing up. "Tenants are getting evicted for having cups in their cupboards. The landlords say it's clutter. They'll say anything. Eventually the tenants just give up," a lawyer for a tenants' rights organization told me. His employer, the Eviction Defense Collaborative, was itself getting evicted from its offices so that the landlord could rent the space to a tech startup.

I chanced upon an antieviction protest at City Hall one afternoon. Some five hundred people swarmed around the grand staircase in the atrium, chanting and waving signs with slogans like CLASS WAR NO MORE. "Our home is for sale. The vultures are circling," one man intoned during a round of human megaphone. Before marching upstairs to deliver a petition, the protesters unfurled a large banner reading NO MONSTER IN THE MISSION.

The monster in question was a proposed three-hundred-fifty-unit luxury apartment complex where rents would start at $5,000 a month. For protesters like Bianca, a Latina single mother of two, "development" meant coercive expulsion. "My building is for sale, so I'll probably be evicted soon," she told me. A native San Franciscan named Kenny lingered alone on the steps. Kenny, middle-aged and black, was newly homeless. He'd been granted a housing voucher through a welfare program, but it wasn't doing much good because he needed to find a place that rented for less than $2,000 a month. "It's too much. They've got nothing for you unless you're already rich," Kenny said. Outside, I met Fatima, a black mother of three who was waving a banner at passing cars. She saw the boom as a purge of the lower classes. "Fifteen thousand dollars a month—who can afford that? Only Googles, Yahoos, Ubers," Fatima told me. "Those big corporations are taking more and more housing, more and more jobs—more and more everything." She wasn't exaggerating: it was possible to spend $15,000 a month—or more—for a two- or three-bedroom luxury apartment in various neighborhoods around the city.

I strolled westward to Hayes Valley, the latest fashionable yuppie mecca, and found a dive bar celebrating its own wake. The Irish immigrant bartender inside told me the neighborhood establishment would be closing for good in a matter of days. What was moving in? I asked. "It'll be another bar," he said, "but with fifteen-dollar cocktails." When I told him I was a writer, he shut up. After another employee had spoken to the press, the owner signed a confidentiality agreement with the landlord. As tech companies established their dominance over the city, more and more mundane aspects of life came to resemble Web-style terms-of-service agreements—unfair, unenforceable, vaguely threatening, and totally rigged. There were even apps for homeless panhandlers to collect Bitcoin, but more popular was an app developed to help the propertied classes report the unwelcome poor to the city's nuisance hotline.

Outside, after dark, I watched a man in a suit pause to hand a few crumpled bills to a hunched beggar woman. His date was not pleased. "God, you're stupid," she snapped.

The growing class divide was written all over the bricks and glass and bathroom tiles of the cityscape. The corporate gentrifiers plastered the skyline with enormous billboards promoting the techie version of domestic bliss, a cross between the households of George Jetson and Ebenezer Scrooge. "It's OK to fire your Robot Butler. He'll land on his wheels," said an ad for Wink, a "smart home" app for people too lazy to press a button to open their garage door, preferring it to rise automatically upon their approach.

The only counterforce to the numbing tide of slick street marketing was, as it always has been, graffiti. However bad the boom was for thousands of long-term San Franciscans forced out by high rents, it at least inspired the city's spraycan artistes. Otherwise sterile yuppie outposts became canvases for elaborate Chicano-style murals depicting the city's working-class purge. The murals were a neighborhood fixture, but frequently updated, and so they, too, began to depict the Man's new manifestations, with tech-worker shuttle buses and condo towers surrounded by the righteous masses. Every cloying marketing slogan was subject to petulant revision by the black marker brigades. A few sarcastic strokes improved the sign outside an ostensibly charitable "economic development corporation" in the Mission District, which was buying up apartments around the neighborhood to renovate as offices:

ROBOT
~~Human~~ Services Agency
Mission Workforce SLAVE Development Center

The Mission longtimers had no sympathy for robot butlers. They worked starvation wages to deliver meals, pour drinks, and mop up messes left behind by the digital colonizers. What did they get in return? Bad tips and an eviction notice.

The well-off newcomers couldn't help but rub it in. Airbnb, which had perhaps more than any other company contributed directly to the displacement of San Francisco tenants by taking some six thousand units off the long-term rental market, addressed its critics with open contempt. Neighborhood activists placed a municipal referendum on the November 2015 ballot that would have forced the venture-capital-backed startup to compete fairly with existing hotels and rental homes. The measure included provisions to ensure that Airbnb hosts paid taxes, stayed up to code, and reported occupancy and earnings. Among other restrictions, it also limited short-term rental hosting to permanent city residents. In response, Airbnb took its lobbying efforts from City Hall to the streets. Before the election, the company bought sneering billboards that advertised how much money they had contributed to the city:

Dear SF Tax Collector,
You know the $12 million in hotel taxes? Don't spend
it all in one place.
Love, Airbnb

Of course, Airbnb had only paid those taxes after a fight.
A second billboard carried on impudently:

But . . . if you do spend all $12 million in one place,
we suggest burritos.
Love, Airbnb

The anti-Airbnb measure was defeated, but turnout was significantly lower than the previous year and the winning side represented a mere 18 percent of eligible voters. Such was the state of
local democracy in San Francisco. "If the poor don't like it, let 'em
buy their own city," one Sharpie-wielding vandal opined on a wall
in the Mission.

As broke as I was, I was still an appendage of the tech industry,
and I absorbed some of the contempt the natives directed toward
newcomers. For those who had trouble picking up on passive-
aggressive West Coast social cues, someone helpfully put up flyers:

NEW TO THE CITY? WORK IN TECH?
YOU'RE A PLAGUE
AND LOCALS
FUCKING HATE YOU
LEAVE

• • • • •

I didn't make the cut for 20Mission, and I couldn't afford to stay in Hacker Condo, but I did manage to find another, longer-term, and significantly cheaper Airbnb that made no pretense of being a collaborative workspace for entrepreneurial techies, although it still attracted those types. This place was in a neighborhood called Excelsior, which means "still higher, ever upward," but that really depended on which direction you were going. For me, every slope ran downhill.

I had reason to suspect that moving into Excelsior House would mean trading sanity for affordability. There was, for instance, the deeply annoying and legalistic "house manual," which forbade, among other things, "hang[ing] out" in the kitchen during meal times. It went on, and on, and on:

> No smoking. No illegal drugs. No parties or
>   disruptive behavior. No pets.
> Must be independent.
> Be financially responsible.
> Please provide your own toiletries.

The rule about drugs could safely be ignored. However, some of the rules, curiously specific and yet forbiddingly cryptic, gave me pause. "Must be independent"? I supposed that meant "No whining." The stipulation that guests "be financially responsible" was strange, considering the rent was paid up front.

The ad also mentioned that I would have to sign an additional contract upon checking in. Whatever. I took heart in the tepid expressions of gratitude found in the online guestbook: "Overall, does the trick," ran a typical comment. And it was hard to argue with the rent: $38 per night, or $1,000 per month. "Your place looks perfect," I wrote to the host, Luna. I paid two months up front and packed my bags.

I arrived midafternoon. The house was a dull military green. It faced a concrete noise barrier that unfortunately blocked what would otherwise have been a clear view of the freeway. The door was secured by an electronic lock with a ten-digit keypad. Luna had given me the code, so I let myself in. There was no light in the dusty hall. The curtains were closed, and the creaky wooden floors seemed to absorb whatever ambient light remained. "Hello?" I said. No one answered.

Inside, there was nowhere to turn. To the left was a locked door—one of the bedrooms. To the right was a tall folding screen. The screen sectioned off what had once been a small living room. Now the room had two cots lined up on either side, leaving an aisle a few feet wide for luggage and maneuvering. I guessed that was why "living room" wasn't named in the short list of designated common areas. I walked down the hall. White printouts were taped in various spots along the walls, which were painted the same dreary grayish green as the exterior of the house. One printout was decorated with catalog photos of surveillance cameras. "Be Aware this area is monitored," it said. There were several copies of this notice in different areas of the house. Google may have brought the surveillance state into my email, but Airbnb put twenty-four-hour surveillance cameras in my kitchen.

The kitchen, by the way, was the best room in the house, full of fresh air and natural light. It was too bad I had agreed not to "hang out" in there.

I found the door to my room unlocked, the keys resting on a desk. Besides a door that locked, the room had several other amenities I'd come to miss, including a mini-fridge and, for some reason, four reading lamps. I unpacked completely for the first time in a long time. Then I decorated my room with a string of festive rainbow bunting my wife had packed to remind me of home. It may have been a claustrophobic dump by the freeway, but it was mine, for now. It even had a window. I pulled back the sheer blue curtain. The view was of another window—someone else's bedroom. A narrow space in between allowed sunlight to trickle down for a few minutes each day. I trusted that the pervasive dimness would keep me focused.

I returned to the kitchen to copy the internet password from one of the printouts taped to the wall. Across the room stood a lumbering figure in a stained white tank top draped loosely over the black curly down that covered his chest, arms, and back. This was Mike. He was a man of middle age, well over six feet tall and pushing three hundred pounds. A bandage covered one of his knees, which bowed gingerly beneath his baggy gray workout shorts, and he walked with a limp. Mike hurt his knee in the navy, from which he had recently retired. But apart from that injury, and his tendency to leave stilted all-caps communiqués around the kitchen announcing impending fridge cleanings and such, Mike betrayed few indications of his martial background. Whatever else had happened to him in the navy, Mike had learned to keep his head down. He was needlessly apologetic and easily startled. "Oh!" he said when I entered the kitchen.

I asked how long he'd been living in the basement. One year, he said.

"How do you like it?" I asked.

"It sucks," he said.

"Oh," I said.

"It's the cheapest place in San Francisco," he said.

"Yeah," I said. "So how is the landlord, Luna? I haven't met her yet."

"In my experience, the less we see of Luna, the better," Mike said.

"Why is that?" I asked.

Mike, suddenly contrite, stammered. "I shouldn't have said that," he said. "Never mind. I didn't say that." He seemed almost afraid.

Luna managed several other properties that were listed on Airbnb, each with its own scattered records of reviews. When I finally pieced them together, I realized why Mike had seemed so spooked. He desperately wanted to move. To do so, he would need Luna's reference. And Luna did not take criticism well. When one former guest complained about the cleanliness of her accommodations, Luna replied, "I guess [she] just wants to destroy my reputation as a host due to her own bitterness." To a couple who likewise found the standards subpar, Luna gave no quarter: "They left the mattress stained, broke the toilet handle, stained the sheets, towel, etc. I would not host them again." When another woman deemed it "sketchy" that Luna was renting out the living room, Luna delivered a coup de grâce: "her behavior was abhorrent . . . she brought 2 drifter guys whom she picked out of nowhere . . . I hope that the information above is helpful to her next potential airbnb host."

Most of these critical reviews actually pulled punches. The broken bed frame murdered my spine every night. The overcrowding was absurd. It sometimes took as long as an hour to get a turn in the bathroom, which was filthy, and where the only roll of toilet paper had MIKE scrawled across the top in Sharpie. The prevalence of misleadingly positive reviews could only be explained by the system of mutually assured destruction implicit in the Airbnb review process. Praise was usually repaid in kind. However, the merest tremble of complaint, however valid, was sure to be answered with devastating slander. One previous guest wrote that when she and her boyfriend accidentally checked out late, Luna "threatened to keep our airbnb deposit unless we gave her a positive review."

"I was not blackmailing her," Luna replied. "She should have followed policy."

In Luna's telling, the restrictive house rules were necessary to restrain her barbaric guests. "People were being too social," Luna complained. Her solution, the common-area curfew, was all too effective. When guests passed one another, they most often avoided eye contact, dashed into their rooms, and slammed the doors.

In all, there were nine people living in four upstairs rooms and the living room. Downstairs, there were three proper bedrooms and I don't know how many people. Across the hall from me lived two culinary students with night jobs in restaurants across the

Bay. In less than six months, they'd already moved between three different Airbnbs. And they'd have to move again in a week, because Luna refused to give them an extension on rent when their paychecks came late. The black woman on the cot in the living room always left early in the morning, returned late at night, and spoke rarely. A South Asian family of three shared a single room down the hall. They spoke no English, so I never got their story. By mid-June most of the rooms were claimed by college boys, all white or East Asian, in town for their summer internships at Google and other tech companies.

Luna claimed she "serve[d] a niche in the airbnb community." Yup. It was the niche once known as "affordable housing," now Slums as a Service.

The daily simmer of demographic malice and spite spilled over in every direction. Which is not to say that everyone was equally to blame. The migratory tech bourgeoisie were naïve at best, bigoted at worst, and generally clueless about their surroundings, even by the standards of twentysomethings from the suburbs. My tech bro roommates were a sheltered lot. Apart from the mysteries of women and the demands of work, their greatest source of anxiety seemed to be San Francisco itself. The city and its people—especially Latinos, blacks, and the homeless—frightened them. "No one told me I'd be sleeping next to a *black woman*," gasped one Google intern, a young Asian American man who occupied the other half of the partitioned living room. It struck me that she probably didn't expect to share a room with a maladjusted racist, either—but it was he who complained to the landlady, and he who switched rooms.

Rarely were such biases so plainly stated. To the spoiled middle-class consumers flooding Silicon Valley and the Bay Area, everything came down to a matter of preference. The assumptions of cutthroat libertarianism were so embedded in the worldview of these lucky newcomers that they spoke as though the victims of tech-fueled displacement and gentrification had chosen to live in poverty and squalor, just as they themselves chose to learn to code, chose a management-track job at a major corporation, and chose to set themselves up for a comfortable upper-middle-class suburban life. "In Mountain View, the houses are so nice. It's like a small town instead of a dirty big city," another Google intern, this one from the Czech Republic, told me. He intended to move out of the city the second he got hired. Yet another stripling, this one working at a bank downtown, had bigger plans. "I'm going to wait until the next recession and buy up all the houses here," he said.

"Yeah, but you don't know when it will be," the Czech replied. "It could be fifty years."

"Five years, fifty years—it will happen. That's what I'm doing," the budding banker said.

These kids knew it was their destiny to inherit the place. Systematically and faster than anyone expected, the city was being remade to cater to the tastes and prejudices of these callow child princes.

Speaking of taste: They didn't have any.

To save money, I took to cooking my own meals most of the

time. This was when I discovered that it was much easier to launch a tech startup if you could afford to always have food delivered and never had to deal with mundane chores such as doing laundry, washing dishes, or buying groceries. As one Twitter wag observed, San Francisco's "tech culture is focused on solving one problem: What is my mother no longer doing for me?"

I never felt older nor crankier than when watching these "digital natives" stumble through the daily rituals of adulthood. One of the kids, an overachieving Ivy Leaguer whose Google internship demanded an advanced understanding of high-level mathematics, was completely baffled when it came to using a simple rice cooker. His helplessness vexed me because he ate rice for most meals. I explained the process: Put in rice, add water, press the button labeled Cook. He grew increasingly flustered, and I suspected he wanted me to make the rice for him. He managed to sauté a boneless, skinless chicken breast, but only by following the instructions on the package to the letter. "How did it turn out?" I asked.

"It's terrible. Bland," he said. "I'm full, that's all that matters. I don't care how it tastes."

When I first heard about Soylent, the startup selling a gooey "meal replacement beverage" powder with a determinedly "neutral" flavor, I wondered what sort of miserable insensates would choose to subsist on such glop. Now I knew. The Czech ate nothing except boiled eggs at home. Another Googler preferred dry pan-fried toast. Mostly, they never cooked at all, because their employers hired people to do that for them.

If the techies shared an enviable certitude regarding their future careers, they were lost as to their personal desires, except when those desires concerned consumer products. I came into the kitchen one night and found one of my roommates at the kitchen table staring intently into some video on his smartphone. Was he watching a movie? No: he was watching shoe advertisements, one after another. Whenever the Czech finished his walk home from his chartered bus stop, he boiled an egg, opened his laptop on the kitchen counter, and loaded his favorite online fantasy-themed card game. "So that's what you do: you just come home, play video games, and go to bed?" another housemate asked. "Basically, yes," he said.

It may have been better for everyone when the overpaid nerds stayed home. "All the young people who live here work in tech and finance. This city has produced art and culture for decades. It's become sterile," said a retirement-age white woman whom I met passing out antigentrification flyers outside City Hall. "Talk about Android phones—the people are androids. They're boring." Some saw a grand philistine conspiracy engineered by the tech giants to destroy the old, simple pleasures and replace them with brand-sponsored, demographically targeted multimedia lifestyle experiences. "They're importing children to destroy the culture," one young but old-school bar owner told me. Such resentments were not confined to those outside the industry. "The internet is dirty, man," said a tech company grunt who wanted nothing more than to be a musician. "I grew up here. All my life. It used to be a great center of culture. Now it's this," he said, miming masturbation with his beer bottle. "Whose app is bigger? Whose dick is bigger?"

Indeed, to overhear the baby-faced billionaire wannabes exchanging boastful inanities in public could be enraging. Their inevitable first question: "What's your space?" Not "How's it going?" Not "Where are you from?" "What's your space?" *Over there across the room*, I always wanted to say. This was perhaps the most insufferable bit of tech jargon I heard. "What's your space?" meant "What does your company do?" This was not quite the same as asking "What do you do for a living?" because one's company may well produce no living at all. One's "space" had an aspirational quality one's day job never would. If you flipped hamburgers all day, you wouldn't say "I'm a fry cook," you'd say "I'm in the carbonized protein space." If you were a gravedigger, you'd say "I'm in the lifecycle fulfillment space." If you were a writer, you would never say "I'm a writer." You'd say "I'm in the content space," or, if you were more ambitious, "I'm in the media space." But if you were *really* ambitious you'd know that "media" was out and "platforms" were in, and that the measure—excuse me, the "metric"—that investors used to judge platform companies was attention, because this ephemeral thing, attention, could be sold to advertisers for cash. So if someone asked "What's your space?" and you had a deeply unfashionable job like, say, writer, it behooved you to say "I deliver eyeballs like a fucking ninja."

In my former life I'd have sooner gouged my own eyeballs out than describe myself in such a way, but in postrecession, postboom, postwork, postshame San Francisco, we all did what we had to do to survive.

III

Gigs Make Us Free

I envied the tech workers even as I pitied them. The paychecks weren't bad at all, and the benefits were downright Dionysian. Their industry was the alien invader that consumed everything it touched. Its radioactive presence may have sterilized the outside world, stifling organic life in all forms, but inside the warm embrace of the mother ship, the worker drones had comfort, stimulation, and plenty.

A corporate recruiter explained to me the forces driving the "perks war," an escalating tit-for-tat of such freebies as steak dinners delivered to employees' desks, free laundry service, free bikes and bike repair, free concierge service, and of course free drinks. "They might get a twenty-dollar steak, but with the extra time they've stayed at work, they've provided an extra two hundred dollars in value to their employer," the recruiter said. Thus the seemingly lavish enticements were a way to attract profit-producing programmers, who were in exceedingly high demand, without offering higher salaries. The perks also provided effective cover for the companies' slave-driving work schedules.

But my intern roommates seemed happy with the arrangement, at least at first. "Everything they say about Google is true," one intern told me after his orientation at the Googleplex. "There are twenty cafeterias, a gym—everything." Early every weekday morning, he and the other Googlers in his neighborhood swiped their ID cards to board a chartered bus parked near the BART station, then rode thirty-five miles to Mountain View. They started working onboard the bus, which was equipped with WiFi, and didn't leave the campus until sometime around 8 p.m., when another bus ferried them home after they ate at the company cafeteria. This was a pretty standard deal at the big Silicon Valley companies. Even rinky-dink startups in SoMa warehouses offered free catering. "The perks, man!" another roommate, a non-Googler, raved after arriving home at 10 p.m. from his first day on the job. "I worked until nine because dinner is free if you work that late . . . And they'll pay for your cab home," he went on. That became his routine, and he never questioned it. Come to think of it, like a lot of his contemporaries, he never questioned *anything*.

In this milieu, a certain tolerance for phoniness was a prerequisite. It was not enough to have the right skills, put in your time, and get the job done—you had to be *fucking pumped* about your job, or else it was time to find a new one. Certain specialties were in more demand than others. Any chump with a humanities degree could talk his or her way into a marketing job, but programmers were harder to come by. One sunny day I followed the waterfront to the event center at Pier 27 and signed in to the DeveloperWeek conference. DevWeek, as everyone called it, was basically a weeklong recruitment fair sprinkled with slideshows and panel talks. It was jarring to see employers desperate to hire, not the other way around. In 2010s America, the only place that was always hiring, apart from Silicon Valley, was the local U.S. Army recruiting center. Hundreds upon hundreds of people had flocked here to look for a better job and still there were not enough applicants to fill all the openings for "Java Legends, Python Badasses, Hadoop Heroes," and other gratingly childish classifications describing various programming specialties. As exciting as it was to plunge into the bustle of a boomtown hiring hall, something about the ridiculous job titles got under my skin. The West Coast techies were alienated from their neighbors, the natives, not only by habit and custom but also by language. Techies would call themselves just about anything to avoid the stigmatizing label of "worker." They could only face themselves in the mirror if their business card proved that they were rock stars or ninjas or something romantic and brave and individualistic—anything but the truth, anything but a drone.

The official language of DevWeek was an impenetrable digital argot. The schedule was packed with events and panels with titles like "Integrating Browserify and Gulp with Sprockets" and "Enterprise Apps Are Not as Boring as You Might Think" (I begged to differ). I didn't understand half of what anyone was saying, but that was okay, because I found so many new things to get passionate about. The convention sprawled through the pier terminal, filling cavernous carpeted chambers and descending to the water line, where tents and portable heaters were erected on cold concrete floors. I flitted from table to table and panel to panel, collecting colorful brochures and absorbing up-to-the-minute jargon. I sampled passions like I was shopping for a new pair of blue jeans:

> I am passionate about the internet of things.
> I am passionate about big data.
> I am passionate about machine learning.
> I am passionate about key-value stores.
> I am passionate about a native ticketing
>   experience.
> I am passionate about an integration
>   platform-as-a-service.

I had an important realization at DevWeek: I wasn't the only one bluffing my way through the tech scene. Everyone was doing it, even the much-sought-after engineering talent. I was struck by how many developers were, like myself, not really programmers, but rather this, that, and the other. A great number of tech ninjas were not exactly black belts when it came to the actual onerous work of computer programming. So many of the complex, discrete tasks involved in the creation of a website or an app had been routinized and automated that it was no longer necessary to possess an extensive or even fundamental knowledge of software mechanics. The coder's work was rarely a craft. The apps ran on an assembly line, built with "open-source" off-the-shelf components. The most important computer commands for the ninja to master were Copy and Paste. Many of the hottest startups were built by patching other people's code together with the virtual equivalent of duct tape and chicken wire.

A little know-how went a long way. Total ignorance went pretty far, too.

At one of the DevWeek afterparties in a bar near the pier, I met a self-assured professional woman who had moved from Texas, where she worked for small startups, to the Bay Area, where she joined a large company. Then something remarkable happened. At the same time she took that new job, she also happened to discover her passion for user interfaces. "UI," she said, "is everything." Although she had no technical background, the large company put the Texan in charge of a team of highly specialized engineers. Thus she had only a limited understanding of what her subordinates did all day. That was by design. "My role is, I'm stupid, I don't know how anything works, and if I can't figure out how to use this in four seconds, it's over," she said. I could tell she was passionate about being stupid.

Tech companies exploited a variety of well-honed managerial tactics to sow mischief and precarity. The largest favored "stack ranking," which pits colleagues and departments against one another in a mad scramble to stay out of the lowest-rated percentile during performance reviews and thus avoid a pink slip. Large and small companies employed "agile" and "scrum" procedures that gave clueless managers a way to discipline and control engineers whose work they could neither reproduce independently nor competently evaluate. The hipper, newer startups, meanwhile, promised fun and flexibility yet delivered a bevy of even more depraved employment practices, from discriminatory hiring to widespread wage theft. Silicon Valley's relentless profit hunger, combined with its mastery of the latest productivity tools and managerial techniques, forced workers to push themselves harder and harder, and to keep smiling about it, until they were all used up.

Tech company employees weren't the only ones stuck on this grueling hamster wheel. Entrepreneurs, the nominal bosses of these companies, ground themselves into the dirt as well for the benefit of their own bosses, the venture capitalists.

Startups promised independence and financial freedom to people desperate for a taste of both. But most startup "chief executives" possessed little of either, for investors typically managed the process from founding to exit. I asked one cheerfully cynical VC over beers, "Are startup founders capital, or are they labor?" It depends, he replied. "Mark Zuckerberg is capital. But for every Zuckerberg there's one hundred guys who basically got fired from their startups. They aren't capital. They're labor," he said. They were ideal laborers, too, being allergic to the concept of solidarity. These founders worked like dogs, and until they struck it rich—which most never did—they often lived in barrackslike quarters not much more comfortable than my own. Somehow it still seemed they had the best deal going.

I found that most startup founders told the truth about their sorry circumstances only while drunk or from behind the cover of anonymity. It was easy to find cracks in the veneer of enthusiasm even on the relentlessly enthusiastic news and discussion website Hacker News. A sample of some questions submitted by different users to the "Ask HN" feature of the site gives the flavor of the stress and anxiety plaguing those who struck out on their own seeking treasure in Silicon Valley:

> Should I pretend that my startup is already successful?
> What should I do if I feel burnt out?
> How many years have you "wasted" on failed startups?
> My startup failed. $9k in debt and need to pay most
> of it in 12 days.
> I Used My Credit Cards to Fund My Failed Startup
> and Now They're Suing
> Startup life: Working hard to enrich other people?
> Have you had trouble getting a job after a failed
> startup?
> Just what exactly is "real-world experience" and how
> do I get it?
> Joining the military?
> About to be homeless, any ideas . . . ?
> How do you fight depression?
> Why keep living?
> Could we crowdfund a therapist who is available to
> depressed hackers?

Here was the story of the 95 percent of entrepreneurs who failed. It was the story of, among others, Adrian—the geeky guy with the giant yellow iPhone holster I'd met at a party regaling passersby with tales from his Groupon knockoff. For all his geekish suave, there was something sad about Adrian. Once fully lubricated, he laid it all out for me. After studying at community college, Adrian worked for years as a manager at a retail chain as well as a restaurant. Those jobs were stressful enough. But as a startup founder he felt constantly on the verge of total burnout. He no longer took time off on the weekends, or put in less than a twelve-hour day during the workweek, without triggering feelings of overwhelming guilt and the subtle scorn of his colleagues, who were also his friends. As for money, he earned less as a CEO than he would have if he had taken a regular job at the company. He had no health insurance, not even Obamacare. His apartment sucked. His litany continued. I tried pointing out Adrian's many achievements: He had found investors! He had raised millions of dollars! He was walking the path to greatness! He was like a role model to millions!

"If I had to do it all over again," he told me, shoulders slumped, "I'd have gone to work for the government."

I wish I had told him then that it was okay to quit. I didn't. I wished him luck. About a year later, when writing this, I decided to see what Adrian was up to.

The news was not good.

Adrian's startup had floundered, as he described in an emotional blog post. He fell deeper into debt and had trouble making rent. Approximately three months after I met him, Adrian walked to a local chain drug store, purchased several large bottles of extra-strength painkillers, returned to his apartment, and swallowed enough pills to end his life, or so he hoped. As it happened, Adrian's online research into suicide methods had turned up false information. Instead of drifting painlessly into a fatal coma, he spent twelve hours writhing on the floor of his apartment in agony, passing in

and out of consciousness. After vomiting, he crawled to his cell phone
and called 911. An ambulance came. More bodily torments followed
in the emergency room, where doctors and nurses probed his ori-
fices and purged his guts in order to save his life. Adrian luckily
survived the hospital without losing a kidney, but his next stop was
a psych ward, where the patients who weren't knocked out on seda-
tives were left to occupy themselves with such delights as puzzles
that had missing pieces. Adrian, already a private cynic when it came
to startup culture, said he learned one thing from his experience:
Corporations don't care about people. But he was glad to be alive,
and working as a headwaiter at a midmarket chain restaurant.

The saddest thing about people like Adrian was that they hadn't
suffered from some outsize ambition. They were only doing what
they were told. Barack Obama's White House had endorsed Silicon Valley's "learn to code" campaign—it was an official government job-creation program. With the traditional U.S. job market
still a smoldering charcoal pit after the 2008 crash, computer programming skills were promoted as one sure way to attain the sort
of prosperity and stability Americans had over many decades
come to expect—nice house, new car, good credit, big TV, full medicine cabinet, all the latest toys, and a retirement plan.

But why, then, were so many programmers who'd "made it" in
Silicon Valley scrambling to promote themselves from coder to
"founder"? There wasn't necessarily more money to be had running
a startup, and the increase in status was marginal unless one's
startup attracted major investment and the right kind of press
coverage. It's because the programmers knew that their own ladder
to prosperity was on fire and disintegrating fast. They knew that

well-paid programming jobs would also soon turn to smoke and ash, as the proliferation of learn-to-code courses around the world lowered the market value of their skills, and as advances in artificial intelligence allowed for computers to take over more of the mundane work of producing software. The programmers also knew that the fastest way to win that promotion to founder was to find some new domain that hadn't yet been automated. Every tech industry campaign designed to spur investment in the Next Big Thing—at that time, it was the "sharing economy"—concealed a larger program for the transformation of society, always in a direction that favored the investor and executive classes.

In the first seven years after the 2008 crash, sixteen million people left the U.S. labor force. And in that same period, thanks to Silicon Valley's timely opportunism, the country gained an endless bounty of *gigs*. Tech startups, backed by Wall Street, swept in to offer displaced workers countless push-button moneymaking schemes—what Bloomberg News called "entrepreneurialism-in-a-box." Need fast cash? Take out a "peer-to-peer" loan, or start a crowdfunding campaign. Need a career? Take on odd jobs as a TaskRabbit or pitch corporate swag as a YouTube "vlogger." Nine-to-five jobs with benefits and overtime may be in the process of getting disrupted out of existence, but in their place we have the internet, with endless gigs and freelance opportunities, where survival becomes something like a video game—a matter of pressing the right buttons to attain instant gratification and meager rewards.

More than a third of American workers now qualify as "freelancers" or "contingent workers"—that is, their livelihoods are contingent upon the whims of their managers. That's because the choice to become entrepreneurs has been made for them. The destruction of social welfare, public education, and organized labor has created what might be called the 50 Cent economy, a system structured to offer only two options: "Get rich or die trying." President George W. Bush called it the "ownership society." Obama, smitten with his Silicon Valley donors, gave us "Startup America." And Donald Trump, history's luckiest winner, reigned over a nation of "losers." Under the latest iteration of the American Dream, if you aren't a billionaire yet, you haven't tried hard enough.

There was no place more appropriate to begin my conquest of the new gig economy than in the proverbial basement—from there, after all, I had nowhere to go but up. The contemporary equivalent of an entry-level job in the corporate mailroom was a work-from-home service called Mechanical Turk, operated by Amazon, the $136 billion online retailer controlled by Jeff Bezos. The idea with Mechanical Turk was to create a digitized assembly line featuring thousands of discrete "Human Intelligence Tasks," designed to be completed within seconds and commensurately paying pennies. Academic surveys found that many Turkers worked more than thirty hours per week for average wages of under $2 per hour. Yet these workers were considered self-employed small business owners. Their work was commissioned by social scientists seeking to cut costs on large-sample surveys, but also by profit-minded companies that hired hundreds of Turkers as needed, instead of a full- or part-time employee. The trick was to break the necessary work into a series of discrete and minuscule tasks appropriate for the structure of Amazon's platform. The jobs that were most easily deconstructed in such a way tended to be internet-based business-to-business services, such as "search engine optimization" marketing or bulk data processing, as well as scammy operations like fake news clickbait factories seeking to profit by arbitraging between the price of labor on Mechanical Turk and the value of a click from an online advertising broker.

Speed, efficiency, and endurance—self-robotization, basically—were the keys to Turking success. Most of the tasks listed on the service were gruelingly monotonous:

- Click on specific Google
  search result   Reward: $0.05
- Looking at a receipt
  image, identify the
  business of the receipt   Reward: $0.01

Some tasks required slightly more creativity:

- Describe the picture in
  a complete sentence using
  10 words or more   Reward: $0.01
- Write 5 alternative headlines
  for the following   Reward: $0.05

When I was a news editor, I got paid a lot more for the same work. But then my work was judged based on quality. Turking was strictly a volume business. Which wasn't to say it lacked personality:

- Teach a computer
  the meaning of family   Reward: $0.65
- Rate dating profile photos   Reward: $0.03
- Flag offensive content images   Reward: $0.01

The Mechanical Turk listings provided an unsettling look at the seedy underbelly of the internet economy, for many websites employed Turkers to serve as on-demand censors. Turkers who signed on for such work sometimes found themselves the unwitting recipients of illegal child porn. This bargain basement labor market, conceived as a vehicle for the realization of free market ideals, had created a strange subculture of digital trash pickers, damaged mentally by the torrent of horrors they endured, and often physically by repetitive motion disorders.

A Turker's life was not for me. I applied but was rejected by some Amazonian algorithm. "Our account review criteria are proprietary and we cannot disclose the reason why," the email said. The lonesome sterility of their presentation made one wish for a crowded old-time union hiring hall—or an unemployment line, for that matter.

There were more entertaining ways to scrape pennies together while facing a lifetime of permanent redundancy. Another website, Twitch.tv, catered to gamers and helped some earn money from their hobby by allowing them to broadcast footage of their gameplay to viewers around the world. When Amazon bought Twitch for $970 million, in 2015, the site had 60 million users—three times the audience of NBC's *Sunday Night Football*. Approximately eleven thousand of those users were earning at least a little bit of money as "Twitch Partners" by maintaining a frequent broadcast schedule and developing a large following. It may not be obvious why anyone would want to watch other people play video games, to say nothing of companies paying people to play them. Twitch should be seen as one part of corporate America's effort to control a new medium that it had created, yet still barely understood. The Twitch Partners were the beneficiaries of a larger effort by marketing departments far and wide to anoint new celebrities who were fit to serve as advertising vehicles to a younger audience that was resistant to more traditional methods. I spent a few days playing computer games and trying to break in to this scene, but it quickly became clear I was well past my prime.

No longer the path to ostracism, video games had become an ever-present feature of daily life for billions of people. This was all the more true in the software industry, where video games were the extracurricular activity of choice. The games by their very design had lessons to teach about risk and reward, about life and work as a series of progressive stages, about acquisitiveness and accomplishment and competition. Therefore it was no surprise that Silicon Valley was intent upon "gamifying" all aspects of human behavior. Corporations were spending hundreds of millions of dollars on "funsultants" who provided advice on "enterprise gamification"—filling the most menial wage labor with "fun"

82   Corey Pein

Pavlovian rewards and punishments. According to the futurist Ray Kurzweil, there soon "won't be a clear distinction between work and play." If that seems far-fetched, consider how successfully Facebook gamified friendship.

Sex, too, became a game, as well as a profit opportunity, on sites like Chaturbate. As the name implied, Chaturbate was Twitch for sex shows, some of which appeared to be staged in actual brothels. Viewers could pay approximately $0.10 to receive a virtual token, which they could then tip to performers, who received less than $0.05 after Chaturbate's anonymous owners took their cut. Apart from the miserable pay, masturbating for pennies was not as easy as it sounded. Camgirls' forums were filled with sad stories about panic attacks, post-traumatic flashbacks, abusive customers, and costly website glitches. "I don't have any real friends," one camgirl wrote. "They are all at university or living their lives or having new relationships and I feel thoroughly forgotten about." While traditional social institutions left such underemployed, undereducated young people behind, the postwork sharing economy came to the rescue by affording them the opportunity to serve as virtual strippers. Who says the tech industry doesn't make room for women?

The sharing economy's greatest success story was a YouTube celebrity for whom work and play and reality and artifice had merged beyond all recognition. There were many dubious aspects of his rise to stardom, not the least of which was his politics, beginning with the name he chose for himself: PewDiePie. It sounds even stranger when spoken, often in a drawn-out, high-pitched whine—"Pew-Dee-Piiiiiieee!" PewDiePie's real name is Felix Kjellberg, and he lives in Brighton, England, same as I once did, but in a much nicer house. PewDiePie's YouTube channel had racked up 10 billion views and 40 million subscribers and counting. And all he did was play video games on camera. PewDiePie shrieked and cursed and made strange burbling noises as he mowed down virtual monsters, to the delight of his young, mostly male following, the "bro army."

Ending most videos with a "brofist"—better known as a fist bump—aimed at the camera, PewDiePie was a kind of surrogate older brother to millions of gamer tweens. His angular Swedish features suggested a fallback career with a third-rate boy band. His pretty Italian girlfriend was also a YouTube celebrity by the name of CutiePieMarzia. Their personality cult wasn't only about good looks and lifestyle envy. PewDiePie was an existential bro, and his persistent whingeing about the vacuity of existence resonated with his screen-addled tween audience. As he put it: "I just feel so empty, you know? Hashtag *relatable*!"

When a Swedish newspaper reported that PewDiePie was earning up to $7 million a year from his videos, he responded defensively to jealous "haters":

> They thought I just sit on my ass all day and I just yell at the screen over here—which is true. But there's so much more to it than that ... It really doesn't matter what you think. Life is not fair. It's just how it is. If you think someone else is funnier, go refresh their videos over and over, because that's how we get paid.

PewDiePie's income was dependent upon the existence of a video game industry that had grown to $61 billion in annual sales. Although a kind of pitchman, he had forsworn sponsorships, meaning his multimillion-dollar income came entirely from his cut of the ad revenue, via Google. Eventually he did take on sponsorships, including from Disney. The money was too good to pass up. But it came with scrutiny, and this was PewDiePie's downfall. He couldn't handle criticism. He grew paranoid. In December 2016, he announced that his benefactors at YouTube were conspiring to knock him off the number 1 spot and replace him with "someone really cancerous"—a Desi Indian woman. "I'm white. Can I make that comment? But I do think that's a problem," a visibly agitated PewDiePie told the bro army. Certain tendencies, once subdued, became clear. He took to sprinkling swastika imagery and audio clips from "Deutschland über Alles" into his video game commentary. He bleached his hair platinum blond and filmed himself giving a Nazi salute. In January 2017, he posted a video in which two shirtless Indian men held up a banner that read DEATH TO ALL JEWS. PewDiePie said it was all just a joke, but Disney yanked its lucrative sponsorship of his channel, and YouTube kicked him out of its "preferred" advertiser program. So his income suffered, but PewDiePie's bro army remained loyal, and each new video he published still got millions of views.

The "Death to All Jews" clip wasn't something PewDiePie had stumbled across on the internet. He had set it up by using a website called Fiverr to hire those Indian men to record themselves holding up a sign with his chosen message. Another sharing economy upstart, Fiverr was a catalog of freelance "gigs," from illustration to translation, all sold at a fixed cost of $5. Launched in 2010 by two Israeli techies, Fiverr raised more than $50 million in investment within five years, on annual revenue of $15 million. Silicon Valley investors praised the founders' "incredible vision" and swooned over the "liquidity, velocity and engagement" the company brought to the global marketplace.

The founders said Fiverr would be the world's next billion-dollar company by disrupting the services sector. "We're not interested in making people slaves until they die," CEO Micha Kaufman said.

Of course not.

The internet had plenty of freelance directories before Fiverr came along. Fiverr's sole innovation was also its crippling limitation. The fixed-fee model created what economists called an "artificial scarcity"—not of goods or services, but of cash. It was like the libertarians' beloved "flat tax," but for wages. Work for fifteen minutes? You made $5. Work for two hours? You still made $5. The consequences were twofold: first, to reduce quality; and second, to lower the cost of labor—not only for those tendering their services on the site, but throughout the broader service economy.

The Fiverr model, by design, constitutes a limited-time profit opportunity for investors, for the only services that make pecuniary sense for sellers are the ones that are the most repetitive and easily deconstructed—and therefore the most likely to become obsolete through automation in the near future. The time bomb nature of this and other sharing economy services suits shareholders just fine, for they will profit at each stage of the process. It is the users—the workers—who will lose the most as technological "progress" comes to the labor market.

· · · · ·

It was remarkable what people were willing to do for $5—more like $3.92 after service fees. A lot of ads promised custom website development. Others offered quick-and-dirty logos, proofreading, or résumé writing. I hoped to forge my place in the strange niche of bargain basement flat-fee consulting. Thousands of people were paying $5 to strangers for direction on matters they found too difficult, too stressful, or too trivial to face alone.

Fiverr's terms of service forbade "nonsense" and "uncool stuff" but the service seemed to tolerate ads like one for an Amazon "Kindle ghostwriting machine"; or another for tools designed "to cheat likes on social networks"; and still another for "a profitable forex cheating strategy"—an obvious scam that Fiverr marked for a while as "recommended." I had entered a murky ethical realm. I didn't get to decide what was cool or uncool—Fiverr did. The penalty for uncoolness was permanent banishment. And I wasn't ready to risk a lifetime in exile.

I scanned gigs methodically. I learned that it paid to overpromise. No matter was too momentous.

· I will teach you to make Life and Death Decisions
  for $5

This gig was listed by a Fiverr-certified "top-rated seller" who claimed experience as a broker of precious metals.

Another popular tactic involved claiming special powers. Heavenly prophets, psychics, shamans—they were all on Fiverr. A "true born Holy Priestess" from Slovenia promised to cast a "powerful

MONEY spell to make you wealthier and rich." Wealthier *and* rich? For $5? Sign me up!

The Holy Priestess enjoyed a 4.9-star rating from two hundred nineteen satisfied customers. To each, she responded quid pro quo with a perfect 5-star buyer rating. Sometimes she even gave a free follow-up consultation. "I used my metal detector," one customer wrote. "Did not find anything." To which the Holy Priestess replied, "The diamond and ruby is lower in the ground."

No wonder she had such stellar reviews. Her looks didn't hurt. The Holy Priestess had snowy skin, round eyes with long eyelashes, finely combed black hair, and bright red lipstick. She could have been a model. Indeed, she was! I found the same portrait on a goth fashion site. More likely, of course, the Holy Priestess was a fraudster who stole the model's image.

Another subset of gigs were topical in nature.

- I will help you Survive the Fatal Ebola Virus
  Epidemic for $5

As far as I knew, there was no cure for Ebola. But who was I to argue with a five-star-rated seller? Could two thousand six hundred seventy-nine customers be wrong? Another gig capitalizing on the deadly pandemic promised "Easy Home Treatment" with over-the-counter drugs. "This is what they are doing in Africa now," the ad said. Alert the World Health Organization!

Still, all was not well in Fiverrville. On the site's discussion boards, sellers swapped stories of unfair competition from scammers, insufficient payments from Fiverr, capricious rules, meager sales, and endless hours. Some sounded genuinely desperate. Fiverr even sent its workers emails about increasing productivity by avoiding depression. Full-time Fiverring took a physical toll, as well, with many slavish gig-peddlers reporting rapid weight gain. "I know what you mean! I bought some jeggings this weekend," one woman wrote. Another commenter saw opportunity. "If anyone is interested," he wrote, "I'm putting together a Fiverr gig where I will be offering online fitness coaching."

Fiverr offered a glimpse at the new model worker: a fat, depressed con artist forever scheming against his comrades, egged on by the distant architects of the virtual marketplace—the only real winners. The company eventually embraced this image and celebrated it with a subway ad campaign featuring a fatigued-looking model with frizzy hair and circles under her eyes. "You eat a coffee for lunch. You follow through on your follow through. Sleep deprivation is your drug of choice," the ad said. "You might be a doer," it concluded. When busyness became a status symbol, the glamorization of exhaustion was inevitable.

A thriving market for testimonials provided a veneer of trustworthiness to . . . whatever the client wanted. The demand for testimonials was driven primarily by other moneymaking schemes on Fiverr and beyond.

One prolific and highly rated Fiverrer, a middle-aged woman going by the name Rhoda Lee, specialized in promoting such frauds. Rhoda was an adjunct college English teacher as well as a "trained, professional actress," with an impressive reel of home-made promo videos. She had one stipulation: "NO DATING SITES OR ADULT SITES." Everything else was okay. Rhoda preferred to

improvise, lending a natural feel to her patter, although any devoted
follower of her work would soon recognize that her endorsements,
delivered as they were through an impressive array of pseudonyms,
were purely transactional:

- Hey, my name is Josephine, and I wanted to share
  my experience using silicone breast forms . . .
- Hey, my name is Erin, and I am very excited to
  be able to share the way I finally took the weight
  off after having two children, using combo
  pilling . . .
- Hey, I'm Nila, and I wanted to offer my very
  positive review . . .
- Hey, my name is Anna, and yes, that really
  was me . . .

Her clients were thrilled. "So natural! OMG!!" wrote one.
Another praised her "authentic real person feel . . . NOT a corporate
mouthpiece." Clearly not. I found her on YouTube as well, recount-
ing another tale of woe with a miraculous happy ending. She
claimed a $79-a-bottle herbal vitamin supplement "effective on all
forms of addiction" had cured her husband's terrible and violent
mood swings after his return from Iraq. Miracle of miracles!

I decided to give Fiverr a try. Setting up shop was easy. I uploaded
a picture of my own smiling face and composed an appealing
self-description.

I am an emergent global entrepreneur determined to change the world through bold, disruptive ideas and the miracle of technology. I have worked at major corporations and small startups. I also have a decade of experience as a multiplatform journalist, writer, editor, and interviewist.

I made up that word, "interviewist." I thought it sounded very cutting-edge and horrible, like "multiplatform."

The next step was to create a gig, beginning with a title. "Choose wisely," the website warned. Each ad could run no more than eighty characters and had to begin with the phrase "I will." I had a fair idea about what I was willing to do. Also what I was unwilling to do. But what was I actually *capable* of doing? The insistent blank space triggered creative paralysis.

I will . . . answer your email?

Terrible idea. I hated answering my own email, so why would I want to answer other people's?

I will . . . wait on hold for you?

Same problem. I would not make my fortune listening to Muzak in Limbo.

I needed to change tack. What was I good at? I was a journalist, but I may as well have claimed ten years as a gravedigger for all the respect that conferred. I had been, briefly and bitterly, a manager. That was it! The public cried out for sage guidance and an iron hand. I could be a Decider.

I will . . . be your boss.

"Too short," Fiverr complained.

I will . . . tell you what to do.

"Just perfect," the computer said.

Still, I needed to specialize. Surely I must possess some useful skill? I pondered. Hmm. In a former life, I wrote reviews. That's how I came up with the idea of selling book recommendations. Sure, people gave those away for free on Amazon, but these would be *personalized*. Even better, I could tell everyone who paid $5 for my advice to *buy my own book*.

Fiverr rejected my first attempt at an ad.

Description contains excessive use of the terms: book

My only recourse was to break out the thesaurus and try again. My revised listing, which was approved, read in part as follows:

Bookstores can be daunting. Reviews can be misleading. Maybe you just don't know where to start—it's OK! . . . Unlike some reviewers, I have read literally hundreds of books.

I wanted to hedge my bets, so I posted a second gig. The basic idea was similar.

- **I will tell you how to vote.**

Elections can pose many difficult questions, chiefly, which of the many competing candidates on the long, confusing ballot deserve your vote?

As an active voter for over a decade . . . I have extensive experience in assessing candidates and their relative merits.

I am happy to ease your Election Day burden. For just $5, I'll help you fill out your ballot . . .

Don't delay! Participate in the democratic process today!

Now to sit back and count the money.

A few days passed with no response. My "analytics" revealed the sad truth.

Clicks	4
Orders	0
Cancellations	0

Zero cancellations! Now there was something to brag about: My customer satisfaction rate was one hundred percent.

But clearly something was wrong with my approach. I needed expert advice—a mentor. Perhaps someone on Fiverr could help?

• • • • •

I found Corey Ferreira through his website, makefiverrmoney.com, which was a marketing vehicle for his e-book, *Fiverr Success: $4000 a Month. 8 Hours of Work a Week.* The e-book cost $17. For $50 more, Corey would throw in one hundred free gig ideas, thirty prerecorded video lessons, an audiobook, and an audio recording of a "webinar." Betting on the empathic bond of our common forename, I emailed Corey to request a Skype chat. He agreed. Then I persuaded him to reveal his secrets for free.

Corey, a Toronto native in his late twenties, had been making money online since the age of sixteen, when he built a website for a friend of his father's and earned $100. Fiverr offered dramatically lower rates, but he saw the service as an opportunity to land more clients. He began by performing simple tasks, like moving a website from one server to another, and upselling his Fiverr customers on more expensive services. It worked. Next he broadened his offerings by aping the top sellers he saw elsewhere on the site, including "technically" violating the terms of service by posting duplicate ads. Although he once advocated a strategy based on volume, with sales targets as high as thirty gigs a day, Corey said he had returned to the concept of upselling.

"People do way too much work for four dollars," he said. No kidding.

Corey joined Fiverr at "probably just the right time"—three years ahead of me. "When I started out," he said, "the slogan was, 'What will you do for $5?' Not anymore." After Fiverr "blew up" as a market for full-time freelancers and entrepreneurs, he noticed it had begun to cannibalize his outside earnings by forcing offsite providers to lower their rates to stay competitive. For instance, he had grown accustomed to online copywriting rates of approximately one penny per word. Fiverr pushed the going rate down to half a cent per word. Over time, the same halving manifested in his overall gross from the site. "I don't make as much money as I used to," Corey told me. "At one point I was making four thousand dollars a month from Fiverr. It was basically my full-time job. I had to put off Web design. Now it's about half that."

Faced with slowing business, Corey adopted a new approach. He could "sell the method." He got the idea from a book called *The Laptop Millionaire*, which describes "a guy's journey from being basically homeless to making money online. One of the things he talks about is making 'information products.'" Hence *Fiverr Success* by Corey Ferreira was born, selling "hundreds" of copies. Many buyers were full-time Fiverrers in places like the Philippines or India, where $5 went a lot farther, he said. The book also marked a transition for Corey, as he spent less time doing the labor-intensive Web design and more time searching for the cold fusion of internet marketing: "passive income." This was shorthand for a variety of techniques whereby one could generate wealth while sitting around doing nothing. Some were proven yet not easily attainable, such as living off the compound interest from one's investments and savings. Others—unlike Corey's methods—were elaborate, unworkable, or illegal, such as pyramid schemes and spambot-powered credit card fraud. Compared to more reliable methods of generating passive income, like inheriting a trust fund, these scams had a relatively low barrier to entry. Either way, the appeal was self-evident. "It comes to a point where trading your time for money—it's limiting, you know?" Corey said. Oh, I knew.

If Fiverr didn't produce a fast fortune, there was always the Next Big Thing. "Fiverr is like the new eBay," he said. His digression took a pensive turn. "I remember when eBay started. I was kinda young. I was already making money then. Everybody was talking about how to make money on eBay. I remember somebody telling me, 'During a gold rush, you should sell shovels.'

"That's kinda what I do with Fiverr," he said.

There was an epiphany buried in Canadian Corey's nostalgia trip. I felt he had let me in on some oracular wisdom. Don't dig for gold: Sell shovels to all the suckers who think they'll get rich digging for gold. To post an ad on Fiverr was to announce one's status as an easy mark. To hawk get-rich-quick manuals to all those eager Fiverrers, however, was to join the exalted ranks of the shovel merchants. My Airbnb landlord, I realized, was a shovel merchant. As was the company that rented me server space for website hosting. As were the "startup community organizers" selling tickets to conferences and networking parties. As were the startup awards shows and Hacker News and the whole Silicon Valley economic apparatus promoting the ideal of individual achievement. We startup wannabes were not entrepreneurs. We were suckers for the shovel merchants, who were much cleverer than the thick-skulled "innovators" who did all the work while trading away the rewards. Selling shovels wasn't the only way to make money in tech, but it was . . . *the Silicon Valley way.*

IV

Selling Crack to Children

For a business incompetent such as myself, this concept of selling a method, rather than a straightforward product or service, was revelatory. I understood this lesson as an extension of that old saying about teaching a man to fish instead of just giving him a fish. Now the idea was: you made him pay for fishing lessons, offering student loans if necessary, and failed to mention that you had already depleted the pool. This was a smart business! In a late capitalist society with dwindling opportunities for cash-poor workers and few checks on entrepreneurial conduct, what could be better to sell than false hope? So many hungered for it.

My afternoon email arrived with a warm invitation to get in on the big grift.

Hello Mr. Pein,
My name is Aron. Lately I thought of an idea for a startup:
An application where ordinary people would be able to
take photos of news events, sports events, fashion events
etc. . . . Since you have already been in an organization
that does similar things, I would be thrilled if you could
join me as a co-founder to this endeavor.

I would love to hear from you as soon as you can . . .

Aron Cohen

It was a strange note. I was cautious. But I was also curious. I did some quick research on Aron. His LinkedIn résumé claimed he had worked for Israeli Army intelligence unit 8200, which is that country's version of the National Security Agency—a sophisticated, secretive, and ambitious electronic surveillance organization that happens to produce a lot of tech entrepreneurs.

Aron looked young, but he was older than me. His photo showed him avoiding eye contact with the camera and wearing a straight-brimmed fedora, a fashion accessory associated with a certain type of charmless chauvinist techie. Aron also expressed an enthusiasm for Bitcoin. I decided to hold none of this against him. He had already shown impeccable taste in potential cofounders. I wrote back.

Hi Aron,

Thanks for contacting me and for the kind offer. Since you have done some research you must know that this is a very challenging area . . . What is your relevant experience? And what is your startup capital?

Corey

Aron was quick to respond. He said he had previously cofounded "a company for value added services for the mobile industry," whatever that meant, only to fall in with "a bad person" who suckered him into some fraudulent scheme. "That evil person stole

3 million dollars from me, that I earned during my whole lifetime," Aron wrote. After the sob story, he got back to business.

> What is the budget that you think that is appropriate for
> this lean startup, bearing in mind that the professional
> force will be rewarded mostly with options/stocks in the
> company?

Aha! Here was a sign that Aron had some real experience running
a tech company: He didn't want to pay his workers.

I knew that greedy people were the easiest to scam. I wondered
how Aron had lost $3 million. I wanted to hear the "evil" person's
side of the story. I did a little more digging and found Aron's name
attached to a curious website. This site featured dozens of blurry
photos of women in their underwear, their faces hidden. The cap-
tions were in Hebrew, so I ran them through Google's online trans-
lator. Evidently these women were all very friendly! "Russia sexy
and horny orgasm rant also awaits you on the phone," one said.

This was a camsite—"a first of its kind in Israel!" Aron was the
registered owner. So my prospective business partner was a cyber-
pimp. But he was so much more! He was also a shovel merchant—a
model technopreneur—and although the connection was not yet
clear in my mind, I had some sense that this dodgy pitchman followed the same basic template as more successful internet entrepreneurs. It would be unwise to do business with Aron, clearly, but
perhaps I could learn from him.

I clicked on another website I found registered to Aron, this
one Bulgarian. It filled my screen with noisy, flashing pop-up ads.

BECOME A SELF-MADE MILLIONAIRE, one ad said. THIS IS YOUR
PERSONAL INVITATION TO EARN YOU TO [*sic*] $1,620.90 DAILY
WITH VERIFIABLE AND UNDENIABLE PROOF! They had my
attention.

The site boasted several videotaped testimonials, which all
started playing at once. These newly minted millionaires were so
excited they were talking over one another. "Hello . . . I'm a self-
made millionaire." "I am a self-made millionaire." "I've been using
AlgoPrime for, I think, seven months now and I'm a freaking self-
made millionaire . . ." One face in the blur of satisfied customers
stuck out. It was a woman. She looked and sounded so familiar.
What was her name? Anna? Josephine? No—*Rhoda!* From Fiverr!
"My name is Susan," Rhoda said. "I'm a stay-at-home mom and, yes,
I'm also a millionaire." There was too much weirdness in this
world. How could the internet be so small?

As the din of testimonials subsided, one voice continued speaking. It belonged to a man who claimed to be the inventor of this
online moneymaking miracle. He said he had built a powerful
trading program for some hedge fund billionaires, who promptly
fired him. In revenge for this treachery, he was taking his secret
and giving it away . . . But I would never find out what happened
next, because I accidentally closed the window on my computer.

The ghost in the machine was looking out for me that day,
because my Web browser immediately served up another, very
similar pitch. This one, too, opened with a series of video testimonials. "Last year I was broke, and lost my house. By 2014, I became
a millionaire," one person said. But how? The pitch continued
with faceless narration from a polished, reassuring male voice.

"Congratulations, you are about to become a millionaire, too," he said. "All you need to do is click your mouse a few times." The appeal was indisputable. I was already spending a lot of time clicking. I might as well get paid for it. "You can join our secret Millionaires Society today, for free. Yes, free. One hundred percent free. No catch . . . Look around you, there's no Buy Now button anywhere." I looked around the screen. So far, this guy was telling the truth.

We're not wannabe internet gurus trying to rip off honest guys like you in order to make a quick buck. Who am I? My name is Brad Marshall, and yes, I'm a millionaire, too.

Brad also wanted me to understand that he was different. "I'm not your average jerk millionaire," he promised. He was *relatable*. "Apart from being a multimillionaire, I'm a member of a small, secret club called the Millionaires Society," he went on.

Nobody out there knows about this secret society, or the system we use. That's why it's so easy and works every single time. You are the first outsider to be let in on the secret.

There was a surreal quality to this semivoluntary online advertising experience. How had I come to this place? What time was it? Was Brad a real person? Or another Fiverr actor? He swore up and down that he hadn't hijacked my Web browser in order to dupe me into some kind of scam. His secret society's system was "one hundred percent legal and ethical," he said. "Our software works. We have nothing to hide." He kept repeating that: "We have nothing to hide." Then why was it a secret society? The pitch moved so relentlessly it was impossible to hold on to such thoughts.

Brad proceeded to deliver a fast-paced demonstration of the Millionaires Society software. "I followed a few simple steps, put two hundred fifty dollars into an account ... Now look at what happens. Within minutes, we went from two fifty to five thousand three sixty-five—in just the time I've been talking to you," he said. "It's that easy." I wasn't sure what had happened, but Brad sounded convincing—and he had spreadsheets. "Now, let me be honest with you: somebody who really cares about you invited you to this membership club," Brad said. How thoughtful! Perhaps it was Aron.

Now that we had established an emotional bond, Brad got to the point. "Remember when I told you that you could join for free? Well, I lied. It'll cost you fifty thousand dollars," he said. Oh.

Now, don't panic ... We're giving you access to an automated system that can make you millions for years to come ... You don't need to know anything about trading ... The software takes care of everything for you.

That meager $50,000 investment would quickly pay off, Brad assured. Before I knew it, I would quickly be matching his earnings of $300,000 per month. The Millionaires Society software was so powerful that "traders from some of the biggest banks in the USA" had once sought to buy it for their own exclusive use. But

Brad had turned them down. "This is just too powerful to let it slip into the hands of the wrong people," he said. I couldn't agree more. Rich people simply could not be trusted with money.

I felt I had gotten closer to solving the mystery of how Aron lost his fortune. I typed "Is the Millionaires Society a scam?" into Google and clicked the search button. A few happy customers said no. But many more told me yes, the Millionaires Society *was* a scam—and that I should try *their* secret moneymaking system instead. I found a YouTube video by a man with a soothing British accent named Steve Dourdil, who broke down the Millionaires Society con job in detail and compared it to other online money-making offers. "Ninety-five percent of them are really lame or just complete scams," Steve said. "A lot of people go around in circles and spend fortunes jumping from one product to the next and never really making any money and winding up going broke." Steve proceeded to explain his own marketing system, the Instant Pay-day Network. "I think you'd be nuts not to check this out if you've been trying to find something legitimate and genuine. All you have to do is click on the link down there, fill out your details on the form down there, and once you've done that, it'll send you to a page with a thirty-five-minute video," he said. "You can start making money from this within days if you want to."

I rebuffed Aron somewhat sternly and he slunk away for good. Whether or not his partnership offer was made in earnest, he'd clearly been involved with at least one online scam. Even if his version of events was true—and even if he wasn't a cyber-pimp—

I was not inclined to pity him. Any scam that depended on the greed of its victims also made them accomplices. Aron's transparent greed revealed his culpability. If, however, as I suspected, his business proposal was merely another ruse—albeit a more elaborate and sophisticated one than the Millionaires Society—then there was actually something compelling about it. For if a chintzy fraudster like Aron could win and lose a small fortune with only an internet connection and an arsenal of psychological tricks, there was no limit to what a powerful corporation might be able to do, given enough budget, ambition, and manipulative technique.

With that thought still rattling in my mind, I went out to yet another techie happy hour, where I met Cyrus and Joe, two guys a few years out of college who worked together in the lower ranks of a tech marketing company in the Financial District. They weren't exactly plugged in to the glamorous side of the business. Their job was "lead generation"—which, as they explained it, meant building lists of email addresses for other companies to spam with bad deals, such as offers of student loans for worthless for-profit universities.

"My bosses are so bitter," Joe said. "My vice president said, 'If you understand the drug industry, you understand the tech industry.' It's a hustle. You've got to figure out how to convince people they want what you've got."

Cyrus corrected Joe's memory: "He said, 'Internet marketing is like selling crack to children.'"

"That's right," Joe said, nodding.

Pushing drugs sounded even more profitable than selling shovels.

My new friends were not merely repeating their bosses' contemptuous catchphrase—they were describing an explicit strategy tech companies used to attract and retain customers. Their job was about more than just identifying potential customers to inundate with offers. It also involved combining sophisticated psychological manipulation techniques with the massive scale and semiautomated targeting enabled by computerization.

I got a deeper look at these methods when I dropped by the annual Startup Conference at the historic downtown Fox Theater in Redwood City. Inside the auditorium, Stanford grad and startup founder Nir Eyal captivated a crowd of several hundred with a distillation of his book *Hooked: How to Build Habit-Forming Products*, which promised to give marketers the key to the unconscious mind.

"It all comes from the work of B. F. Skinner," Eyal said. Skinner, best known for his operant conditioning experiments on animals, denied the existence of free will and human dignity, once writing, "The real question is not whether machines think but whether men do." Skinner's monstrous theories inspired Anthony Burgess to write the horrifying scenes of psychological torture in *A Clockwork Orange*. Here, however, Skinner was a hero. With creative applications of the latest research in neuroscience and behavior as well as evolutionary psychology, startup marketers could make users respond as predictably as lab rats. "What we now know is that the *nucleus accumbens* does not stimulate pleasure per se," Eyal said, referring to a particular region of the brain. The key, he went on, was to trigger "the stress of desire" and then to capitalize upon "the anticipation of the reward." This tension "is endemic to all sorts of habit-forming technologies," he said—especially Facebook. Zuckerberg's titanic offspring had already made news for running a secret scientific experiment that manipulated users' emotions through the selective editing of material that appeared on their "news feeds," and would soon face congressional hearings for its role spreading foreign propaganda in the 2016 elections. But the Startup Conference crowd had no inclination to dwell upon the nightmarish possibilities of these methods. Their concerns were pedestrian and practical.

Eyal presented several categories of virtual tchotchkes companies might offer in exchange for people's money or attention. One category he called "rewards of the tribe," which he described as "things that feel good, have an element of variability, and come from other people"—like Likes. Another category: "rewards of the hunt," which involved "the search for resources" such as food. "In our modern society, we buy these things with money," Eyal said. The addictive power of slot machines offered one example of how marketers could manipulate people's animal instincts. Video game companies like Zynga had taken those Pavlovian processes to a new level, bringing players to the peak of excitement and then hitting them up for cash, which is sort of like a mystery movie that pauses itself mid–plot twist and demands that you insert a coin.

I wasn't qualified to judge the neuroscientific basis of Eyal's pitch, but pop-sci of this sort sent my bullshit detector whooping like a klaxon. Whether or not his theories worked, it was disturbing to hear such an eagerness to exploit human behavioral tics for the sake of profit. Was this how Silicon Valley intended to make the world a better place? Was there anyone they *wouldn't* empower with these manipulative tools, for the right price?

"There's one more thing I'd like to discuss: the morality of manipulation," Eyal went on. "I know what that nervous laughter is about . . . I know some of you were thinking, 'Is this kosher?' If you had that response, bravo." Eyal conceded that digital gadgets may be "the cigarettes of this century," but said he was optimistic that these addictive products could be used for "good" and to "help people live healthier, happier, more productive" lives.

Eyal wrapped up with a slide of Mahatma Gandhi, although El Chapo might've been a better choice. "I encourage you to build the change you wish to see in the world," he concluded, then basked in applause.

As impoverished and self-serving as it was, Eyal's lecture was the first and perhaps only time I heard the word "morality" emerge from the mouth of a Silicon Valley stage speaker. Most people in the industry were convinced that their work was moral because it increased consumer choice and therefore freedom. New technologies were evidence of progress and therefore innately good. And any criticism of the industry's practices or motives therefore threatened freedom and progress. Nowhere were these attitudes more plain than in the industry's propaganda apparatus known as the tech press.

What a sad heap it was, the tech press—an interchangeable assortment of sycophantic blogs, gee-whiz podcasts, and thinly veiled advertising supplements, whose producers had neither the aptitude nor the inclination to really dig into their subject. Most of the thousands of pieces of tech-related "content" inflicted on the public during my time in Silicon Valley could have been replaced with a single book I found on a shelf at Urban Outfitters called *Get Shit Done*. Its authorship was attributed to a company called Startup Vitamins that sold motivational posters. Thumbing through its pages, I realized this book distilled every vapid and hollow slogan promulgated by the boom-time tech press. "Less meetings, more doing. Passion never fails," the book began. The rest of the pages were filled with alternately hectoring and platitudinous quotes from billionaire executives like Bill Gates ("I never took a day off in my twenties. Not one.") and Elon Musk of Tesla Motors ("Optimism, pessimism, fuck that; we're going to make it happen."). With rare exception, the tech press—by which I mean both the trade press focused exclusively on the tech industry and the tech sections of general-interest news organizations—functions as an appendage of the Silicon Valley marketing machine.

I got some historical perspective on the subject talking to Gregg Pascal Zachary, a journalist turned academic who walked away from covering the tech industry just as that beat was growing increasingly lucrative. But according to Gregg, it was also becoming less and less ethical. He covered Silicon Valley at the *San Jose Mercury News* in the 1980s, then wrote for the *Wall Street Journal* from 1989 until 2002—in time to catch both the birth of the Web and the inflation and implosion of the dot-com bubble. When Gregg got started on the beat, the tech industry was scarcely covered outside electronics hobbyist and trade magazines. That began to change in the 1980s, when, fueled by booming markets, the mainstream press began to expand its coverage of business, finance, and industry. Business editors in those days "were usually sports reporters who were such bad alcoholics they couldn't make it anymore. I'm not even joking," Gregg says. "They essentially let the companies write all the stories."

By the midnineties, when Netscape kicked off the first internet boom with its breakthrough $3 billion public stock offering, that had changed. Reporters who were already famous began searching for ways to "glom on" to the hot new tech trend. Among those was Gregg's colleague at the *Journal*, Walt Mossberg, who then covered the State Department but carved out a new space for himself as a reviewer of gadgets and software. But Mossberg's column became a hit and created a new (lower) standard for mainstream press relations with tech companies. By 2000, Gregg says, the tech press was completely co-opted by the industry, caught in a pincer grip from two directions. First, by well-known, award-winning journalists who covered figures like Steve Jobs as though they were rock stars—and second, by "former trade journalists who . . . got in through the trade world, moved up the food chain, and were never trained in adversarial journalism. They don't even know what it is."

Furthermore, most tech reporters understood that they could eventually make a fast and easy jump to a better-paying gig with a tech company if they played nice. "Part of the seduction is, if you just keep your head down and don't cause any trouble, there's some half-million-a-year, giant-paying job waiting for you," Gregg says. "Look at Michael Moritz. He was a Silicon Valley reporter. Now he's one of the richest people in the world." Moritz came up at the same time as Gregg and wrote an important early eighties profile of Steve Jobs for *Time* magazine—and subsequently the first book about Apple's history, titled *The Little Kingdom*. Moritz parlayed the connections he made as a journalist to a partnership at Sequoia Capital, which in turn landed him a seat on the board of Google and eventually a personal net worth of more than $3 billion.

Since Gregg left the business in 2002, a new problem had emerged. The relative power of the traditional press was eclipsed by that of the tech companies themselves. Because social media companies like Facebook commanded such massive audiences, they could essentially force print and broadcast news organizations into harmful distribution partnerships. Old media companies were finding it harder and harder to get people's attention despite spending more and more time and effort on social media. Eventually they even adapted their work to feature more prominently on platforms like Facebook and Twitter, hence the profusion of cloying headlines ending in stock formulas like "You'll never believe what happened next!" Finally, Facebook offered to host publishers' stories directly on Facebook.com, rather than on their own websites. Practically speaking, this arrangement means publications are paying their employees to write for Facebook, which retains the lion's share of advertising revenue as well as exclusive control over audience data. More significantly, it also allows Facebook to gain some editorial influence. "How can the *New York Times* cover Facebook when Facebook is actually a significant source of revenue for the *Times*—such a significant source of revenue that they had to admit it to the Securities and Exchange Commission?"

Gregg says. And, increasingly, the same investors who bankrolled the tech companies were funding their own media organizations. Old-media companies soon found they were losing staff to higher-paying, venture-backed startups like BuzzFeed, which discouraged internal dissent with a "no haters" hiring policy and bet heavily on "sponsored content"—ads disguised as articles. This new wave of "digital-first" media startups was characterized by an overwhelming focus on "metrics" and traffic targets, as journalism became just another item in the tech company product catalog. "When Yahoo put together a newsroom, nobody's covering Yahoo anymore. Because it's like, 'Hey, I might get hired by Yahoo at twice the salary. I'm principled, but not self-destructive,'" Gregg says.

The new tech media establishment introduced foreign customs to the culture of newsrooms. Challenging authority was out. Sycophancy was in. It had always worked that way in Silicon Valley. A TechCrunch writer described the pressure to me as indirect but correlative: The least critical reporters got the most access from companies they were supposed to cover. Unlike government agencies, which were subject to public records laws and accountable ultimately to voters, private companies could control what the public knew about them by limiting who spoke to the press and on what terms. And if tech press editors cared more about being the first to report the specs of say, the next iPhone model—rather than, say, Apple's labor practices or its global efforts at tax avoidance—reporters had every incentive to make nice with industry public relations people, who were always happy to pick up the bar tab, anyway.

I'd seen the obsequious behavior of the tech press at the Startup

Conference. A panel of experienced reporters and editors dutifully took the stage and told a roomful of founders and investors
how to better promote their startups. It should have occurred to
them that giving such advice was not the job of a journalist. It was
the job of a publicist. Out in the hall during a break, I met one of
the panelists, a former *Wall Street Journal* reporter who'd gone on
to edit CNET, a large and well-established tech site owned by CBS
Interactive. In the course of our conversation, I made a critical
remark about Facebook's manipulation of users' news feeds. He
responded with the company line, a fine example of the sort of
circular reasoning that eliminated the need for moral judgment.
"Facebook is a reflection of what you see on the internet," he said,
"so if you don't like what you see on Facebook, it's your own damn
fault." I knew that his argument was bogus—Facebook's story
selection algorithms came with the biases of the engineers who
designed them built in. But in the mind of this high-level tech
journalist, there was no reason to doubt Facebook's assertion of
political neutrality, or question how the unexamined race, class,
and gender biases of its designers might have influenced the decisions they made as programmers, and thus the daily media intake
of billions of users.

At times, examples were made of those who departed from the
script. This rarely took nudging by the industry—like overzealous
hall monitors, the tech press policed their own. I met tech reporters who regarded sharp critics such as Evgeny Morozov as "cheap"
and "nasty," practically spitting his name. Anything but cheer-
leading was grounds for suspicion. Every moderately skeptical
tech reporter I met had a private stockpile of anecdotes about

company press reps threatening his or her editors—sometimes subtly, other times brazenly—with retaliation after receiving even slightly critical coverage. The publicists would often demand the assignment of reporters known to be more pliable. Or else they'd threaten to blacklist the publication. This kind of thing did happen in other areas of journalism. The difference was that in the tech press, it was not seen as a scandalous breach of ethics, but rather accepted as the way of the world. Since I'd written a number of censorious articles about the industry over the years, I feared people in Silicon Valley might not want to talk to me. But I was only flattering myself, for I had never drawn blood. Besides, very few techies were avid readers. A surprising number barely followed the news about the companies that employed them.

But when a powerful person in the Valley seriously resented his own press coverage, the offending writers would be made to pay. Never was this made more clear than with Hulk Hogan's successful privacy lawsuit against Gawker Media in the spring of 2016, infamously bankrolled in secret by the billionaire VC Peter Thiel, who regarded Gawker as a "terrorist" organization. Although the East Coast press saw Thiel's subterfuge for what it was—an attack on free speech—Valley players and even some in the tech press rallied behind Thiel, believing, as his fellow billionaire VC Vinod Khosla, put it, that disfavored "journalists need to be taught lessons." It worked. After Gawker filed for bankruptcy, a larger corporate media property, Fusion, bought its assets and immediately shut down the flagship site, Gawker.com, for fear of further legal harassment.

· · · · ·

The tech press has come to occupy a strange place, for its function is more than symbiotic—it is integral to the industry. As all forms of media and commerce are gradually digitized, every manner of company aspires to become, in one sense or another, a tech company. And in Silicon Valley's current iteration as an internet-focused startup creation machine, these companies are fueled by the same basic resource: "eyeballs." The fate and fortune of tech as an industry now relies on the vagaries of the human attention span. Advertising is everything.

When a tech company captures an audience, it gets more than the opportunity to sell products and ideas. It also harvests the discretely quantified and collated bits of individual user data that people hand over, wittingly and unwittingly, as they stare at their computer and smartphone screens. As valuable as this information is for what it reveals about individual consumer habits and preferences, it's even more precious in the aggregate, as so-called big data, which can be used to predict political shifts, market trends, and even the public mood. Who knows, wins, as the old military adage goes—and this is equally true in the world of business. Watch the video, click the link, fill out the form—this is the labor that tech companies turn into profits. The people who carry out this labor consider themselves customers, but they are also uncompensated workers. The process whereby eyeballs get turned into money is mysterious, but not totally opaque—just discouragingly complicated and boring.

I spent two dismal days popping in and out of sessions at the

Ad:Tech conference trying to get a better handle on this process. The conference, at the Moscone Center in downtown San Francisco, was a sprawling affair attended by thousands of smiling sharks from all corners of the advertising industry. In the expo hall, vendors peddling unregulated dietary supplements competed with dodgy exhibitors promising to "buy and deliver" Web traffic. Without rampant, unchecked fraud, I came to realize, the entire digital media business would collapse.

Fraud was the hot topic that year, because digital ad buyers were starting to wise up. More than two decades after the arrival of the commercialized Web, a trade group finally funded a proper scientific study on the problem of online ad fraud. The study found, among other things, that marketers were losing $6.3 billion a year to various forms of fraud, much of it staged by organized criminal networks. In outline, such scams allow fraudsters to siphon the fat from corporate ad budgets by employing bots that pose as genuine consumers to click on ads. The crooks are able to grab a piece of the money advertisers are paying out because online publishers— that is, people who run websites on which the ads appear—receive a cut of the money paid to online ad sellers by the companies that buy ads. The crooks are even able to redirect ad revenue from legitimate publishers to their own fraudulent sites through a process known as "injection," or to generate bogus clicks by hijacking users' browsers with automated hacking tools. Several experts at the conference told me the study lowballed its multibillion-dollar estimate of industry-wide fraud losses and that the real figure was multiples higher.

In other words, online advertising—the basis for the attention economy that fueled all speculative investment in digital media, from giants like Google on down to low-rent email marketers— was a racket. In the case of Google, an ad buyer will fill out a form saying what search keywords they'd like to associate themselves with, so that when a Google user types in, say, "soap," they might see an ad for Irish Spring. On Facebook, it would work a little differently. There, ad buyers are able to specify a certain demographic they want to reach—say, expectant mothers with household incomes of $80,000 a year and up, or people with bachelor's degrees who drive secondhand cars in the Cleveland, Ohio, metro area. This kind of targeting is the core promise of digital advertising. But during the course of the Ad:Tech talks, I came to see that the promise was a sham. The old knock on print and broadcast advertising was that half of ad budgets were wasted, but no one knew which half—the ads went out to everyone. Online ad targeting was supposed to change that by essentially surveilling users and letting advertisers see who actually viewed their ad and did or didn't buy their product as a result. In reality, though, the new data collection tools didn't work nearly so well as was promised. A full half of ad budgets was still getting flushed down the toilet.

The mechanics of the fraud are complex and technical, but it boils down to this: Companies that place online ads think they are paying based on how many potential customers will see their messages, but the ads are ineffective in actually reaching consumers. Companies in fact frequently pay for ads that are "seen" only by automated computer programs known as bots, or by low-wage workers toiling in offshore "click farms." The bots and click-serfs drive up costs for advertisers by faking "impressions" on their online campaigns—meaning that any time an ad is recorded as being seen or clicked on, Google, Facebook, or whoever sold the ad charges the client.

While everyone at the conference was eager to talk about fraud, few were willing to discuss its implications. That's because the profits from fraud widely benefit both of Ad:Tech's namesake industries. Furthermore, the biggest victims of the fraud are not always the most sympathetic figures. They are often major corporations like PepsiCo or Procter & Gamble, who are scarcely liable to notice a few million skimmed from their gargantuan marketing budgets quarter after quarter, even if it adds up to a total marketwide loss of $6 billion and change annually. The beneficiaries of the fraud are not limited to ad firms and ad-backed tech giants like Facebook and Google, who book revenue from every ad sale, impression, and click whether it comes from a genuine human or a penny-sucking fraudbot. The Wall Street and international investors in the tech companies have also benefited from the drain on corporate budgets. If online ad fraud is as prevalent as I heard at Ad:Tech, it follows that the overall revenues of the dominant ad-based internet companies—chiefly Google and Facebook— are significantly inflated by bogus transactions. And that's a big deal for the stock markets as a whole. A few percentage points could be the difference between a profitable quarter and a confidence-destroying slowdown in growth. There is no suggestion that either Google or Facebook is actively engaged in bot fraud or other deceptive practices, and both companies do a certain amount to police illicit use of their platforms. However, it is not in the interests of the tech companies or their investors or their business partners to aggressively police unlawful and deceptive advertising practices, which were not limited to bot fraud but also manifested as online scams like the Millionaires Society and even more nefarious enterprises. The discovery in 2017 of mind-warping child abuse videos with millions of recorded views—real or not—on YouTube Kids seemed to be a low point. Google promised to address the problem. However, the pandemic spread of gross-out bargain-basement Web ads demonstrates how dependent online media businesses are on dodgy gray- and black-market operators. Anyone who's been online in recent years will recognize the ubiquitous block of faux news headlines and prurient trompe l'oeils from companies like Outbrain and Taboola, which promise celebrity peep shows and offer "one weird trick" to solve just about any problem. Such lowest-common-denominator marketing props up the whole of the internet. And no one has any incentive to improve the quality, trustworthiness, or fairness of the new media ecosystem. The online ad monopolists, Google and Facebook, have grown too big to fail. They are so important to the fortunes of every other media business that no one wants to scream too loudly about the fraud problem lest they trigger a landslide that wipes out their own fragile patch of turf.

The same applies to the ad monopolists' business partners in the wider economy. Thus, various industries with little in common apart from their reliance on online advertising have become complicit in an almost pyramid-scheme-like system. But, I realize, for publishers—a term of art that now applies not only to media organizations but to any company that maintains a website, blog, or social media page—to adhere to a strict standard of lawful, ethical behavior is to commit commercial suicide. "If you clean all of the bots off your platform, your clickthrough rates are going to drop," Michael Tiffany, chief executive of the White Ops security agency, which led the ad agencies' fraud study, says. What this meant was simple: "Your numbers will go down."

And if there's anything corporate culture cannot tolerate, it's numbers that go down.

"It's all about getting the chart that goes up," a disaffected social media marketing expert told me over drinks. "There's a whole industry devoted to making charts that go up." To illustrate his point, he pointed me to the *Guardian* newspaper's now-defunct "partner zones" program, which afforded large institutional advertisers the opportunity to pay massive sums to the newspaper in exchange for the right to post promotional "news" stories on its website—a form of "sponsored content," in the industry's parlance. To create the all-important "chart that goes up," the clients would then pay Facebook to generate traffic to their advertorials. Ostensibly this traffic came through "organically" promoted links targeting genuine potential customers who are so enchanted by the serendipitous appearance of an online advertorial that speaks to their personal desires that they make a conscious choice to click, read, like, and share—or so the story goes. However, the expert, who was a friend of mine, had noticed that a suspiciously high percentage of the paid traffic came from far-flung, low-wage countries such as Bhutan. So the new model supporting digital media was for floundering corporations to pay to place stories about how awesome they were, which publishers would then promote by buying phantom readers. "Then the advertisers can go to the boss and say, 'Look, we got an article in the *Guardian*,'" my friend the marketing cynic said. Those phony measures of success supplied fodder for still more charts that went up—these ones for internal consumption, and used to justify the marketing department budget to higher-ups.

But wasn't it obvious that nobody was really reading all that crap online? "There's nobody more gullible than a marketer chasing a trend," he said. And no one cared about the truth so long as the charts kept going up.

Here was a socioeconomic explanation for why the tone at the Startup Conference, at Ad:Tech, and at basically every public function I'd attended since setting foot in California was so relentlessly, insufferably upbeat: The system demands positivity. To speak of a chart that went down—to admit so much as a glimmer of pessimism—was beyond comprehension. It was simply taken for granted that the tech industry itself was a kind of perpetual motion machine driving humanity to ever greater heights. And that unshakable optimism extended to everyone who participated in the industry, even as a hanger-on. I once met a gaggle of Aussies who'd paid thousands of dollars out of their own pockets for airfare and registration to attend an annual Apple convention called the Worldwide Developers Conference, or WWDC—or, in this crowd, "Dub Dub."

"Was it worth it? What do you get out of it?" I asked.

"What do you mean?" one of the Aussies gasped. "It's Dub Dub!"

On another occasion, at a different tech conference, I met two partners who ran a small design studio in Memphis. They had paid their own way—$225 each for tickets to the conference, plus travel expenses from Tennessee to Silicon Valley, which turned out to be a lot more than they'd counted on. But it was all worth it, they said, just for the chance to soak up the go-getter passion. The desperate insistence on "productive" activity and "inspirational" talk minimized the possibility of intrusive, doubtful thoughts. I was choking on positivity. I developed a deep, torturous craving for truth, or at least something a little more downbeat—perhaps a conversation that consisted of something besides phony encouragement. I had not heard from my pothead Rhodesian entrepreneur friend, Lawrence, in a long time. I needed a new misfit mentor.

V

It's Called Capitalism

I found him at the strangest time. I was trapped at a conference party in some bloodless Valley suburb hours from my Airbnb and wanted nothing more than to strangle with his own lanyard the next guy who tried to hand me a business card. I sought refuge next to someone who looked almost as miserable as me. He sat alone at a small table, a tired-looking bearded man in a beige suit and plaid sweater. I claimed an empty stool. "I'm on vacation," the bearded man growled. Nevertheless, he had spent all day at this conference, skipping nary a session. He took a sip of honey-colored beer from a sturdy glass stein. His name was Ghazi Ben Othman. He told me he worked as head of strategy for a $250 million Saudi-owned private equity fund that invested in technology companies around the world, and also ran a "Shariah-compliant" fund for startups based inside the kingdom, some run by women.

Ghazi possessed a wide repertoire of shrugs, each loaded with subtle shades of meaning. As I guessed somehow from his body language, he had a notably different outlook from that of the other investors and tinkerers and climbers I had met. Silicon Valley was "the most brutal capitalistic machine there is," he said. "The strong get stronger and the weak get crushed. It's very Darwinian."

Ghazi's awakening as a Silicon Valley cynic followed several career shifts. Trained as an engineer, he had moved to the finance side of the tech industry, first as an analyst, then as an investor, bouncing around until his current employers from Saudi Arabia hired him as their representative in Silicon Valley. In an industry overrun with early-twentysomethings, Ghazi was a literal gray-beard. Over the course of his career, he had observed and participated in several boom-and-bust cycles. Experience lent him foresight. Ghazi seemed to me like some dark seer in the wilderness, consumed by visions that he shared with passing strangers such as myself. It was simply delightful to spend time with someone who validated my persistent sense that something was seriously wrong here.

As a venture capitalist, Ghazi may have developed a jaundiced view of the business side of tech, but his was the anger of the righteous, for he had once been an engineer, and as such he remained a believer in the power of progress and innovation, the twin shibboleths of the Valley. Yet he was not so blinded by faith as to miss the patterns and signs.

In Ghazi's telling, each tech boom began with a constant and a variable. The constant was easy financing, whether from government-subsidized borrowing or unsophisticated investors. The variable was whatever Silicon Valley was trying to sell at the time. In the early nineties, the boom was about hardware. IBM and Apple had found a way to commercialize military-funded computer research by churning out personal desktop computers and accessories. "Back then, Silicon Valley was small," Ghazi said. "It was focused almost exclusively on the technology with very little thought on how to market it." Then, in the late nineties, came another commercial boom, also underwritten by government research: the internet. This time, something changed. Wall Street got involved.

"All of a sudden, Silicon Valley got the first taste of the big money," Ghazi said. Certain venture capital funds, such as Kleiner Perkins and Sequoia, grew large and powerful—even more so after the bubble popped in 2000. The big crash cleared out the competition. While industry down cycles drove lots of people out of business, the surviving players claimed even more ground. This pattern went back a long way. In fact, as my subsequent research revealed, it went back to the beginning.

The vaunted forefathers of the internet were a clever lot of schemers whose transgressions were forgiven, per American custom, once they got rich. Consider the career of Vinton G. Cerf, who developed the internet "packet" protocols still used today. In grad school at the University of California, Los Angeles, in the late 1960s, an old high school pal got Cerf involved with a Pentagon-funded project called ARPANET, the precursor of today's internet. Cerf began following the money into the private sector as early as 1982, when MCI Communications hired him to lobby his former public sector colleagues to allow the company unprecedented access to the publicly owned internet, giving it a jump on all potential competitors. Until then, the internet was reserved for "academic and research activities." Commercial use was forbidden. Over time, the military ceded control of the internet to the National Science Foundation, where networking division director Stephen S. Wolff was bent on

privatization. Wolff oversaw "a backroom deal" that effectively gave
managerial control of the internet to a corporate consortium dominated by MCI and IBM (where Cerf had also worked). Wolff's gift
of invaluable public property to private interests was his own
unilateral decision, made without consulting anyone. Later, the
federal Office of the Inspector General found that the early privatization process presented clear conflicts of interest and that
Wolff's NSF department made "no effort whatever to seek competition." Investigators complained that a "lack of documentation"
forced them to "reconstruct the reasoning behind the decision from
interviews," which predictably led to "inaccuracies." Wolff craftily
defended his cloak-and-dagger approach as an effort to prevent
the abuse of federal open records laws. Not long after, Wolff followed Cerf into the private sector and joined San Jose–based Cisco
Systems, a $49 billion hardware company that remains the world's
largest provider of internet infrastructure.

No politician or other official was ever sanctioned for this plunder of public assets. The propriety of the matter was rendered moot
by the presidential administration of Bill Clinton and Al Gore,
two great friends of the telecom industry who led the political
campaign to cement internet privatization as the law of the land.
While still in government, Wolff scoffed at warnings that his policies would enable a powerful new set of monopoly corporations.
"Might telcos become dominant? Of course there is such a dan-
ger," Wolff argued. "But remember, if they employ illegal means of
increasing market share, we have laws against anticompetitive
behavior. I doubt that they would do something questionable and
walk away unchallenged." In America? In Silicon Valley? Never!

The privatization led by Clinton and Gore enabled the dot-com
boom of the 1990s as well as the bust that followed. Once more, the
best-connected insiders emerged from the chaos in an even stronger position. Ghazi was working as an investment analyst during
the boom, but his former company promoted him to VC only after
the bubble popped. This meant he missed his first chance at easy
money. In 2005, there was another great inflation, this one fueled
by social media companies like Facebook. The dot-com boom had
lasted only five years. The social media boom—which was called,
for a while, Web 2.0, and closely followed Google's massive 2004
initial public stock offering—was going strong for more than a
decade by the time I met Ghazi. Some things hadn't changed
since he first arrived in the Valley. It ran on the same old mix of
government-subsidized research, cheap labor, and a regulatory
outlook inherited from the Ronald Reagan era that permitted
corporations to unload the costs of doing business on customers,
employees, taxpayers, and the ecosystem.

But some things had changed, Ghazi said. Silicon Valley had
grown more volatile, more ruthless and ravenous for the blood of
virgin entrepreneurs. "The machine is so efficient now, spinning
so fast, that either you get crushed or you get in and are connected
to everything all at once," he told me. I couldn't tell whether he
meant this as a warning or an enticement. All the same, I could
feel the whirling sensation he described. I was constantly talking
to people who believed success could strike anyone at any time, and
also surrounded by people who were, like myself, one accident away
from going broke and getting crushed. There were winners and
losers and no in-betweens here. Ghazi's Silicon Valley was as

frightening as it was dazzling. It was shiny and fast, felicitous and cruel. The wheels spun faster, faster, faster, and the Silicon Valley corruption machine kicked into overdrive. "You make it sound like Las Vegas," I said. "It's Las Vegas with card counting," he replied. But that wasn't quite right, because card counting gave the player an edge over the house. It was more like Las Vegas with an even bigger house edge and a gambling commission that was hand-picked by the casino bosses.

For all they had in common with the dodgy gambling moguls of Las Vegas lore, the Silicon Valley tycoons had achieved a more convincing patina of legitimacy—which was strange, considering how far they try to push the limits of established law. Indeed, flagrancy is at the very heart of their success—the secret ingredient.

A scan of the biggest winners confirms this view. In the first phase of the tech boom, Google started out by "borrowing" Stanford's computing resources—at times, consuming half of the network capacity of the university, where the founders were grad students—in order to "crawl" and "cache" (read: copy and paste) webpages without permission and irrespective of copyright. Google used this questionably sourced data hoard as the basis for a business selling ads to dodgy businesses such as get-rich-quick schemers and mail-order prescription drug dealers, among others. Before its IPO in 2004, Google issued stock options worth $80 million to employees in violation of SEC registration and disclosure requirements because it failed to disclose the arrangement to potential new investors. But the company emerged "unscathed" after promising in a settlement to behave in the future. Google also rigged the results of its chief product, the search engine, while insisting the results were somehow algorithmically pure and beyond reproach, as a multiyear investigation by the European Commission concluded in 2017. Eventually, the wheezing Federal Trade Commission launched an investigation and produced a report detailing Google's practices. As reported by the *Register*, FTC investigators "recommended the watchdog take action. However, the FTC's political appointees cut a deal with Google instead." (The terms called for Google to provide websites more opportunities to "opt out" of granting Google rights to certain copyrighted material while permitting it to carry on with the most controversial and profitable practice of promoting its own services above competitors'.) As Google grew, it also shrank—small enough to fit inside a mailbox in Bermuda, where it funneled $14 billion in annual profits via an intricate series of transatlantic shell companies that allowed it to avoid an estimated $2 billion in taxes every year. "It's called capitalism," chairman Eric Schmidt said when questioned about it. Google set a high bar for rule breaking that its $275 billion Web 2.0 cousin, Facebook, tried mightily to surpass. Mark Zuckerberg may have committed multiple violations of felony hacking laws in the early days of the company. According to the *Harvard Crimson*, he stole student photos from Harvard networks, broke into email accounts, and vandalized a competing startup. As Facebook amassed data on millions and then billions of people, it "monetized" the information in unsavory ways. For instance, in 2015, the company began selling its customer data trove to banks and insurance companies, who might use it, among other ways, as a basis to deny services to poor people, minorities, and the disabled. Then there was the time Facebook ignored federal laws requiring "informed consent" in its secret behavioral experiments. The only reason anyone noticed was that the findings got published in a research journal. You can bet Facebook won't make that mistake again!

Amazon, the $259 billion "everything store," may have benefited from the sale of unknown quantities of "gray market" and "e-fenced" goods that were allegedly counterfeit or stolen, according to press reports and the book *Black Market Billions* by Hitha Prabhakar. Furthermore, Amazon faced allegations of abuse of employment laws. Amazon's salaried cubicle jockeys got it almost as bad as the warehouse temps, who were so overworked and toiled in such miserable conditions, that the company notoriously hired private paramedics to park their ambulances outside one of its facilities waiting to treat the next batch of employees who collapsed as a result of heat exhaustion. In Germany, Amazon hired menacing black-clad security guards employed by an outfit with neo-Nazi ties as modern-day Pinkertons to police its warehouse workers. And until the spring of 2017, founder Jeff Bezos refused to collect hundreds of millions of dollars in sales taxes in many jurisdictions, thus starving state and local governments while furnishing extra cash to crush the competition.

The pattern continued with eBay, the grifters' paradise; Craigslist, which profited from the promotion of prostitution and discriminatory housing arrangements (although a judge found Craigslist not liable); and PayPal, which partnered with offshore gambling operations, fought attempts to regulate it as a bank, and settled various money laundering charges. Netflix, like most major corporations these days, faced an antitrust complaint, which it beat, as well as alleged Americans with Disabilities Act violations. (An appeals court ruled the ADA did not apply to Netflix.) LinkedIn—which set a historic sales price record following Microsoft's $26 billion buyout in 2016—conducted a galling spam campaign that was critical to its growth and settled a class-action lawsuit over it for $13 million. TripAdvisor was officially sanctioned in the UN for misleading advertising, and settled a claim that it classified its employees as independent contractors. Groupon settled various consumer protection lawsuits.

This outlaw tradition carried forward to the second wave of postmillennial unicorns, which picked up unstoppable momentum in 2004 or 2005. Uber, the unlicensed taxi service launched in 2010, proved once and for all that a few people really can change the world using nothing more than powerful connections, billions of dollars in capital, and a willingness to trample long-standing norms such as the nigh-universal requirement for taxi companies to obtain operating permits and insurance and to certify their drivers for the sake of public safety.

In the early days, the company operated under the name Uber-Cab, promoting itself as a "one-click" service to hire "licensed, professional drivers"—a misleading claim, as the company itself was unlicensed and recruited anyone who happened to own a car. By classifying its drivers as "independent contractors" rather than employees, the company shrugged off the burden of minimum wage laws, payroll taxes, health insurance, and other obligations. This brazen startup raised $50 million in several early investment rounds, then pressured state regulators and elected officials until its service was effectively legalized. With its "break laws first, buy influence later" strategy proven, Uber's next round raised an astonishing $258 million with help from Google, which needed to "disrupt" the rules of the road if it hoped to gain approval for its driverless cars. The cash windfall fueled Uber's global expansion. Its CEO and cofounder, Travis Kalanick, was a big fan of the novelist Ayn Rand, and at times his behavior seemed to imitate one of Rand's infinitely selfish antiheroes.

Uber tried to subvert resistance wherever it launched by ingratiating itself with politicians. Usually, it worked. In Portland, Oregon, it hired the services of a powerful local political consultant who had managed the election campaigns for the mayor, a key city councilor, and many other statewide power players. After the councilor and the mayor met secretly with Uber reps at the consultant's home—in violation of city lobbying rules—the city, lo and behold, cut Uber a break. While that was going on, Uber was actively circumventing Portland regulators using special software called Greyball, which it had designed to identify and avoid local taxi inspectors when they tried to hail an Uber car. Similar intrigues followed Uber around the country and the world. To grease the skids in its global expansion, Uber hired David Plouffe, who managed Barack Obama's 2008 presidential campaign and advised him in the White House as head of public affairs. After a year, Plouffe joined Uber's board and was replaced in the public affairs job by Google's longtime head of PR, Rachel Whetstone, a Tory power broker and personal friend of former British prime minister David Cameron. Incidentally, the UK was one of the first places outside the United States where Uber was legalized.

Teaming up with the lobbying industry was only one aspect of Uber's expansion strategy. It also plotted skulduggery such as covertly tracking the movements of suspect journalists as well as digging up dirt on the personal lives of known critics and their family members. The company broke laws in so many places around the world, someone started a Wikipedia page to keep track.

Uber didn't give a flying fuck about the law. That's what made it so successful.

Most people think of "cybercrime" as credit card fraud, identity theft, and the fencing of stolen or counterfeit goods. And indeed, these are multibillion-dollar globalized businesses. But the greatest rewards for shady online startups accrue to those who can conceal or deny the illegality of their conduct by "going legitimate." There are several time-tested ways companies can go about this.

The first and best way is for an ambitious startup to get really big, really fast. The best defense against legal criticism and excessive regulatory scrutiny is an enormous bank account. As Uber showed, politicians can be used to minimize any consequences for past misconduct. The second path to legitimacy is to work the most complex and ambiguous areas of the law that will not invite intense scrutiny from authorities and regulators. No startup should skimp on the legal department! The third way such a startup can maintain its patina of legitimacy is to focus on laws that are, for whatever reason, difficult to enforce—for example, the laws of a hostile foreign country. This was the idea with ZunZuneo, a now defunct Twitter-like service secretly contracted by the United States Agency for International Development in 2010 to undermine the Castro government in Cuba. As the Associated Press reported in a 2014 exposé on ZunZuneo, the company's *yanqui*-backed founders ran the service using shell companies in Spain, the United Kingdom, and the Cayman Islands. The strategy shielded them from Cuban authorities as well as European internet regulators.

Among the first to publicly recognize the internet's potential to help companies evade regulations was a law professor named A. Michael Froomkin, who presented a paper on that subject at a Harvard symposium in 1996. Froomkin wrote that "the multinational nature of the Internet makes it possible for users to engage in regulatory arbitrage." What that clever coinage refers to is the practice of using the internet to make money doing something that might be illegal if you did the same thing without using the internet. The VC Marc Andreessen, who made a fortune in the early nineties as a cofounder of the once dominant Web browser Netscape, revealed regulatory arbitrage to be a crucial plank in the strategy of his investment firm, Andreessen-Horowitz, in a 2014 interview with Bloomberg News. Andreessen enthused that tech startups could "reinvent the entire system" of finance and commerce. "To me, it's all about unbundling the banks," he said.

There are regulatory arbitrage opportunities every step of the way. If the regulators are going to regulate banks, then you'll have nonbank entities that spring up to do the things that banks can't do. Bank regulation tends to backfire, and of late that means consumer lending is getting unbundled.

What exactly is "unbundling"? Andreessen's buzzword simply means taking a regulated service provided by traditional banks, such as making cash loans to individuals, and offering the same service online, where legal precedent did not apply and where regulators were often poorly prepared to police. Startups can offer deceptively low price points for consumers and higher profits for investors precisely because they do not follow the same rules as offline competitors—rules that were designed for the protection of investors and consumers alike. Prior to the computer age, "unbundled" lending went by many names: usury, gouging, loansharking. But old-fashioned brick-and-mortar loan sharks didn't enjoy advantages like ample VC funding and catchy dot-com domains. All that was old is new again, and with Wall Street in great disrepute, the tech-focused venture capital firms can pass off "peer-to-peer" lending and "microloan" schemes with outrageous fees and effective interest rates as a humane alternative to traditional banking. The only innovation such startups have offered is an exciting new way to get screwed.

The wildly successful cowboys of the tech industry imperium set a clear example for up-and-coming entrepreneurs. Sites like Hacker News and Product Hunt, where newly launched startups seek publicity and investment, are full of barely disguised efforts to get rich through "regulatory arbitrage." With a quick search I found dozens of examples of startups whose founders knew, or were warned, that they might be breaking the law. Bitcoin Fax built a service to "send faxes anywhere in the world with no sign up required" and payment accepted in Bitcoin. One reviewer recognized the likely customer base immediately: communications for "highly illegal" transactions involving drugs or child pornography on the Deep Web, where Silk Road once thrived. Another startup, Burner, built an app supplying unlimited temporary phone numbers. A reviewer on HN likened the choice of name to "carrying around a 10 foot sign saying 'Department of Justice, come and get me!'" (The company later amended its terms of service to clarify that it would comply with law enforcement requests for information, and may keep copies of users' phone records and text message to that end.) Several startups, like Fleetzen, Ghostruck, and Wagon, launched "Uber for cargo" services to provide uninsured amateur truckers for hire. "Load sizes, damage, loss, personal injury. This is going to be a problem very quickly," one Fleetzen reviewer wrote. "All of which make this a great opportunity," another replied. Uber, of course, already had plans to break into trucking.

The conventional wisdom held that illegal conspiracies were best conducted in secret. But the tech boom that began in 2005 changed all that. Startup entrepreneurs describe their schemes in detail to investors hoping to buy in to the next epic heist. Should these founders run into any trouble, the investors have the money, know-how, and connections to fight the law and win. It's the perfect crime—when it works.

In a 2013 *Shark Tank*–style live investor pitch, the founder of a startup called Zenefits, Parker Conrad, feistily promised "to *mess stuff up* for two very large industries"—insurance and human resources. "If you're an insurance broker," Conrad explained, "we're going to drink your milkshake." The catchphrase was borrowed from the ruthless oilman portrayed by Daniel Day-Lewis in *There Will Be Blood*, who uttered it shortly before murdering a business rival. Investors loved the concept. As Conrad explained, it was clearly illegal for insurance brokers, who helped companies choose insurance policies for their employees, to give "rebates" of their "very generous" sales commissions to insurance providers. (He never explained *why* it was illegal: because brokers who received kickbacks from insurance companies would have every incentive to push worse policies on their clients, ultimately screwing over everybody who paid premiums.) However, Zenefits found a loophole. It was, in Conrad's opinion anyway, not explicitly illegal for a broker—which Zenefits was—to provide its clients with free software and services—as Zenefits did—while at the same time receiving compensation from insurance providers that might otherwise be illegal. Because its clients weren't paying Zenefits to act as an insurance broker, the compensation was kosher . . . or so Conrad hoped. In most states, insurance regulators failed to notice Zenefits' egregious end run around consumer protection rules. But Utah regulators did notice. They cited the company for violations and were all set to ban it from doing business.

"I felt like I'd been punched in the gut," Conrad recalled in a recorded interview. "This was just, like, something completely out of left field, where suddenly there's this government agency that's like, you know, telling us we're not allowed to operate." It's fair to say Conrad's mellow was thoroughly harshed. "At the time, we were a really small startup and, you know, it didn't *seem* like we were doing anything wrong or anything illegal, and so it was quite upsetting," he said. "I was like, 'Uh-oh, maybe we're going to be in really big trouble here.'" It didn't help, perhaps, that he had announced his intentions onstage at the highest-profile startup competition in the world, TechCrunch Disrupt.

But where there was cash, there was hope. Coached by the investors who had poured $84 million into the startup, Zenefits "went to the mat" with the government of Utah. Zenefits staged a petition and made itself a techie cause célèbre. Then the company hired "some folks" in Utah, as Conrad put it, to "kind of help us out on the ground and make introductions so that we could sort of plead our case to the various different legislators." Those folks included at least five lobbyists, including the former deputy mayor of Salt Lake County ("a confidant to many lawmakers"); the former head of the state's largest political fundraising committee; and the former executive director of the Utah Republican Party.

After successfully beating back the pesky regulators in Utah, Zenefits joined the unicorn herd with a $4.5 billion valuation in 2015. The management reportedly blew a lot of that money on motivational bacchanals that were debauched even by Silicon Valley standards (before the company laid off nearly half its staff, employees were reportedly asked to stop leaving cigarette butts and used condoms in the office). Conrad resigned as CEO in 2016 after regulators in other states brought the heat. His successor, David Sacks, claimed that "an internal investigation brought to light deficiencies" in company practices—although of course it was state regulators who first pointed out those unlawful "deficien-cies." Sacks then said Zenefits was rebranding as the Compliance Company and would use its experience to help clients stay out of trouble with regulators and avoid waste, fraud, and abuse. There was a neat irony to the new brand message, considering everything.

Studying the example of all these successful tech companies helped me better understand the day-to-day work of startup found-ers and venture capitalists, stripped of jargon and euphemism: Entrepreneurs devised new ways to break the law, while investors spotted and bankrolled the most promising schemes. That was the secret of the Silicon Valley shovel merchants.

Loopholes, like veins of ore, could be depleted, as I had previ-ously discovered at the Collaborate convention, which billed itself as a chance for people in the startup scene to "build valuable new relationships" with people in government, and vice versa. I attended a session on the Small Business Innovation Research (SBIR) grant program, created by Congress in 1982, ostensibly to underwrite state-of-the-art scientific and technological research by small businesses—although applicants were often expected to partner with big contractors such as Lockheed or Booz Allen Hamilton. This grew into a $2.5 billion government venture capital fund, about half of which was controlled by the Defense Department and focused on startups that private-sector VCs might deem "too risky." In recent years, military grants had funded incredible break-throughs, such as the Energetically Autonomous Tactical Robot (EATR), a very special war machine. As its developers explained, EATR recharged its batteries by extracting energy from "biomass" and "other organically based energy sources," such as plants—and, presumably, should the mission call for it, people. Hence the name. The grant program official listed several other success stories, including Biogen, a $10 billion pharmaceutical company, and iRobot, maker of the Roomba vacuum cleaner.

The session, which dealt with techniques for obtaining an SBIR, was conducted by a gregarious man with a flashy gold watch who'd made a career gaming the system. His name was Eric Adolphe, and his company was called Government Proposal Solutions. Once "flat broke," he won an SBIR on his first try. "I didn't know anything," he recalled. "I was desperate, I submitted, and I won." Partnering with a company then called GRiD Computers to obtain funding from NASA, he had helped develop an early touch-screen tablet computer. That first SBIR led to another, and another. Congress increased the program's funding, and Adolphe made a killing. "My company went from zero to a hundred million," he said. "Me and my CTO had a bet to see who could win more SBIRs. That's what kind of a sick guy I was." Now he wanted to share.

Adolphe's grant-winning strategy began by dotting every *i* and crossing every *t*. "Machines are deciding what's compliant," he explained. "If you miss a page, or you didn't follow some instruction, you're out of luck." He also tried to get inside the heads of the bureaucrats who held the purse strings and parrot back whatever their requirements needed. Whenever the government presented some requirement that would seem to disqualify him, he found a work-around. "I learned the game," he said. "Every SBIR I went after, I had a PhD on my team. They said, 'Well, he's got a PhD on his team, he must know what he's doing.'" Usually, he went on, this "team member" was some random Joe with a PhD whom Adolphe had taken out for doughnuts for a couple of hours. Everyone laughed. "They are now doing audits," he said somberly. "It didn't used to be that way." Alas. Later on I met a VC who said this particular gravy train had long since pulled out of the station. "SBIRs became the business model of some companies," the investor said, "but the authorities have started to catch on." No wonder Adolphe had gone into business selling his secrets—they were obsolete!

At every turn, my research and experiences would bear out the cynical assessment Ghazi shared with me over drinks. Still, I had more to learn.

As Ghazi want on, my beer glass grew warmer. There was another thing to understand, he said: "Investors are like sheep."

"How are they like sheep?" I asked.

Ghazi asked if I'd seen the VC panel at the conference we'd attended that day. I had. It was an exceedingly dull pitch competition involving three startups and twice as many investors. "The moderator asked, 'Would you invest?' The woman said, 'I'll wait for someone else.' She didn't want to be the first to make a bet," Ghazi said.

Even with small armies of highly educated analysts at their disposal, Ghazi explained, most VC shops were not actually qualified to assess the technical merits of all the various startups looking for money in Silicon Valley. It took only one big hit—one ride on a unicorn's back—to make an investor's reputation. But with billions of dollars at stake, careers could be ruined as quickly as

they were made. This contributed to the high-rolling "fail fast"
mentality among VCs, which in turn kept them primed to make
snap judgments based on stereotypes and superficial information,
delivered via PowerPoint. It also forced them to rely heavily on
ideas and models with which they were already familiar. "At VC
shops, we looked at four hundred deals per year. That's one per
day, so you're talking about a few slides at most," Ghazi explained.
Here was another reason why so many startups seemed alike in
mediocrity—they didn't win the support of investors by creating
innovative products that offered new and better ways of doing
things, but by crafting formulaic, whiz-bang PowerPoint presentations to impress MBA-credentialed sheep.

I found it hard to believe that the actual merit of a company or
product—factors like its design, programming, or engineering—
were never taken into consideration.

"So is engineering *never* a factor?" I asked.

Ghazi shook his head. Neither was having revenue, or customers. In fact, the *last* thing that mattered in Silicon Valley was
technological innovation. Marketing came first and foremost. The
actual products of the tech industry—computers and software—
were less important than the techniques used to sell those products, and to sell shares in the companies that made them. The
portfolios of venture capital firms were composed largely of go-
nowhere companies built on bluster. There was a paucity of genuine innovation among these companies, because incremental
advances in technology were less reliable generators of profit than,
say, finding clever ways to rip people off, or exploiting regulatory
loopholes. The overwhelming majority of VC-backed startups

were destined to flame out quickly—or, at best, to sputter along for a few years producing modest annual returns of, say, 1 percent. This was not necessarily a problem, at least from the investors' point of view. Ghazi explained that 60 percent of a venture fund's earnings typically come from 10 percent of its investments, and "everything else is crap." Thus financiers were almost guaranteed to profit, eventually. The odds were much worse for entrepreneurs, who were almost certainly doomed even if they secured VC funding. A 2012 Harvard Business School study of two thousand venture-backed companies found that more than 95 percent failed. "You don't hear a lot about the failures," Ghazi said.

He was right. Techies only talked about their past failures as a necessary prelude to their present success. But most failures were permanent, and founders didn't easily bounce back. I contemplated those numbers from the Harvard study. If 95 percent of startups failed, that meant 5 percent of startups received most of the attention from inside and outside the industry. Which meant that the mediated image of Silicon Valley bore little resemblance to the reality. I was living the reality. The reality was that almost everyone was a loser like me, trying to break through.

We were chum. Fodder. Marks. Ghazi shared with me his pity for "fresh-off-the-boat" entrepreneurs who lacked elite connections and still believed the hype about meritocracy, opportunity, collaboration, and geek camaraderie. As Ghazi saw it, one single factor determined who even got the chance to join the 5 percent of winners: "It's about who you know," he said. "Go to Stanford, and if you have a bad idea, it will get funded."

One company, which the *Wall Street Journal* called "The

Epitome of a Stanford-Fueled Startup," encapsulated in every
respect the sham of the Silicon Valley meritocracy, from its charmed
beginnings to its ignominious downfall. This company, called
Clinkle, secured investors before settling on a product. Clinkle was,
in the words of its founder, Lucas Duplan, "a movement to push the
human race forward," but beyond that no one seemed quite sure
what the company was all about. Duplan was a nineteen-year-old
Stanford computer science major and an insufferable showboat.
No need to dwell on Duplan's shortcomings, however—the important thing is that his academic adviser was Stanford president and
Google board member John Hennessy. Along with Hennessy, several professors backed Duplan's charge into the private sector,
endorsing what the *Wall Street Journal* called "one of the largest
exoduses" in departmental history. More than a dozen students
abandoned their studies to work for Duplan, who rented a house
to serve as Clinkle's headquarters-cum-dormitory with money
invested by his parents and a VC firm, Highland Capital.

With the prestige and power of Stanford's leadership behind
it, and still without a solid business plan, Clinkle raised $25 mil-
lion in seed money to develop some sort of app that would exist
somewhere in the "mobile-payments space." The predictable squan-
dering of that impressive sum was chronicled with due skepticism
and schadenfreude on Gawker's Valleywag blog and elsewhere,
though many a suck-up rose to Clinkle's defense. Employees were
resigning in frustration even before pictures emerged of Duplan
posing like P. Diddy with handfuls of cash. Layoffs followed. Panicked investors called in a series of experienced managers as "adult
supervision," one of whom quit within twenty-four hours. Long

overdue and well over budget, Clinkle eventually launched a digital payments service, and later pivoted to a digital twist on an old-fashioned lottery. Clinkle became a punch line and Duplan a pariah. But the real blame belonged to some members of the Stanford administration and the sheeplike VCs of the Valley. It seemed to me that they were the ones who were seeking to exploit the bountiful energy of relatively naïve tuition-paying kids to make a fast buck on pointless, unworkable, and otherwise dubious investment schemes. The dropout entrepreneurs were just eager saps who, when handed shovels, dug holes for themselves.

Stanford produced another infamous example of Silicon Valley cronyism: Theranos, a much-hyped medical startup hawking what it characterized as a miraculous low-cost blood testing service. Its founder, Stanford dropout Elizabeth Holmes, talked a great game. She dressed in black turtlenecks that drew inevitable comparisons to Steve Jobs. Holmes was another wunderkind from central casting, who, having charmed the likes of Henry Kissinger into joining the Theranos board, became the world's youngest female billionaire. Unlike Clinkle, Theranos received uniformly fawning press, including a cookie-cutter profile by Ken Auletta in the *New Yorker* magazine that praised her spartan determination to build "a world in which no one ever has to say goodbye too soon." It was all laurels and roses for Theranos and Holmes, until a series of investigative articles—again in the *Wall Street Journal*— revealed that its product, a blood testing machine, was worse than useless and that government regulators were threatening to bar Holmes from the medical industry. However, the feds ultimately let Theranos off the hook by accepting its promise to stay out of the blood testing business for two years. The company fended off lawsuits from shareholders by agreeing to compensate them with some of Holmes's own shares in the company—essentially, by increasing their cut of the profits from the fraud. Under the logic of capital, even a disgraced company such as Theranos could still be portrayed as a success. A friend of mine who evaluated tech company investments for a large pension fund once explained his employers' mentality to me. He said it didn't matter whether a new technology actually worked. What mattered was that other investors thought it could work. If they did, their confidence would cause the company's value to increase regardless of its actual merit. "Everything is sales," my friend said. The trick was knowing when to buy shares and when to unload them. That was why it helped to have inside information.

What Ghazi described was a patronage system, one with an informal and constantly shifting but nonetheless inescapable hierarchy. This, of course, was very much at odds with Silicon Valley's outward image as a collaborative meritocracy of geeks whose lofty ideals and mental discipline put them above petty interpersonal politicking. The patronage system kept insiders relatively safe from outside threats, such as small-shareholder revolts and regulatory inquiries. It didn't just pick winners—it created them. "That's how Sequoia and Andreessen get hit after hit. They get to see the best ideas first and everybody else gets sloppy seconds," Ghazi said.

He paused and took a big drink. He wanted me to understand that the tech industry did not *endure* boom-and-bust cycles—it was dependent on them. The outside world understood Silicon Valley by the wealth of its winners and marveled at their miraculous triumphs. However, as Ghazi saw it, the system could not function without a far greater number of losers. This might not seem like such a revelation to anyone versed in the theory or practice of capitalism, but in this context, Ghazi's point was not only profound but heretical. The rhetoric and the motivating spirit of Silicon Valley emerged from the win-win booster fantasies of free market ideologues, though it was slathered in a veneer of altruism and progress. To suggest, as Ghazi did, that the economic pie had only so many slices to go around was to undermine the entire Silicon Valley enterprise, which had made so many people here rich and which many more imagined would make them rich as well.

But Ghazi sensed a turn coming. The speculators were getting nervous. The easy money for startups was drying up. Only the most coldly disenchanted and obsessive—and the best connected—would know what was coming next. Yet many of Ghazi's colleagues and friends were still drunk on the Kool-Aid. One, sharing his firm's analysis of the situation, had recently told him, "We don't see this bubble as ending." To which Ghazi replied, "Look, by definition it has to end." Anything, from a federal budget cut to a student loan crisis, could precipitate the next bust. Regardless, the fallout, Ghazi said, will be familiar: employee layoffs, along with tersely worded shutdown notices to users and pennies-on-the-dollar buyouts to save face for founders and investors. "I've seen it three times. People literally pack up their stuff and leave," Ghazi said. By the end of 2015, few startups sought to make initial public offerings, and the cleverest unicorns were hoarding cash in "war chests," as

Ghazi put it, instead of torching it on booze cruises and ad campaigns.

"Whenever you hear people say 'No, everything is fine, it's not going to collapse'—that's when something is going to happen," Ghazi said.

His doomsaying made me feel both vindicated and anxious. Vindicated because, as I had suspected, Silicon Valley was a top-to-bottom racket. Anxious because I sensed I had come too late. However, the situation was not yet hopeless, my fate not yet sealed—I still had an unbeatable combination of Yankee pluck, lowborn grit, and chemical confidence.

VI

Failing Up

I'd had enough of circling the fringe. I wanted inside. I wanted to pitch my incredible startup idea. I wanted to hear an investor say, "You're a rock star, here's a check for five million dollars, come back for more when you've spent it all." I wanted the money and the glory.

I wanted something else, too. I wanted to burn it all down. I wanted to humiliate these venal fools. I wanted to compensate myself for all the boredom I'd endured traipsing from bar to club, from conference to conference, from Pointless Product Launch A to Pathetic Networking Party B. I wanted to get rich, and I wanted to defeat the rich. I wanted to poke the beehive and gorge on the honey. Most of all, I wanted to prove that I was more worthy than all these dumb-luck techies by tricking them into paying me to prove how dishonest and manipulative they were. All I needed was an idea. It had to be the right sort of idea, something that was just a little too stupid, or a little too criminal. It had to be a scheme so risky, and yet so potentially profitable, that Valley VCs would find it irresistible.

Or something like that. Unfortunately, I didn't have any ideas that fit the bill. So I set about looking for successful ideas to rip off. The difference between mediocrity and genius could sometimes be a minor tweak. Twitter was popular . . . Tweakr? Twitter for meth enthusiasts? No . . . too many liabilities. And according to *Vice*, all the tech-savvy tweakers were already using Tumblr to compare their paranoid delusions and to share thoughts like "I have hives because of this meth binge and I'm so fucking itchy." Stonerr, then? Twitter for potheads? Redundant. "Twitter is . . . a horribly mismanaged company—probably a lot of pot smoking going on there," the VC Peter Thiel said once on television. What about Facebook for people without friends? I could call it . . . Strangebook? But it would be hard to beat RentAFriend.com, which claimed half a million users. Facebook for animals? People liked to post pictures of their pets. Why not let the pets do it themselves? I was late once again. The pet-sharing space was crowded with competitors like MySocialPetwork.com, Petwink—"for passionate pet owners"—and Petbu, which promised to help "make your pet famous." I needed to come up with something entirely different, yet samey.

I browsed the tech press for inspiration, returning, as ever, to Hacker News, the internet home page for people who were convinced they were the world's smartest people, and I found an essay by the website's founder, Paul Graham, called "Before the Startup." That seemed to describe where I was. The essay was adapted from a guest lecture Graham delivered to his business partner Sam Altman's startup class at Stanford. "The way to succeed in a startup is not to be an expert on startups, but to be an expert on your users and the problem you're solving for them," Graham wrote. I was an expert in nothing, which in Graham's formulation put me at a slight advantage over people who were experts on startups. "The dangerous thing is, faking does work to some degree on investors," Graham wrote. "If you're super good at sounding like you know what you're talking about, you can fool investors for at least one and perhaps even two rounds of funding." Did I need more than one or two rounds of funding? Not really. This was encouraging.

I felt even better about my prospects after learning that I didn't really need an idea. In 2012, Y Combinator, the investment fund behind Hacker News, announced in an online post that it would begin accepting funding applications from teams who didn't even have ideas for their startups. "So if the only thing holding you back from starting a startup is not having an idea for one," the investors wrote, "now nothing is holding you back." I knew the spendthrift reputation of venture capital, yet I was still surprised to learn that some of the most prestigious investors in tech were funneling millions of dollars in capital to kids who showed up for their interviews without so much as an idea. What did they care? It wasn't their money. Like private stockbrokers for startups, VCs managed large pools of funds. Which is to say, the investors had investors. Often these were big institutions like foundations and universities—Stanford, naturally, was a major player—as well as pension funds.

Because such people expected results, the VC industry couldn't appear *completely* irresponsible. Therefore, Y Combinator presented a flimsy rationale for its lax investment criteria in the same online post:

A lot of the startups we accept change their ideas completely, and some of those do really well . . . The other reason we're doing it is that our experience suggests that smart people who think they can't come up with a good startup idea are generally mistaken. Almost every smart person has a good idea in them.

Incredibly, technology had advanced such that I didn't even need to think of a name for my startup with no idea—I could simply order one up with the touch of a button. Several startups existed to generate names for other startups, such as whatthefuckshould Inamemystartup.com, which suggested DownLaunch, Growth-Boost, SnapSlice, Spotlr, and Starterfyer. These were all serviceable but lacked the je ne sais quoi my brand would require.

After careful deliberation, I settled on Monkeywrench International. It was simple, powerful, and suggested multiple possibilities for an adorable mascot. Most important, as every do-it-yourselfer knows, a sturdy monkey wrench is the most versatile item in any toolbox. To further establish my bona fides as a technologist and entrepreneur, I spent a few hours building a small website. It had just the right look for a circa-2015 startup—a bold palette, free of adornments. Leaning back in my desk chair, I regarded my creation admiringly. Here was what the tech entrepreneurs would refer to as my "minimum viable product." Visit us online at monkeywrench.international!

My next challenge: to devise a succinct, memorable expression of the essence of a company with nothing to offer.

Then I remembered reading something about the VE firm Andreessen-Horowitz, which, much like my new company, I thought, produced nothing at all of value. I had read that Andreessen-Horowitz's motto was inspired by an obscure and archaic Trotskyite buzzword: "permanent revolution." Salvaged from the forgotten struggle for a classless society and reclaimed for the new era of capitalist dominion, the old Marxist dogma gained a crisp motivational pizzazz. Taking a cue from Andreessen-Horowitz, I consulted Mao: "A revolution is not a dinner party, or writing an essay, or painting a picture, or doing embroidery; it cannot be so refined, so leisurely and gentle, so temperate, kind, courteous, restrained and magnanimous. A revolution is an insurrection, an act of violence by which one class overthrows another." There was my slogan: Disruption is not a dinner party.

Disruption was everything. A tech company's worth was measured by its disruptive potential. If your startup wasn't disruptive, you might as well go back to your freshman dorm and switch to an English major. A "disruptive" company had the potential to take over an entire industry, as medieval scriptoria were disrupted by movable type, the infantry charge by the machine gun, knowledge by Google, and so on. The spurious notion that there was some discernible Law of Business Administration to be found within such miscellaneous instances of human behavioral change dated to 1997, when a Harvard Business School professor published his theory of "disruptive innovation." Another Harvardite, Mark

Zuckerberg, enshrined disruption as the operating principle of Facebook, commanding employees to "move fast and break things." Later techie manifestos boiled the scholarly pretense down to its vulgar essence: "Break shit." I needed to look like someone who was ready to break shit. I procured a bright yellow T-shirt that proclaimed, in big block letters, IT'S TIME FOR PLAN ฿—Bitcoin, of course. I wanted disruptive business cards, but I was on a budget. To save money, I bought some reflective silver stock on Amazon and made them myself. After printing, I cut the cards into small rectangles with an X-Acto knife so that they resembled pocket mirrors used for snorting cocaine—a favorite productivity booster in Silicon Valley's executive suites since the 1980s. Each card bore only a single line of text—my new email address, futurebillionaire@aol.com. I completed the ensemble with a slick cerulean blue jacket I found at Nordstrom Rack for $26.

Soon I would be ready to hit the scene. I just needed that elusive *idea*. Perhaps I was wrong to focus on quality, when quantity would suffice. The internet came through again. I quickly found a half dozen startup idea generators. My favorite was ItsThisForThat.com. Every time you clicked the refresh button, it spat out a new idea.

- Neural Network for Pets!
- Wearable Computer for Ex-Convicts!
- 1-800-Flowers for Medicinal Marijuana!
- Snapchat for Adult Dancers!
- Foursquare for Attractive People!
- Social Game for Social Outcasts!

The site delivered pitchable ideas in minutes. There was a problem, however: these ideas, absurd though they seemed, had already been done. To wit:

- Neural network for pets? *No More Woof* is "an electronic device that promises to analyze dogs' brain waves and translate a few of their thoughts into rudimentary English."
- Wearable computer for ex-convicts? The *3M One-Piece GPS Offender Tracking System* allows police to "efficiently track offenders virtually anywhere, anytime, at varying levels of intensity through a single, compact, body-worn unit."
- 1-800-Flowers for medicinal marijuana? *Eaze*, backed by Peter Thiel, offers "easy, quick, professional marijuana delivery" on demand.
- Snapchat for adult dancers? It's called *Snapchat*.
- Foursquare for attractive people? *Instagram*.
- Social game for social outcasts? *Foursquare*.

Truly, there is nothing new under the sun.

I cursed my rotten luck as I walked along Market Street past the fortresses of the fortunate. As I neared Uber's headquarters, a motorcycle peloton rolled past. I saw a fleet of cop cars parked along the street, not far from four big black buses that idled curbside. A small formation of riot police stood blocking the middle of the road. What was all this fuss? Then I spotted a man holding a hand-painted sign that read UBER APP=INSURANCE GAP. He was the last cabbie standing following a protest involving one or two hundred licensed taxi drivers earlier that morning. The protest was timed to catch the attention of a visiting delegation from the U.S. Conference of Mayors—hence the buses. "They're here because Uber is buying them lunch," the cabbie told me. He was riled up. "I don't mind competing with Uber in a fair fight. They just don't want to pay for licensing and insurance. It's not hard to get. Any idiot can do it. They just don't want to pay," he said.

Cabbies weren't the only workers caught in this bind. Most of the startups pitched as "Uber for X" boiled down to "Cheaper Labor for X," and they had the same effect of depressing wages across an industry, just as the VC money Uber used to subsidize its cheap fares undercut taxi drivers who hoped to earn a decent wage.

That angry cabbie was my muse.

His problem was the solution I'd been searching for. He'd given me an idea: What if there was a way to *increase* the cost of labor? The cabbie belonged to a union—as did all the others who had protested that morning. Through history, unionization was the most reliable way for workers to earn *more* money for *less* work.

That was it. My world-changing idea: labor unions.

An app for organizing . . . But how could it be monetized? Who would pay for it? Unions? No. Corporations? No. I had it: *The competition.*

Here again Uber pointed the way. The company had run an ingeniously underhanded dirty tricks campaign against its largest rival, Lyft, by ordering, then canceling, thousands of rides. The hope was that Lyft's drivers, frustrated by the cancellations, would come work for Uber. Then there was Operation SLOG—"Supplying Long-term Operations Growth"—a "marketing program" revealed by the *Verge* that involved undercover recruiters equipped with "burner phones, credit cards, and driver kits," charged with hailing rides on Lyft and then persuading the drivers to defect to Uber.

"Not only does Uber know about this, they're actively encouraging these actions day to day and, in doing so, are flat-out lying both to their customers, the media, and their investors," one whistleblower told the *Verge*. Operation SLOG reportedly began with in-person meetings between drivers and Uber high-level marketing staff, and the ongoing encouragement included emails with pep talks and follow-up instructions. And indeed, the public uproar against Uber's campaign did little to stop the company's momentum toward a public stock offering at a valuation of $68 billion—making the company worth as much in investors' eyes as BMW, and more than GM, Ford, or Nissan. Apart from a fleeting barrage of finger wagging by ineffectual do-gooders such as Juno and Lyft, the company's campaign of competitive sabotage was an unalloyed success. Perhaps the only thing keeping other startups from adopting similar tactics was a lack of know-how. And a sense of propriety. Which was not a problem for me.

My idea was truly disruptive, in the sense that it was both dubiously legal and potentially profitable. I sought to apply proven methods of corporate subversion to a market that was woefully neglected by established players in the tech industry.

The idea was so simple, I was surprised it hadn't been done
yet. If Uber could use stealthy labor-organizing-style tactics in its
campaign to poach drivers from Lyft, why shouldn't Lyft retaliate
by covertly funding an actual employee union drive at Uber? Come
to think of it, why shouldn't *any* company that wanted to gain an
edge over a competitor do this? It made intuitive sense on a business level, especially given how focused most American companies were on near-term results. In the long term, of course, the
idea had the potential to turn the rapacious tendencies of capitalism against itself, by tricking corporations into underwriting the
growth of the labor movement. Monkeywrench International was
going to disrupt labor organizing and oligarchic capitalism *at the*
same time.

The best part, given my limited resources, was that there was
no app, as such, to build. The technical details could wait until I
raised a round of seed funding. Before proceeding, I needed to
decide what to call this new product. The first name that came to
mind was Laborswarm. I quickly rejected it as too insectoid in
favor of a less creepy brand moniker: Laborize. The dot-com domain
was available for only $10. I bought it right away and got to work
building a snazzy landing page. First I found an old and hopefully
out-of-copyright black-and-white photograph of a workers' march.
The image was from a May Day parade in Minneapolis in 1937,
three years after the Teamsters led a three-month general strike
in that city. A banner at the focal point of the original picture said
FOR A UNITED LABOR MOVEMENT. I Photoshopped a new slogan
in its place: ORGANIZE THE COMPETITION. I thought that got the
concept across.

I filled out the rest of laborize.com with descriptive slogans: "Their solidarity is your opportunity," "Labor agitation anytime, anywhere," and "strikes as a service." I added more photos from other historical strikes and riots, concluding with an image of Bolsheviks rallying outside the Winter Palace in St. Petersburg in 1917. With a few clicks and taps, the site went live online. Looking at what I had achieved, I was no longer worried about dying alone in a grimy cage. In less than one day's time, using only my wits and a MacBook, I had constructed the world's next great startup—the Uber killer—my golden ticket to the Millionaires Society—the engine of revolution—Laborize!

I ran my startup idea by Ghazi, hoping for a stamp of approval from the cynic who inspired it. I knew he wasn't going to invest, but I wanted his advice. He was happy to oblige. I gave him the spiel. Then I asked, "How do you think that's going to go over with VCs?"

Ghazi laughed and laughed. There were tears in his eyes. "They're going to think you're joking," he said. "They're going to think, 'This guy is trying to expose us for backing this thing we know goes on all the time.'"

Well, I was, and I wasn't.

Pitching was agony. I loathed every second of abjection involved in soliciting investors, but I had no intention of giving up before I had done so. Most of the time, I feared I'd never earn another dime. In my optimistic moments, I was terrified that someone might actually write me a check. Suppose I took money to build a flagrantly illegal startup. Suppose I then ran into trouble with, say, the United States Department of Justice. What then? I could say that it was all a joke. Ha-ha! Although even if I escaped criminal prosecution, my investors could still claim I'd defrauded them. At which point I could only give their money back and hope they had a good sense of humor. I had prepared a number of unconvincing excuses for these eventualities, modeled on the example of the tech titans who preceded me. If Laborize's users or clients did something untoward, I said, that was their business and their responsibility. I was merely providing a *platform*. And certainly I would forbid illegal activity on this platform while encouraging users to report it when they saw it. This was pretty much how Craigslist, among others, washed its hands of illegal postings while simultaneously benefiting from their presence. Anyway, I figured, how could I be accused of promoting unlawful behavior when I knew next to nothing about the relevant laws?

Considering how poorly thought through my criminal conspiracy was, I suppose I was fortunate that I couldn't get the time of day from any serious investors. Any number of sympathetic strangers who endured my pitch offered polite encouragement, such as the hard-line libertarian Stanford economist I buttonholed at a panel who told me Laborize was intriguing and "just might work." But in retrospect, I was merely culturally confused, and should have understood that Californians always delivered the brush-off with a smile. Wishing someone good luck was one thing, but writing that person a check was another.

Based on the endless succession of half-baked startups that were getting funded, I had assumed I would have little trouble arranging a meeting with investors. But based on the total lack of response to my cold email campaign, I would have had better luck posing as a Nigerian prince. I tried being clever. I tried being funny. I tried being obsequious. I tried piling on the buzzwords. I tried dropping names. No one bit. So I escalated. Twice I ventured downtown to simply barge in to VC headquarters and talk my way in to a meeting on the spot. Each time, I handed one of my mirror-backed cards to the receptionist and asked her to pass it on to an investor with whom I had "been emailing." One woman complimented my chutzpah, which was a small consolation, truly—but at least I had provoked a response.

Again, I escalated—this time to a heist. Why not simply crash someone else's meeting with an investor? My target, an incubator called Runway, was in the Twitter building on Market Street. On a previous visit—for the panel where I'd met that Stanford economist—I had spied a bulletin announcing the office hours for one Kyle Anderson from Greylock Partners. I marked the date in my calendar, and when the time came, I successfully bluffed my way past security. Luckily I arrived during a shift change, so the guard was busy chatting with her friend. Upstairs in Runway, I wandered around the rows of mostly empty desks and peered into conference rooms looking for Kyle, but he was nowhere to be found. Finally I found someone to ask about Kyle's whereabouts. "A lot of people aren't in today," he said. "The Warriors victory party was last night." As a favor of sorts, I sent Kyle an email letting him know that even though he had apparently blown off his Friday afternoon commitments, I would still be open to the possibility of an investment from Greylock. Funny enough, he never wrote back.

Perhaps I would have better luck establishing relationships with monied techies in a more intimate, well-lubricated, convivial setting? Acting on a tip, I ventured out to Sand Hill Road for what was described to me as the hottest night out in Menlo Park: Cougar Night. This, I learned, was a tradition at the Stanford University–owned Rosewood Hotel, dating to 2009, with several interruptions related to public accusations of prostitution. The men who showed up were too old to be classified as cougar bait, but I can confirm that the debauchery of Cougar Night lived up to the legend, with all the fervid groping of last call at a British nightclub combined with the hyperpreppy attire of a velvet-rope club in New York's Meatpacking District and the tangible awkwardness of any Silicon Valley social event. At one point, I found myself talking to an abrasive fashion designer who had recently dumped her boyfriend. He ran "this bullshit startup," she said. "He had a bad logo and no revenue plan." Everyone was a critic. Finally, before the last train left for San Francisco, I had the chance to buttonhole a VC in line at the bar. He nodded, glassy-eyed, as I delivered my pitch. Although only in his thirties, the VC, a former engineer, had grown jaded. "It almost doesn't matter if you build a better mousetrap," he said. "It's all this other shit"—like slick branding, good timing, personal connections, and, of course, dumb luck. So much for that plan. I realized I'd come to Cougar Night for all the wrong reasons.

Ultimately I resigned myself to embracing the last resort of all fresh-off-the-boat Silicon Valley entrepreneurs: I could pay to pitch my idea to investors. From a distance, this practice might have seemed strange, even backward. After all, whenever a startup takes off, the investors make far more money than the founders. It seemed investors should be paying to listen to founders, not the other way around.

Of course, there was a market basis for this counterintuitive custom. Everybody had an idea, but only a few people had money to burn. The imbalance, even more acute in boom times, provided a nourishing environment for intermediaries to grow, flourish, and skim from the endless stream of startup hopefuls. While advance-fee "casting workshops" for actors and artists were illegal in California, their tech industry equivalents thrived. One such go-between boasted prestigious affiliates including a noted member of the Harvard Angels investment club who was also a trustee of the Computer History Museum, as well as a partner from Pillsbury Winthrop Shaw Pittman LLP, a top corporate law firm established in the 1860s to cash in on the California gold rush.

This outfit, called VC Taskforce, charged $105 for the chance to pitch an investor panel for two minutes, followed by eight minutes of questions and "feedback." It occurred to me that if I ever tired of the founder's life, I should hang a shingle as an investor and charge $630 an hour to sit around listening to other people's ideas. In the meantime, I looked for a cheaper ticket.

Many pay-to-pitch events were framed as competitions, and they were held on a regular basis around the Bay Area. I registered for Startup Weekend, an outfit backed by Google and endorsed by the Obama White House. I paid $29.70 to join a competition of startups conceived, designed, and pitched to a panel of judges over three days. Win or lose, I figured the bottomless pizza-and-beer buffet alone was worth the price of admission.

My destination was Galvanize, a chichi startup "campus" that charged premium rates of $550 per month for an unreserved seat at a table, or $750 for a desk of one's own. The self-described "front door of the tech industry," Galvanize stood opposite a muddy construction site ringed with a chain-link fence, where homeless people lived. I loitered outside. Down the way, I saw a big cardboard box shuddering and rocking side to side. A boot emerged, then another, then the complete pair of legs. When the man inside emerged in full, he methodically flattened the cardboard, then packed away his belongings in a sack. Thus encumbered, he proceeded slowly in my direction. I gave him a couple of dollars in seed money, then turned and entered Galvanize.

Inside, I found a registration table with an array of lanyards attached to blank name tags, along with a Sharpie. Startup Weekend suggested entrants choose from one of three descriptive titles: DESIGNER, HACKER, or HUSTLER. I wrote COREY PEIN, HUSTLER on my name tag. Just then a trio of slick dudes in nice suits lined up behind me. "Husslahs!" one whooped, grabbing a marker. Indeed. This clearly wasn't their first pitch competition. Before I could say hello, the Husslahs were off schmoozing. This meet-and-greet time was used to scout potential teammates for the startup competition. Our task as hustlers was to work the room, describing our ideas to the people with actual skills (the designers and hackers) and persuading as many of them as possible to join our group in the competition. Once teamed up, we would then develop a PowerPoint presentation (or "pitch deck")—and hopefully, by the end of the weekend, a working prototype. The ideas were supposed to evolve depending on who joined up for any given team, but it clearly paid to come prepared. I chatted with whoever the Husslahs ignored. As a result I found myself talking to a shy twenty-year-old computer science student visiting the city from Tuscaloosa, Alabama; a skittish Android developer from Pune, India; and an easygoing restaurateur from South Florida who had merely tagged along with friend. If these were to be my teammates, we would be Team Underdog. So much the better.

The line for pizza and beer was growing, and the chairs, arranged in concentric semicircles facing the podium, were filling. A bearded hipster—the emcee—bounded to the fore and called for attention. "Hey, are you guys ready for Startup Weekend?" the emcee asked. "Whoo!" the audience replied. The emcee, Frank, who let it be known that he preferred to be called a facilitator, began by announcing, "The mission of Startup Weekend is to inspire change in the lives of entrepreneurs. It's a movement around the world." I zoned out, waiting for the pablum to pass. On any given weekend, Frank said, seven or eight far-flung groups were doing just the same: conceiving, building, and pitching a tech company with a group of total strangers.

This Startup Weekend had a theme: "Hack immigration." Mine wasn't an "immigration" startup, strictly speaking, but I figured I could fudge that. Outsourcing, trade, and international labor issues in general were core to the Silicon Valley profit model, as the opening panel made clear. The speakers included startup founders who happened to be immigrants; veterans of major corporations such as Goldman Sachs; and a couple of immigration lawyers, one of whom spoke about "finding creative pathways around our laws." The marquee name, however, was Todd Schulte, president of Fwd.us, a "full stack advocacy organization"—that is, a lobbying group—founded by Mark Zuckerberg with support from other tech tycoons, including Bill Gates and LinkedIn's Reid Hoffman. The organization launched with $50 million in cash, giving it instant name recognition and access in Washington, D.C., and spent nearly $2 million on lobbying in its first three years. Schulte, who overlapped with Zuckerberg at Harvard, had been promoted to lead Fwd.us after the board forced out founding president Joe Green, who'd lived in the dorm next to Zuckerberg at Harvard. I discerned a pattern in these high-level appointments. Schulte was one of the most obnoxious tools I had the displeasure of encountering in San Francisco. He had arrived with a sizable entourage. When he was called to join the panel, one loyal aide blasted the fifteen-year-old hip-hop hit "Who Let the Dogs Out" from a smartphone speaker while the rest of Schulte's pack whooped and cheered.

A dutiful subordinate posted Schulte's photo to Twitter. He later added the approving caption "Thought leaderin'."

"My job, and our job at Fwd.us, is to pass comprehensive immigration reform," Schulte began. The sole panelist who carried his alcoholic drink onstage, he punctuated his points by tilting a beer bottle toward the audience. "We're going to have a system where more high-skilled immigrants can come to this country," he said. *Tilt.* "We are not going to deport eleven and a half million people," he went on. "No credible person in Washington thinks this." *Tilt.*

Schulte was so, so smug and so, so wrong. He spoke just weeks before Donald Trump launched his successful bid for the Republican presidential nomination, a campaign based almost entirely on a xenophobic pledge to deport millions of immigrants, whom the Trumpists slandered with the most obscene racist stereotypes.

"By the way," Schulte went on, "both parties have huge incentives to get this done." *Tilt.* His organization's strategy, cynical and yet naïve as it was, aimed to appease Republicans by pushing high-tech border surveillance—a sure boon for Silicon Valley's federal contractors—while bringing corporate-friendly Democrats around to its proposals for a new "entrepreneurs visa." The Zuckerberg-backed group also lobbied for an expansion of the existing H-1B specialty workers visa, the lucky winners of which live in perpetual uncertainty and are exploited mercilessly by tech industry labor brokers known as body shops. Schulte shared the stage with one such labor broker, whose company played "matchmaker" for San Francisco startups seeking "high-talent workers" from abroad. "Kick-ass policy changes . . . that's what my man Todd is working on," she said. Another panelist, a former Skype executive and Andreessen-Horowitz "entrepreneur in residence" from Estonia, now leading an immigration startup in Palo Alto, had grandiose designs that went far beyond ass kicking. "We want to make every single government in the world compete for every single citizen," the entrepreneur, Sten Tamkivi, said. I looked around. Tamkivi had blown minds with this nonsense. But his startup was so modest in scope that it made a mockery of his fantastically ambitious rhetoric about supplanting the global reign of nation-states. The startup, Teleport, supplied globetrotting "digital nomads" with personalized advice, such as how to find work in a new city and what neighborhoods to consider gentrifying. As he saw it, governments had a solemn obligation to compete for tech "talent" by offering favorable immigration policies and plentiful WiFi. It was a global race in which the position of the United States "if I may say, is falling sharply every year." On that point, he was correct, but it was not because the government didn't do enough to champion the cockamamie libertarianism of hucksters like Tamkivi. Still, after hearing this plan to refashion the international order as an upscale shopping mall for governments, I feared my own outlandish startup might come off as too pedestrian.

The panel petered out. There was a break. I was sick of beer and pizza. Then Frank the facilitator called for attention. It was time. The format he described was simple. Everyone who wanted to pitch an idea would get in line. Each person would have sixty seconds to sell the audience on their startup. Afterward, people would vote for their favorite ideas by attaching sticky notes to sheets of butcher paper. Everyone who pitched got three votes. The voting interval would offer another chance to recruit teammates for the weekend, although surely the Husslahs were ahead of me there. "Ten to fifteen" projects would make the cut, and those teams would spend the rest of the weekend brainstorming, building their apps or websites, and, on Sunday night, presenting to a new panel of judges, who would pick three winners. Prizes would include in-kind services from Galvanize and the sponsors, as well as publicity for the winners' new companies.

A lot of people wanted to pitch. I hurried to join the line. There were a few people ahead of me, which was fine. I didn't want to go first—not because I was nervous, necessarily, but for strategic reasons. The room hadn't settled yet, and whoever pitched first would need to shout over the mingling crowd. And I *was* oddly nervous.

First into the maw was a timid young Android developer pitching an app called Visa Doctor. The concept was, uh, unclear. "I will need a back-end developer, designer, and growth hacker. Together we can build mumble mumble mumble," he concluded. Everyone applauded. "Yay," the woman in line behind me said. The next idea was a service whereby prospective U.S. citizens could upload videos of themselves, which "verified citizens" could then watch and rate in the manner of stupid pet tricks on YouTube or prospective Tinder dates. Inevitably, if this startup ever took off, the most photogenic migrants would be let in and the ugly turned away. The crowd seemed to like it. But the next pitch beat them all. The presenter had a thick, indeterminate accent. His app would help arrange marriages between would-be migrants and citizens in their country of choice. He called it "Greender, the Tinder for green cards," which got a big laugh, either because no one knew such marriage arrangements could be illegal or because everyone did. Fortunately, I didn't have to follow Greender. I didn't really catch the pitch before mine because I was studying the notes on my phone. Sixty seconds passed in a blink and someone handed me the microphone.

My time had come. I was ready to blow minds. Who let the dogs out, indeed? Who? Who?

"Hi," I said. At this moment, before this audience, I hoped that the banal cynicism of my ideas would mask their more subversive aspects. My goal was to make a startup designed to encourage corporate cannibalization sound entirely normal and safe, yet exciting and profitable. I paused to take a breath and, hopefully, to build anticipation. I put my phone away. I didn't need notes. All I had to do was open up.

My practiced pitch spilled out in a hyperactive babble. To my own ears, I sounded like a coked-up sociopath, which was kind of what I was going for. It's not important what I said. What's important is that I tried. And people seemed to like it. They clapped, anyway. I thought it went okay. I retreated to the audience in such a hurry I almost forgot to hang a piece of butcher paper on the wall so that people could vote for my startup.

I watched the remaining presentations from a safe remove. There was an app to deliver home-cooked immigrant food to restaurants, taking advantage of an obscure exemption in California's food inspection laws—"Uber or Airbnb but with immigrants' food," the presenter said. A do-gooder wanted to build some kind of worker-owned sharing economy cooperative, but the details were so fuzzy, I wasn't sure what it would actually do. A whacked-out dude pitched a startup called "New Political System . . . the killer app for your political life," which was similarly mushy when it came to specifics but earned a round of applause nonetheless.

Before the voting commenced, I counted twenty-three startup proposals. It seemed I barely had to canvass for support, because people kept coming over to to ask questions about my presentation. A couple of Web designers from Oakland offered their assistance. Others had questions about the legality of my project. Fortunately, I was prepared. "We're going to rely on users to flag anything illegal," I said. "Just like the prostitution ads on Craigslist."

"You could always pay people in Bitcoin, too!" one curious Weekender interjected.

"That's right!" I said. People *got* it. Mercenary attitudes were so common in Silicon Valley that no one lectured me about propriety. People mainly wanted to know how I intended to get away with a patently unlawful conspiracy. This was a reasonable concern. One of my inspirations, Ross Ulbricht, was sentenced to life in prison for operating an illegal drug market called Silk Road. Accessible only through the Pentagon-funded Tor network—also known as the Dark Web—Silk Road allegedly processed more than one million transactions comprising $1.2 billion in revenue over two years. Ulbricht, a former Eagle Scout, was just about my age. He'd built Silk Road at the Glen Park public library in San Francisco, where I sometimes worked. In a tearful plea for leniency, Ulbricht apologized and told his trial judge, "I'm not a self-centered sociopathic person." But prosecutors showed how Ulbricht had tried to hire a hit man from the Hells Angels to kill another drug dealer who'd threatened to extort him. In reality, Ulbricht was plotting with and against undercover federal investigators who already had him surrounded. A month after the feds shut Ulbricht down, another former Eagle Scout from Texas launched Silk Road 2.0. Ulbricht's successor, a twenty-six-year-old SpaceX employee and Mission District resident named Blake Benthall, lasted less than two months before his arrest on charges of "drug dealing, computer hacking, money laundering, and trafficking in fake identification documents." Benthall awaits trial as of this writing. The prosecuting U.S. attorney, Preet Bharara of Manhattan, made a statement intended for overzealous entrepreneurs:

"Let's be clear—this Silk Road, in whatever form, is the road to prison."

Less than two weeks after my debut on the San Francisco shark tank circuit, another Silk Road–inspired startup, called Open-Bazaar, secured a $1 million seed investment from prominent VCs including Union Square Ventures and Andreessen-Horowitz.

Reality had outpaced my dark and fevered imagination once more.

All was not lost. I could still vote for myself. My face flushed with shame as I pressed a sticky note onto the wall. Hopefully it would encourage others to do the same. I agonized over what to do with my remaining two votes. What was the cultural expectation here? Should I vote for myself again, or would that be tacky and uncollaborative? I gave my remaining votes to Greender, the green card marriage app, because they had outdone me without really trying, and to New Political System, because why not?

When the votes were counted, I got eight, not counting my own. I would've needed at least five more to make the next round. Alas, I'd failed to make an investor connection at one Caligulan meat market.

The next cheap pay-to-pitch ticket was in San Jose.

This event cost $30 and afforded founders a ninety-second opportunity to pitch two investors. I had never heard of the investors or of the organizer, a startup called Lifograph, so I turned to the website, which featured an introductory one-minute video. It had all the elements of a standard-issue startup reel—a peppy acoustic guitar soundtrack, simulated Web browsing, and a fictional protagonist whose problems are solved by the product—yet with each of these elements, something seemed amiss. The narrator, for instance, had a British accent and sounded confused. He paused in all the wrong places and yet maintained an unnerving level of enthusiasm. "Hi! This is *Andy*. Andy's running out of money. Bootstrapping his *tech startup*!" the narrator began.

Lifograph billed itself as "the encyclopedia of people and companies in Silicon Valley and tech." But it wasn't an encyclopedia. It was a penny shopper combined with a pay-to-pitch racket. The Startup Showcase on Lifograph's website featured an app-based cannabis delivery service called Highspeed and an "employment-guaranteed degree program" called European Leadership University, based in Turkey. It cost $70 to be listed alongside these fine companies, inclusive of a custom-made pitch video. I passed. The Lifograph website also featured a number of blog posts, almost half of which were about Steve Jobs. One post was authored by Manny Fernandez, a small-time investor whom I would be pitching at the San Jose event. Manny did not waste his readers' time by padding his Jobsian advice with an introductory paragraph. Instead, he plunged straight into a numbered list of tautologies.

1. BE A LEADER
Steve Jobs was a college dropout, but he was a leader. He was able to rally up investors and employees to create an amazing product.

Leadership is something you develop over time. You have to embrace the idea of being a leader, then get followers to support you.

172 Corey Pein

You can't put a price on advice like that.

The other investor/judge at the San Jose pitch event was to be Istvan Joyner, a computer science PhD and former Google middle manager turned VC. Joyner worked for a low-profile $100 million investment fund owned by an alleged "patent troll," InterDigital, Inc., although the company disputes this characterization. This litigious outfit made hundreds of millions of dollars a year by acquiring patents—more than twenty thousand in all, "including the fundamental technologies that enable wireless communications"—then licensing the right to use those technologies to companies such as Apple and Samsung. Or else.

I knew that Manny and Istvan would be harsher critics than the jury of peers I'd faced at Startup Weekend. But given their connections, I knew the rewards could outweigh the agony of it all.

As I reviewed the outline of my pitch over the smeared remains of a mezze platter, I sensed the onset of what would become a truly evil pressure headache. Within a few minutes, my eyeball was ready to shoot from its socket and go splat against the window. This was terrible timing. As my bus rolled past the sparsely tenanted strip malls on the road to San Jose, I winced portentously in pain.

Outer San Jose saw American architecture at its most beige. The downtown bustled with midmarket consumerist prosperity, as though city planners had somehow ripped a suburban shopping mall from the early 1990s, plunked it down along a light rail line, and added a few contemporary touches such as pricey vintage clothing stores and headache-soothing craft breweries, one of which I visited to kill some time before the big event. The streets were clean and smooth. Even the skater kids wore gold watches.

The pitch session was being hosted at yet another incubator, this one called Founders Floor. I expected another fashionably austere space with cold, hard floors and exposed ductwork. But this was not San Francisco. Founders Floor was a stiflingly passé purgatory of thin carpeting, low ceilings, and subliminally flickering fluorescent lighting. It felt like the kind of place where someone was going to ask me to pee into a cup or fill out a Myers-Briggs personality test. The one decorative flourish that caught my eye was a slightly smaller than life-size wall decal of Leonard Nimoy giving the Vulcan salute.

The San Jose tech scene was less nerd-chic than nerd-core. It could even be called dweeby. The attendees were a clean-cut bunch who quickly took their seats in tidy rows. Many wore eerily similar blue-and-white plaid shirts. It was good that I had dressed up a little. I should have shaved and gotten a haircut. This was also the first tech event I had attended where alcohol was not served. Fortunately, I carried a flask. The entrée was rubbery chicken that slid with a sickening plop into the garbage can. I hated to do anything on an empty stomach, but it would be better to pitch hungry than to projectile-vomit on the investor panel.

I took a seat near the back of the room, near a potbellied guy who ran an email spam filtering service. Part of his secret sauce was scanning the text of inbound email for references to African royalty. In the seat to my left I met a young startup founder who had enrolled at Founders Floor at the behest of the Korean government, which wanted him to learn the art of pitching Silicon Valley investors.

At the front of the room stood Lifograph founder Déa Wilson, a peroxide blond émigré who called herself "Ms. Silicon Valley." She was the bubbliest Romanian I had ever encountered, but then she had been living in California for quite some time. "Come on, let's put on some trance music," she said. The deejay responded by calling up some screeching, sullen electronica. "Maybe next time," Déa said. "Maybe next time we'll put together a song, everybody will be dancing, we will start with a band."

"*Woo-hoo!*" she shrieked without warning. "Let's get a little warmed up. Can I hear *woo-hoo*?"

The audience responded with a tepid "*Woo-hoo.*"

"You guys need more beer, I guess," Déa said. What beer?

"*Woo-hoo!*" one guy in the back shouted.

Déa introduced her sponsors, the first of whom was a mobile app developer seeking new clients. "Lately I've been focusing on niche apps," he said. "These are not billion-dollar apps. They make ten, twenty, thirty thousand dollars. I know it's not a lot of money, but for some of us it's decent change."

"Sounds like it pays better than being a startup entrepreneur," Déa said. There was that Romanian fatalism! I gathered Déa wasn't getting rich running Lifograph, now that she was pouring cold water over the dreams of those who'd forked over money to be there. The pea-soup fog of optimism in Silicon Valley was so dense that Déa's little crack, this minor demonstration of vulnerability, came off as genuinely transgressive.

The sponsors duly acknowledged, Déa introduced Manny and Istvan, the investor-judges, who sat on stools at the front of the room. Istvan was somewhat reserved, but acrid whenever he spoke. Manny, who had a less impressive CV, compensated with showmanship.

"How many people here are raising money? Raise your hands," Manny said.

"Everybody," Déa said, surveying the room.

"Oh, wow," Manny said. "I'm excited about this. I'm kinda tired. But no excuses in the startup world." He related a self-congratulatory anecdote that alluded to his secret moneymaking formula and concluded, "Follow me on Twitter." With that, it was time to pitch. First in line was a slight young immigrant named Harold. "*Woohoo* for Harold!" Déa said. Harold pitched a $3 disposable smartphone battery booster. Istvan loved the pitch but suggested that Harold should make his cheap, disposable junk product *seem* more environmentally friendly, somehow.

The next presenter pitched a home appliance called Pharma-Bot, which dispensed prescriptions in the right dosage on the right day. It had other novel features as well. "A pharmaceutical company can use the PharmaBot as a direct portal access to consumers," she said. "Refills for all medications in the PharmaBot can be directed to a pharmaceutical's brand." Which, I gathered, meant that this invention provided companies a way to push overpriced name brand drugs over cheaper but otherwise equivalent generic medicines in the name of convenience and progress. "This would be a billion-dollar win." It was easy to see how Big Pharma would win. Now here was an idea that I thought radiated evil. I thought it would be a sure hit. I misjudged.

Manny didn't like the presenter's delivery—and he really didn't like the way she kept her eyes on her notes. "I cut a check recently to an entrepreneur that had a lot of passion," he said. "People say, 'Why did you invest?' Well, you know: large market, early market, had a great team. But his *passion* was *contagious*. Passion is the transference of enthusiasm. You cannot get passion by *reading*."

"I was going to say that as well," Istvan said.

A medical doctor pitched a new breathing tube he had invented, which he said would reduce fatal surgical infections. He had already raised $350,000 and wanted another $1 million to shepherd the device through federal regulatory review. While it wasn't a flashy consumer product, it seemed like a solid pitch targeting a proven market—certainly it was more useful than, say, PharmaBot—and he clearly had passion. "We'll be able to save many, many lives," the doctor said.

"We don't invest in that area," Manny said flatly. So much for saving the world with technology.

My headache returned. I was famished. I was in the sixth row, the second to last. It could be two hours before my turn came around. It would be a struggle to stay alert. Few presenters brought energy to the floor. Istvan and Manny shot down one pitch after another. I tried to study the nuances of their responses in order to tailor my pitch to their individual tastes. This was a fool's errand. The judges tended to echo one another's advice, which sometimes meant contradicting advice they'd given earlier. Both men, however, could be relied upon to state the obvious in a blunt and often condescending fashion.

When a woman pitched an app intended to help parents bond with their children, Manny humiliated her by calling for a show of hands to demonstrate there was no market for her product (in an audience of single young male coders). To another female presenter he found too talkative, Manny said: "Investors like startups that are coachable . . . If you're always chiming in, you can't get their wisdom." Istvan could be just as cutting. When a man's pitch sank into a swamp of buzzwords, he interrupted. "Who understood what his company does?" Istvan asked, calling for a show of hands. "Not a lot of people. I wouldn't have raised my hand."

Over time, I noticed a few recurring themes to the investors' advice. Dumb everything down. Focus on the big payday. Fudge when necessary.

By the time Déa summoned me to the fore, Manny and Istvan had crushed the dreams of at least two dozen entrepreneurs. In order to endure what was to come, I had convinced myself I might be an exception. I had memorized my pitch. I paid heed to the judges' advice and would talk dumb and fudge where necessary. I had a big idea but a modest "ask." It was my turn. My chance.

Ninety seconds goes by much more quickly when it's *you* yammering on. It felt exactly like a dream, except that I was fully dressed.

"Hi," I said. "I'm Corey. I'm here to build a business."

I don't know if everybody saw the news from Paris today: a massive taxi protest targeting Uber. Thousands of taxis shut down the city. There was violence. It was not pretty. If I'm Uber, I'm not really happy about that. If I'm a taxi company, maybe. If I'm Lyft—I'm intrigued! This might be good for me. My brand is clean. It's not tarred by these protests.

I hoped that by summoning images of flaming tires and broken glass, I had captured their attention.

That's really our target market for the company I'm launching now, which is called Laborize. It's a unique SAAS offering—Strikes as a Service. Basically—

I heard tittering from the audience. I tried to roll with it.

You're laughing . . . But we offer our clients a competitive advantage by organizing campaigns at their competitors' workplaces—increasing their costs, demoralizing their workforce, and distracting their management.

Manny and Istvan watched with stone faces. I turned toward the crowd.

Um, yeah. My background: I'm a recovering journalist with a technical background. This will be my third startup. I launched one, failed. Um. Second one, I was in management. It was acquired. This is my third go.

I forgot what was supposed to come next. Oh, yeah:

Labor. Worldwide, it's an $18.5 trillion market, minimum. That's according to the OECD. We want, eventually, a piece of all of that. And, uh—yeah. Raising a seed round, two hundred and fifty K. Hire lawyers, organizers, sales, engineering . . .

With only moments to close the deal, I lost the ability to form sentences. A heckler came to my rescue. "Do you hire union work-ers?" someone shouted from the back of the room.

"No, we *create* union workers! For the competitor," I said.

That was it. My time was up. The seconds passed like hours as I awaited judgment. Istvan was the first to break the silence. "So, I didn't actually hear a product. It sounds like a service," he said.

"Yeah," I said. "Strikes as a service."

"Which is not, you know—it's not software as a service, but I guess it's still SAAS. Nevertheless, this is not going to fly with a VC because it's not scalable. VCs rarely, if ever, invest in service companies that require, you know, humans. That's the biggest thing I see here."

I didn't argue, but I knew he was wrong. Uber definitely required humans, for instance. And Uber was then the biggest VC-backed IPO around. Nobody said, "It's not scalable." In retrospect, I think Istvan just said the first discouraging thing that came to mind.

Manny stared blankly at a point in space somewhere across the room and up toward the ceiling. He puffed his cheeks in baf-flement. "Are you on strike?" Déa asked. "Speechless," a color com-mentator in the audience said. Finally, Manny weighed in. "I think that you talked about a large market," he said, "but you didn't talk about how are you going to get into that market. What are you going to do—is it X, Y, Z—to gain that market?"

I had to admit, he had a point. I didn't talk about any of those things. I probably could've made room for at least a word on the practicalities.

"Don't get confused: 'Oh, you know, this is a trillion-dollar market or a billion-dollar market.' Rubber bands are a billion dollars, toilet paper, bottles. How are you actually going to get a piece of that?" Manny went on. "It's like walking down to Wells Fargo and saying, 'Wow, there's a lot of money in there.' There's a lot of money in the market, but how are you going to tap into it? Starting with one dollar. How are you doing that? Put that in your presentation."

"Yeah, I left it out. I'll be happy to talk to you about it later," I said.

"I look forward to it, Corey. Thank you so very much," Manny said.

"*Woo-hoo*! Strikes as a service," Déa said.

"It's very unique," someone said as I yielded the floor.

By the time I returned to my seat, the guy who had been in line behind me was already pitching. "Has anyone here *not* purchased something online because they wanted to try it first?" he said. The words barely registered. I had gotten a *"woo-hoo."* I had gotten "unique." And I had gotten their attention. But these investors wouldn't be opening their Rolodexes up to me, much less their checkbooks. Had I humiliated anyone, save myself? Not really. But I had generated a certain amount of discomfort, and perhaps that was good enough for now.

The remaining presentations passed in a melancholic blur. I didn't even catch who wound up winning the grand prize: "a free demo table ($130 value) at a future Lifograph event."

"Let's say a big *woo-hoo* for everybody!" Déa said.

"Woo-hoo!" everybody said.

Potbellied Spam Man offered consolation. "I loved your presentation. I don't know if it's a business, but I loved the presentation," he said, when the time came to mingle. "You should expand into, like, Occupy Wall Street and other places. 'Protest anything,' you know." His next advice was more counterintuitive, but totally genuine, and it had to do with finding the right mindset to deliver a pitch: Just assume you are a "total loser," doomed to fail. It had always worked for him. "A lot of times it's, 'You've got to love yourself, you've got to be confident,'" he sneered. "Well, what if you don't love yourself and you're not confident?'"

A man in a green shirt came over to share his thoughts on Laborize. "I'm sorry I was laughing," he said. "I thought it was a joke for a second. But it's obviously a relevant issue. And I hope you didn't think it was rude."

"Oh, not at all," I said.

"You had the clearest presentation," the man said. Unfortunately he wasn't who I needed to impress.

A cocksure European founder interjected.

"Every venture-backed company is gonna hate you," he said. "I wouldn't support it." Encouraging union membership, he explained, would be "very harmful for the economy . . . like, I don't know, dealing with guns." But even though he made clear his distaste for the idea, Cocksure still offered some encouragement.

"The idea is crazy," he told me. "It actually may work." I thought so, too, of course.

"But I wouldn't look for VC funding," he went on.

"Crowdfunding?" I said, anticipating his advice.

"Actually," he said, "you could convince the unions."

That actually wasn't a bad idea.

I *should* pitch Laborize to the unions.

• • • • •

First, I would need to retailor my pitch. On one level, Laborize was a sensationally cynical gambit designed to generate wealth for a single individual: me. But on a deeper level, it was a sensationally cynical gambit designed to trick the capitalist elite into underwriting their own downfall, a bet that the tendency to favor short-term gains, combined with the usual element of schadenfreude, would outweigh their long-term interest in suppressing the labor movement. The potential was immense. Consider: If Laborize took off in one industry—leaving one dominant, nonunion player atop a wheezing mound of unionized rivals all hobbled by rising pension costs and endless grievance proceedings—other industries would follow. Soon every company would feel compelled to fund a hostile unionization campaign targeting their competitors—lest the competition beat them to it. If all proceeded as dictated by the laws of reason and economics, eventually every company except one—the last Laborize client—would have a workforce composed of militant trade unionists.

I had no contacts in the local labor movement, such as it was, but I found a likely mark thanks to a timely *SF Weekly* article about a unionization campaign at the Google Express warehouse in Mountain View. Google Express was a home delivery service intended to compete with Amazon, with reportedly comparable working conditions. Leading the campaign was Teamsters Local 853, which had previously organized employee-shuttle drivers for Facebook, Apple, and Genentech. "We're kind of turning into the tech union," the local honcho, Rome Aloise, told the paper. I looked up Rome Aloise and found that he was a bigwig in the International

Brotherhood of Teamsters who happened to be running in the national leadership elections on a slate led by James P. Hoffa, son of the late Jimmy. I called Rome and made a date for the following week at the union's office in San Leandro. As far as he was concerned, I was just another journalist who wanted to interview him about his tech worker organizing. I don't recall mentioning Laborize when setting up the appointment, and if I did, I spun it as an afterthought.

It was sunny and warm when I rode to meet the Teamsters. I set my borrowed bicycle against a bench in a pleasant little park in San Leandro, unpacked my picnic lunch, and checked Twitter. By chance I spotted a news update from a local freelance reporter:

BREAKING: #SF tech buses run by Bauer protested by teamsters in labor dispute, at Valencia street

Those had to be Rome's guys. He had said something was in the works. Bauer was an outfit that ran many of the shuttles that ferried techies to and from their apartments in the city to their offices in the suburbs every day. For the Teamsters, it constituted a soft target.

I pedaled along the cracked streets, dodging broken glass and freight trucks, to a busy industrial district lined with run-down warehouses, where I found the fortresslike red brick headquarters of Teamsters Local 853. I locked my bike to an iron gate outside. White lettering on the tinted glass door listed the pillars of the union's organization: wholesale liquor vendors, milk drivers, construction workers, and builders. A colorful mural of striking workers livened up the vacant lobby. I climbed a narrow staircase and was buzzed inside the offices by a middle-aged lady wearing a windbreaker. She ushered me into an unlit conference room where a portrait of Rome, square-faced and curly-haired and wearing a suit and tie, hung on the wall. The man himself arrived after a few minutes. Rome was built like a truck. I bet he scared the techies. However, his foul mouth put me at ease.

"You had an action this morning?" I said.

"Yeah, we did," he said. "We shut down Bauer—a couple of their buses—this morning in San Francisco over on Twenty-Fourth and Valencia, which is one of their last stops before they go onto the campus of Cisco."

Organizing tech company shuttle drivers had been a public relations blessing for the Teamsters, whose label was tainted by historic associations with organized crime and public corruption. "Because of the names of the companies we're dealing with, people are interested," Rome told me. "If we were just talking about Loop Transportation"—Facebook's shuttle contractor—"or Compass Transportation"—which ferries workers for Apple, eBay, Evernote, Genentech, Yahoo, and Zynga—"nobody would give a shit about it. We've gotten international press over this. It's been amazing."

We talked about his organizing work for quite some time, maybe an hour. I sensed Rome was eager to wrap up the meeting. My window was closing. I began babbling about my experiences chasing venture capital. "I've been pitching people my startup ideas, and most of them get shot down," I told Rome. He listened good-naturedly but with growing fatigue on his face. "So," I said finally, "the idea is a startup that gets a corporation to fund an organizing drive at their competitors."

"Which is illegal as shit," Rome said.

"But so is Airbnb!" I protested. This was imprecise. Like Laborize, certain aspects of Airbnb's business may have been illegal in certain places at certain times, one could argue. Either way, this wasn't going well.

"Yeah, yeah. But listen," Rome said, "there's a big difference in enforcement between the city of San Francisco and the Departments of Labor and Justice." I had to admit he had a point there. If anyone knew about dealing with pressure from the feds, it would be a high-ranking Teamster. Even Uber didn't dare thumb its nose at the FBI. Rome seemed taken aback. "There is no union official— because, it's absolutely—you can't—I can't—you know," he stammered.

Sometimes, Rome said, the unions did try to pit companies against one another. And sometimes the companies were even willing to play along. But the rules governing such self-interested corporate collusion with organized labor were incredibly restrictive. "You cannot take any money from an employer to do anything, other than dues that they deduct from their employees' checks," Rome explained. "Technically, anything over twenty-five bucks is a violation of federal law." What's worse, the government enforcers with the Justice Department had "gotten really chickenshit" of late, pursuing even the most petty violations. This news did not bode well for Laborize. "I guess I'd better find some good lawyers," I said.

"Yeah. Yeah. You're going to have a problem with that one," Rome said.

And so I left the Teamsters' red brick bunker having maintained my perfect record of failure. Laborize had been roundly rejected by representatives of both capital and labor. Which was just as well, really.

Six months after I met with him, the federally appointed panel overseeing the Teamsters organization charged Rome with various corrupt practices and abuses of office. A review turned up all kinds of dirt on Rome, including allegations that he'd tried to rig union elections on behalf of his allies and engaged in acts of nepotism. Among the charges was an alleged act of racketeering, in which Rome accepted gifts from a liquor distributor on the other side of a Teamsters contract. The gifts in question: tickets to the 2013 Playboy Super Bowl party in New Orleans. Rome's career was "likely over" on account of the alleged "massive corruption violations," according to Teamsters for a Democratic Union, a member-run reform group. At the time of this writing, hearings were ongoing in his case and Rome had established a legal defense fund.

I rode the BART as far as Fremont, then pedaled the rest of the way back to Mountain View—past the fetid marsh, along the tall bridge over the Bay, through the cracked concrete of East Palo Alto and across the color line into the leafy yuppie wonderland of Palo Alto proper, where I paused for a hard-earned refreshment. I could not have picked a better place to witness the spectacle of swaggering twenty-one-year-old techies wearing T-shirts being served $18 cocktails by unctuous fortysomething bartenders wearing waistcoats and bow ties. My $14 Sazerac tasted smooth enough. Something else must have left the bitter taste in my mouth.

Spurned and alone, I sought solace once more in consuming the freebies at a nightclub in SoMa. Tonight's spendthrift host was a startup that sold software to other startups so that they could build apps. A velvety lounge near the dance floor had been outfitted with a Connect Four board larger than a chest of drawers, as well as a pile of oversized Jenga blocks, each roughly two feet long and six inches wide. Jenga really drew a crowd. Dozens stood watching as small teams took turns stacking the blocks higher and higher until the inevitable climax when everything came crashing down on the dark crimson carpet.

Leaning back against the wall watching this Sisyphean effort, I spotted a familiar ballcap bursting with black curls. It was Lawrence. My friend! I stepped carefully around the Jenga players and sat on the bench by his side. He didn't notice, for he was already deep in conversation. "I'm Jewish. Did I tell you? My mother is a Russian Jew," Lawrence was telling an uninterested huddle of fresh-out-of-college techies.

"Hey! Lawrence!" I said. He turned to me and smiled. "My man!" He apologized for having lost my number. Something went wrong with his old Obamaphone, he said, but he'd since gotten a newer model. We toasted serendipity and watched the rookies try their hands at Jenga. Two young women, cautious but steady-handed in approach, took the wooden tower to precarious new heights.

At several tense moments, the tower seemed sure to fall. The women's hesitancy grew with each turn. An impatient young man, who seemed to be a co-worker of theirs, valiantly invited himself onto the team. Soon after he took over the block-stacking duties, the tower came tumbling down. A chorus of sympathetic groans rose in unison from the assembled onlookers. Lawrence was unimpressed. "They were playing too conservatively for my taste," he said. "I'd be stacking them every which way—this way, that way." He was not the kind of guy to let a thing like gravity keep him down.

Lawrence stood, eager to put his radical Jenga strategies to the test. He laid one block down on its long side, then balanced a second block on top. However, in a twist that upended conventional Jenga wisdom, the second block was oriented vertically, like a skyscraper. Lawrence then attempted to add a third block. His unorthodox structure collapsed instantly.

I asked Lawrence how his stealth pot-leaf game was coming along. He said he was focusing on a new project. It was called Fridgetopia. The idea had come to him in a psychedelic reverie. He had opened the fridge one night and seen all the various bottles lined up like soldiers. The milk had gone bad, and the other bottles, after organizing among themselves, led a successful revolt. What emerged was a perfect utopia—Fridgetopia—a land of peace and plenty where nothing ever spoiled, although it was somewhat chilly.

I listened, rapt, as Lawrence described in minute detail the various factions that formed and the dramatic series of intrigues that took place before the epoch-making refrigerant revolution. I was not prepared for what happened next: Lawrence asked for my help writing a book about Fridgetopia. "It won't take none of your time," he said.

That was how big offers often came in Silicon Valley, unexpectedly and in a casual setting—or so I had heard. I told Lawrence that it sounded like a worthwhile project but that I was pretty busy with my own startup (and book). Fortunately, there were no hard feelings. Lawrence was a professional. He understood my reasons, and he accepted my reply with characteristic grace. "I forgot your name, to be honest, bro," he said. "I don't pay a lot of attention to people's names that I meet at these things. But you had good energy."

"It's okay," I said. I shared the news of my recent entrepreneurial setbacks. "I pitched my startup. It didn't make the cut," I said.

"No one does, man," Lawrence said. "I don't believe in luck or karma or any of that. I believe you materialize what's inside, out in the world." Soon enough, he was ready to move on to the next tech party, which would be his third that evening. I bade him good night. I couldn't keep up. Who was I kidding?

VII

The Aristocracy of Brains

The best part about the torpid mixture of indifference and contempt that greeted my ideas in Silicon Valley was that it brought a swift end to my entrepreneurial folly. This meant that I would soon have plenty of free time to contemplate and investigate the greater injustices I'd witnessed, many of them perpetrated by a managerial class that was convinced its cutthroat profiteering made the world a better place. Even better, it meant that soon I wouldn't need to spend one more second in an airless conference room listening to some techie talk about his passion for sales metrics and his grand plan for a me-too smartphone app designed to make corporate advertising even more inescapable and corrosive than it already was. I found it taxing to spend so much time with such hysterical optimists—that was why I so valued my fleeting interactions with Lawrence. I'm not saying he would've made the world's greatest roommate, but he was fun in small doses, and his idiosyncratic illusions were not the kind of pipe dreams that threatened to enslave the populace. I did not, however, believe his New Agey woo-woo about manifesting success by cultivating inner peace. When it comes to the question of why some feast on caviar and champagne while others starve in the streets, I'm inclined to agree with Rome, the union leader: The answer comes not from within, but from without. Politics made this world, even the digital parts.

In a land of righteous engineers, this simple observation constitutes a kind of heresy. Lawrence's belief in material success as a manifestation of inner clarity, conviction, or drive was shared by just about everyone in the Bay Area tech scene. Silicon Valley prefers to tell its story in terms of individualistic entrepreneurial achievement against the odds, marked by dramatic moments of insight, in the mythical tradition of Isaac Newton and the Buddha—not as I see it: as a twisted multigenerational shovel-selling enterprise that goes all the way back to the Gold Rush. Code is pure, but politics is messy. Although a klutz with computers, Rome understood the nature of the tech industry more clearly because he did not shy from the gritty work of sorting out who gets what, when, and how. "We had to straighten out this congressman here who said something real positive about the sharing economy," he told me at one point in our conversation. "We said, 'What the fuck? Don't you understand what it is?'"

"What did you tell him?" I asked.

"We said, 'This isn't any *sharing* economy—this is taking the responsibility of employment away from employers and putting it one hundred percent on people's backs.'"

Rome's diagnosis was so simple and succinct, even a member of Congress could understand it. Of course, such hypocrisies are not confined to the phony "sharing economy." They span the industry. Similarly, sympathy for the tech company perspective spans American political institutions, beginning with both major parties.

"I look at the Democrats as the mafia," Rome told me. "They make us pay them for protection but they don't do shit for us. And the Republicans are out to kill us, so we have to support the Democrats to keep what we've got." It's no surprise so many politicians line up to serve as flunkies for corporations, which have unmatchable budgets and long-term domination strategies, rather than supporting workers, who are wholly outmatched. Organized labor is at a structural disadvantage. The government frowns on solidarity, yet it smiles on all manner of corporate con jobs—like the startup bubble itself. Tech companies in particular—thanks to the deep pools of financing available to them and, more important, their invaluable data hoard—approach politics from a position of strength. Yet they also possess the obsessive mentality of tinkerers, and cling to the aggrievement of self-declared outsiders. The combination of power and geekery has produced some bizarre outcomes, and some even weirder ventures in practical change.

I saw this firsthand when I attended a conference talk featuring a man named Tom Chi, who had recently left a high-level position at Google X, the company's far-out research and development division. "My first day," he recalled, "all I had was a one-page document from Larry and Sergey. And all it said was: 'What would it take to get Google inside your brain?'"

"Don't be scared," he added. Cue nervous laughter.

Chi's latest project was a startup focused on "radically shifting large organizations." It was a semisecret project. "This has been stealth for a while," he said. He didn't reveal his partners, but he did share the name of their mysterious venture: the Factory.

Chi said the Factory was inspired by a recent scientific paper that had determined that seven hundred thirty-seven specific organizations influenced 80 percent of the global economy. Most of these organizations were large multinational corporations like General Electric, Procter & Gamble, Sony, Verizon, Nike, Keurig, and Wells Fargo. (Also Google, which Chi left out for some reason.) "If you want to change the world," Chi said, "the most important thing is to influence the mindsets of the leaders of those organizations." This was the stealthily revolutionary mission of the Factory.

What Chi described was not some mundane leadership retreat. Neither was it a glad-handing holiday for the private-jet set, like the Davos or Aspen conferences. The Factory recruited only from those organizations with tremendous global influence, and then only from the ranks of senior vice presidents and higher, Chi said. "We do these intense two-day events. At eight a.m. on the first day, we take them into the park and they do military-style boot camp exercises," he continued. During one such regimen, "two people threw up. It's no joke." He proceeded to describe the Factory's twenty-five-thousand-square-foot mansion in San Francisco and to explain how the concept was inspired by Buddhist notions of "minimizing attachment." He also mentioned a curious ritual called the Crucible. Long story short, the idea was to take these powerful people, break down their egos, and remold them. "This is the new disruption. Influence the influencers," Chi said. "The populist phase of Big Tech is over."

Foolishness or not, the Factory represented earthly desires that Silicon Valley elites were usually too embarrassed to admit, let alone discuss in a room full of strangers. Clearly, beneath all the claptrap about conscious capitalism—the latest buzzword for "mission-driven" corporations—and saving the world, blah blah blah, there lurked a tenebrous techie will to power. To understand it, I needed to get closer to the leaders of the industry. It was time to venture south, to leave the relative splendor of the city for the sprawling suburbs. Once again I found myself in need of housing. The best combination of price, location, and comfort I found on Airbnb was titled "Garden tent near Google, w/Bfast!"

Enjoy sleeping al fresco, but want the convenience of a shower, breakfast, and easy access to the G-plex and major transportation? Queen airbed or XXL Mayan hammock for sleeping. Fire pit and Wi-fi too!

Yes, it was a tent. On the other hand, it was August. Most important, it was only $35 per night. The Mayan hammock clinched it for me. I packed my bags again and moved on to Mountain View, the home of Google and "the heart of Silicon Valley." At least I might get some fresh air in the tent. And breakfast was included!

It was around 7 p.m. when I left San Francisco. The Fourth Street Caltrain station was mobbed. A railway worker shouted over the din: "You can have a couple, but drunken behavior will not be tolerated . . . We will call police . . . Please don't swear in front of the children." All this was to no avail. The train south was a shit-show packed with whooping techie kids who tore open cases of beer like they were Christmas presents, turned the dining trays into poker tables, and blared bad pop music through the cabin.

Perhaps the techies knew the threat to call police was hollow. In the sort of subtly discriminatory double standard that was typical on the West Coast, it was illegal for the major-league-sports-loving rabble to drink on "post-event" trains, but legal for the mostly white, well-off techies who made the daily reverse commute to the suburbs to drink on the Caltrain, at least before 9 p.m. My train crawled and I didn't arrive in Mountain View until 10. My fellow passengers boozed it up the whole way, of course. The transit plaza teemed with more drunken, lanyard-wearing princelings and princesses. As I approached the taxi stand, two white Google cars pulled up simultaneously to an intersection. One was a Street View surveillance vehicle. The other had a label on the side that said SELF-DRIVING CAR, so it must've been a prototype. I took an old-fashioned taxi that got lost on the way to my new home. When I arrived, the host, Jeannie, was out wandering the unlit streets looking for her cat. It being late, she showed me outside to the tent straightaway.

I tiptoed around fallen seeds and dried pine needles in the dark summer night. The Coleman looked roomy, as advertised. And, peeking inside the tent flap, I saw that it had amenities Jeannie had neglected to mention, such as built-in cupholders. Fortunately I had packed a corkscrew as well as a flashlight, with whose bright white beam I traced the curve of a red extension cord, that vital lifeline to internet-enabled distraction. I found the plug end of the cord resting on a chair outside the tent, along with a small cockroach. The roach stood frozen in the harsh incandescent glare. I sent him—or her?—a telepathic peace offering: He would not summon his friends, and I would not try to smash him. I took off

my shoes and fumbled inside. My foot sank deeper than I expected
into the depleted air mattress, and I nearly did a face plant, but
luckily I managed to avoid bringing the whole rig down in a dusty
racket. Another coup!

Even with its foibles, the tent was the most comfortable place
I stayed in all my California travels, which said more about the
quality of Airbnb's offerings than it did about this particular tent.
I slept soundly until 4:51 am, when nature called. I fought the urge
as long as I could.

I stepped softly through the garden and carefully slid open the
glass door. A black cat, in from the streets, sat watching my every
move. I tiptoed through the living room toward a curtain draped
over the bathroom hall. A great big bearded man in shorts darted
through the curtain, startling me terribly. A burglar? Nay, he was
Jeannie's boyfriend, which meant that I, not he, was the strange
man wandering through the house in the dark.

I crawled once more inside the tent and understood the pain of
the family dog, banished from the warm house every night. At least
the dog could pee outside without shame. As I closed my eyes in a
vain effort to fall back asleep, I heard rustling and coughing from
Jeannie's room. The walls were thin. Presumably, she could hear
my every move, too. I lay still. As the sun rose, I found I could hear
the goings-on throughout the neighborhood.

A car engine revved.

A bird chirped.

A squirrel bombarded the tent with acorns from the tree up
above. Either that, or it was beginning to rain.

In the morning, I found Jeannie inside preparing fruit and

pastries to share. She introduced me to her other Airbnb guest, Francis, who was occupying the second bedroom of the tiny ground-floor apartment, and her insubordinate cat, Horace.

"Is Horace a YouTube star?" I asked.

"I have yet to monetize my cat. That's the last piece of the puzzle, I guess," Jeannie said, bobbing a string in front of Horace's face.

Despite having an undergraduate degree from Yale, a law degree, a full-time job as an intellectual property attorney at a large class-action firm, and several freelance gigs, Jeannie was barely getting by. An overseas investor had recently purchased her single-story apartment complex and raised her rent by $600 a month. Her neighbor, the former groundskeeper, lost his job at the same time the rent increase hit. Two other tenants on the property had their rent go up by $1,000 a month. "In the law they call that 'constructive eviction,'" Jeannie said. Renting out a tent in her backyard was not something she'd always dreamed about.

Francis, the other guest, who was currently staying in the indoor bedroom, was an Englishman from Portsmouth, a town I knew. He was about to move to London to take a job with a startup that projected Web streams on walls at tech conferences. It sounded stupid, but I congratulated him all the same. This was his dream vacation in America—his "techie pilgrimage" around Silicon Valley. So far Francis had visited Steve Jobs's old house; the garage where Apple cofounder Steve Wozniak built the first Apple computer; the Xerox PARC laboratory, where many modern features of consumer computers, such as the graphical user interface, had been invented with government support; the Hewlett-Packard campus; and the Googleplex, which was a stone's throw from Jeannie's place. Marveling at the many golden-hued wonders over every desiccated California hilltop, Francis saw signs of genius everywhere he looked. "I met a deaf guy at a bus stop," he said. "He had invented a new kind of paper!"

Jeannie sounded a skeptical note. "Then again, if he's got such a wonderful idea," she said, "why's he taking the bus?"

She was right, but her point raised some obvious and disconcerting follow-up questions, chiefly: If I was so smart, why was I living in a tent? We parted ways for the day. I was on a pilgrimage of my own, to learn what I could about the politics of this place. First, I walked to the Computer History Museum and spent hours taking in the wonderstruck exhibits on robots and rockets and video games, underwritten by the likes of Microsoft and Google and presented with the critical distance of a panel talk at the Consumer Electronics Show. Perhaps I would learn more outside in the sunshine.

I wandered around, enjoying the weather and wondering when I would see the eponymous mountain. I spotted a flyer on a staple-studded bulletin board. It sought volunteers with "healthy brains" for unspecified experiments at Stanford. All of the slips were taken. I walked toward the Googleplex over twelve-lane roads and past sprawling acres of surface parking without passing another pedestrian. The most amazing thing about Mountain View was that for all the billions of dollars in wealth that had flowed here, for all the new construction and the growing population, it still resembled a section of the Universal Studios backlot from the

Leave It to Beaver era of car-friendly domestic idyll. I reasoned that this could only be the case because the people of Mountain View, or at least the influential ones, liked it that way.

Google—now restructured through a holding company called Alphabet—is the world's largest and most important tech company, with $90 billion in annual revenues; seventy-two thousand employees comprising the top graduates in computer science, engineering, business, psychology, and semiotics; and proprietary databases housing the archived private correspondence of some 500 million Gmail users (along with anyone who happens to email them), plus detailed consumer behavioral profiles of many, many more internet users; and a running log of whatever any one of those users happens to be thinking about at any given time, as evidenced by the individualized records of Web search queries, which Google's vast network infrastructure processes at a rate of forty thousand every second.

Contrary to its reputation as a quirky corporate Xanadu, the Googleplex looks like pretty much any other dismal suburban office park. Visitors tend to fixate upon the candy-colored bicycles and the matching outdoor furniture, such as the jaunty patio umbrellas strewn about the sprawling campus, but I knew that the real story hid behind the blackened windows of the squat office buildings. Inside those walls, a secretive, ambitious, and in many ways malevolent project of world-historic scale was under way. All of the things worth loving about life—millennia of arts and culture, the feelings of freedom and surprise, the body and the spirit—were being systematically deconstructed and digitized. Anything in the world that could be duplicated on the internet was being duplicated on the internet, and the internet was unquestionably Google's domain. While the organic originals withered away for lack of attention, the pixelated substitutes were given away—ostensibly for free, but at a high cost to the privacy and independence of everyone who accepted Google's bargain. This company staked its claim over "the world's information," which is to say, over everything. But hey, the perks! The cafeteria is legendary.

Among the most valuable information Google captures is the physical geography of the planet. Its innocuous white sedans are constantly driving up and down city streets and country highways, and thus far have collected over twenty petabytes' worth of digital photographs—enough to fill my laptop hard drive forty-two thousand times—for the eye-level feature of the Google Maps service. But the cars do more than take pictures. For some time, Google's cars also spied on the internet traffic of any unprotected wireless networks they happened to pass by—a practice called "war-driving." In so doing, this mammoth corporation, which tracked its users' behavior more efficiently and comprehensively than any totalitarian government in history, dispensed with the fig leaf of consent implicit in its one-sided "terms of service" agreement. It reasoned that an unlocked door was an invitation to rifle through someone's drawers. And although Google eventually lost a civil lawsuit alleging it violated the federal Wiretap Act—Google claimed the data collections were inadvertent—the company's business was unaffected.

On my stroll through the riparian remnants of Mountain View, I noticed a number of big beautiful "heritage" trees along the public right-of-way marked with yellow ribbons for removal, no doubt to make room for more gaudy plastic furniture. Past the Google-plex, the dirt path connected to a barren concrete "wildlife corri-dor" where electric skateboards were more common than mammals or birds. To the east, I saw a vast parking lot ringed by concrete barriers and fencing topped with barbed wire. This was part of the federal complex that housed the NASA Ames Research Center and a strange little outfit called Singularity University, which was not really a university but more like a dweeby doomsday congre-gation sponsored by some of the biggest names in finance and tech, including Google. The Singularity—a theoretical point in the future when computational power will absorb all life, energy, and matter into a single, all-powerful universal consciousness—is the closest thing Silicon Valley has to an official religion, and it is embraced wholeheartedly by many leaders of the tech industry. But more on that later!

Along with the cloistered military agencies that underwrote the research for the smartphone, the personal computer, and the internet, these institutions—yes, even NASA—shared a set of over-arching goals: to extend the reach of machines to all spheres of human activity; to ensure those machines remained under pri-vate control, unaccountable to the public at large; to automate the countless individual political and economic decisions that consti-tute a nominally free society; and, oh yes, to get richer than the Medicis. The tech tycoons who ruled this land elevated their pro-fane designs with a sacred mythography. The Singularity was its theological expression, but they wrote their own history, too, as I had seen at the Computer History Museum. Their preferred dis-course was reverent contemplation of the lofty arc of scientific progress and homilies on the fortitude of a few pioneers of industry—Father Gates, Saint Musk. What time had they for the vulgar problems of the misfortunate many: housing, wages, police, debt, drugs, disease? Here was the dream of a new order that was at once futuristic and antiquated, a feudal fantasy played out on a sci-fi stage that looked deceptively like any boring stretch of asphalt in America.

To get a deeper view of Silicon Valley's history, I rode my bicycle to Palo Alto, registered for a guest pass at Stanford's main university library, and ventured into the stacks. Here I learned that the university's namesake, Leland Stanford, was a corrupt and loathsome man, an incompetent egotist who was responsible for a great deal of human suffering. No one knows how many of his Chinese workers died building the railroads—but their bones came back from the work camps by the carload. Founding Stanford president David Starr Jordan, for his part, taught a required course on evolution in which he promoted white supremacy, and he authored a eugenics pamphlet titled *The Blood of the Nation: A Study of The Decay of Races Through the Survival of the Unfit*. In a speech to the Stanford class of 1907, Jordan described his ideal man: a "freeborn maverick" (of Anglo-Saxon lineage, of course) who in every respect lined up with the mythic archetype of the heroic Silicon Valley entrepreneur. It was this sort of man Stanford University aimed to produce—for it was such men as these that the frontier forefathers of Silicon Valley deemed destined to rule. "An aristocracy of brains is the final purpose of democracy," Jordan declared—equality was for saps, as he saw it. He blamed poverty on bad breeding. Progress therefore required thinning the human herd and protecting "the stock of freeborn races" from "mulatto taint." Such ideas formed the basis of California's cruel and backward eugenics experiment, which the German Nazi Party used as the basis for its own racist and ultimately genocidal legal framework after gaining power. Connections between the Californian intellectual vanguard of the eugenics movement and the most aggressive political expression of that movement in Germany continued through the twentieth century. For instance, the noted Stanford professor of chemistry Robert Swain, following a visit to Hitler's Germany, gushed over the "marked development and progress" and the "peaceful and confident German people." And connections persisted after the Second World War as well. For decades after the Nazi defeat, elite scientists and engineers in this placid stretch of California farmland—such as William Shockley, the Nobel Prize–winning inventor of the semiconductor and Stanford University professor who is widely regarded as the founder of modern Silicon Valley—carried the torch of eugenics. One of the earliest Silicon Valley power brokers, Otto von Bolschwing, also happened to have been an ambitious and influential Nazi SS officer who reported directly to Adolf Eichmann, the Holocaust's logistics director. After the war, von Bolschwing hooked up with the CIA, which brought him to the United States, and in 1969 he joined a Sacramento investment firm, TCI, with subsidiaries in Palo Alto and Mountain View. Now, in the internet era, the tech tycoons of Silicon Valley, many of them educated at Stanford, have founded companies that provide an ideal organizing platform for white supremacists, neo-Nazis, and all manner of hate groups. Even if this owes more to an earnest, misguided sense of libertarian free-speech absolutism rather than sinister cryptofascism, the result is the same: social media platforms like Facebook and Twitter have done little to stop racist hate groups from using their services to organize and spread noxious propaganda. Google has obligingly indexed the ravings of Holocaust deniers, giving their deadly lies equal weight, and sometimes top billing, in search results. For decades, the world made it a taboo to share fascist ideas, and as a result, those ideas remained deservedly obscure—until Silicon Valley once again disrupted the norm.

The sun was setting by the time I made it back to Mountain View, and the streets were tinted deep purple. After crossing the Caltrain tracks, I took an odd turn onto Stierlin Road and saw the blue and red flashing lights of a police roadblock. I pedaled toward an officer standing in the middle of the street. He was armed with an assault rifle, which seemed a bit excessive. He raised his free hand to stop me. Nearby stood dozens more local police and private security guards. Some wore combat fatigues; others were heavily armored in riot gear. Reinforced sport utility vehicles blocked traffic from the surrounding streets. The policeman was polite enough. He said I'd have to push my bike along the sidewalk or find another route. It was a strange scene. There was no crowd. The streets were quiet, and there was no yellow tape indicating a recent crime scene. What is all this all about? I asked.

There was a visiting dignitary, the policeman said. Who? A "controversial" politician from Europe, he said. I pushed on, toward some dapper-vested parking valets bearing refreshments. The lot outside the meeting hall was full; the bumper stickers suggested a gathering of the National Rifle Association. But the valets didn't have much more information for me. They used that same word, "controversial," to describe whoever had come to speak. I did some quick research on my phone and learned the truth about the guest of honor. "Controversial" was a pretty sorry euphemism for the leader of a glorified neo-Nazi party whose elected members had been spotted throwing Sieg Heil salutes. Seven decades after a former Palo Alto mayor and Stanford president praised "progress under the Hitler regime," hundreds had gathered in Mountain View to fete yet another repulsive fascist leader from Europe.

Here is what they were hearing inside the IFES Portuguese Hall that night, in a talk sponsored by the Conservative Forum of Silicon Valley:

We are all the victims of Islamization. Look around you. This building is surrounded by heavily armed law enforcement officers. This gathering here tonight is heavily protected. Why? We are no criminals.

I will tell you why: Because Islam has entered America and is taking over Europe . . . Islamic neighborhoods are expanding . . . Europe is becoming a continent of head scarves and mosques . . . We all have a problem. It is called Islam. The problem is growing. And we cannot afford to ignore it any longer because our existence is at stake.

Here, in the United States, you have a problem with

illegal immigration from Mexico. Just imagine if Mexico were an Islamic country and there were millions of Islamic immigrants crossing your border. That is exactly what is happening in Europe right now . . .

Our political leaders, your president Barack Obama, Britain's prime minister David Cameron, German chancellor Angela Merkel, my own Dutch prime minister Mark Rutte, they still say that Islam is a religion of peace.

Let me tell you: They are wrong!

So, let us stop bowing to Islam! No appeasement anymore!

The jihadis and their sympathizers do not belong in our societies.

I say: Let us reclaim our freedom!

The speaker was the leader of the far-right Dutch Party for Freedom, Geert Wilders, an aggrieved descendant of Indonesian colonizers and, by his own description, a freedom fighter assailed by threats from Islamic terrorists, with whom he equated the religion itself. *Newsweek* described him as "Islam's arch-nemesis in Europe" and a potential future prime minister of the Netherlands.

The demagogue's visit came in August 2015, when his opponents in the Dutch Labor Party were not yet afraid to call him a fascist. It had been only two months since Donald Trump announced his U.S. presidential campaign, which was then seen by the liberal and conservative establishments alike as an odd joke. Naked racism from the mouths of serious political candidates was still vaguely taboo at that moment. But when it came to tolerating the rhetorical adaptations of resurgent fascism, Silicon Valley was once again on the cutting edge.

"If I were to become the next Dutch prime minister," Wilders told the audience in Mountain View, "here is what I would do: Guarantee freedom of speech. A European First Amendment." Out of the other side of his mouth, he said, "I am fed up with the Koran . . . Why don't we ban that miserable book?"

No protests greeted this man. Wilders came to Mountain View as an honored guest—protected, at public expense, by an overwhelming show of force. After reaffirming his belief that one million residents of the Netherlands should be forcibly purged from the country, he posed for pictures with members of his smiling, gun-brandishing security detail and exchanged warm pleasantries with his audience.

I had put up with a lot of stupid bullshit over my months in Silicon Valley—had even done my part to contribute to it. I'd supported slumlords, fraudsters, and phonies with my own money. Instead of calling out people's ignorant and toxic views on race, sex, and class, I'd taken notes. As a journalist, my job was to observe and report. As a fake entrepreneur, my job was to kiss ass and make friends with all manner of villainous creeps.

But goddammit I drew the line at fascists.

It was not as though all the tech dudes in Silicon Valley—or even a double-digit minority of tech dudes—would've cheered along at that fascist rally I stumbled across. Indeed, rank-and-file tech company workers, like many in their age cohort, proved to constitute an important base for the Bernie Sanders campaign in 2016. But as heartening as it was to see the youthful peons of Google and Apple kicking in $25 or $100 to support an avowed democratic socialist, a harrowing countercurrent was gaining force.

Indeed, as I discovered from months of deep and unsettling research into the seedier corners of the internet, a nerdy sociopathic cabal of reactionary insurrectionists, some in positions of influence, groused that Hitler got a bad rap and dreamed of goose-stepping jackboot parades along the Embarcadero. This clique, a subset of what came to be called the alt-right, seemed to me a small and impotent minority. And yet the echo grew louder and louder—and soon more would hear it. Soon more would witness and shudder before the thing I had only just glimpsed: the emergence of determined fascist movement builders, taking their online organizing into the real world. Theirs was a vast but slapdash network of alienated, underemployed man-children; tortured, gynophobic gamers; and upwardly mobile, right-curious tech dudes. Emboldened, they crawled from underground online haunts like Stormfront and the 4chan forums into the light of day and, after Trump's election, to the city square—in Berkeley, Portland, New York, Charlottesville. They waved war flags adorned with strange idols like Pepe the Frog and chanted paeans to Kek, an ancient Egyptian god adopted by internet racists. They fought with students, activists, and anyone else who opposed their white nationalist vision. They threatened to kill me and my wife in our home.

Before the world could wake up to their existence, the jackboot techies would have their "god-emperor" in power. He, too, arrived like an echo from the past—an unabashed racist pushing a stabbed-

in-the-back story of national decline, who advocated mass deportation of a disfavored ethnic minority, promised wider wars and
the seizure of "spoils" on foreign soil, and whom even imperialist
conservatives denounced as an authoritarian despot in the making.
Sub rosa tech-world fascism was no longer a subculture—it was
the culture. Or at least the dominant strain.

What kept me awake at night, staring at the domed ceiling of
my tent in Mountain View, was not so much the formerly isolated
weirdos of the online alt-right, but their more powerful enablers,
and all the other tech dudes who began nodding in agreement
with recycled fascist ideas. It was hard to know their numbers.
Even as tech company managers espoused a commitment to liberal
principles, and employees evinced a burgeoning curiosity regarding social democratic reforms—like most people of their generation,
young techies had student loans—anecdotally, racism, misogyny,
and protofascist talking points were more pervasive inside tech
companies than elsewhere in corporate America. Google certainly
had no qualms about hiring 4chan founder Chris Poole, even
though the website he created became the central organizing platform for the alt-right. A year later, another Google employee, James
Damore, was fired after news reports revealed that an essay he'd
written and shared internally attacking the company's diversity
policies had attracted many aggrieved white male cosigners.
Regardless of the exact fascist headcount at any one Silicon Valley
corporation, the noxious ideas they harbored were, thanks to the
magic of the internet, suddenly everywhere and impossible to
ignore. Most of the time, they appeared in more palatable and
genteel formulations. These were ideas about racial purity and

supremacy, recast as a humanitarian crusade for "biological innovation" and the scientific freedom to conduct unfettered genetic experimentation; about the social virtues of total surveillance, recast as openness and transparency; about the rightful primacy of technicians and capitalist tycoons; about the decadence of artists and intellectuals.

If, as Google's Tom Chi had said, "the populist phase of Big Tech is over," I wondered, what nightmare comes next?

In March 2014, a Google engineer named Justine Tunney created a strange and ultimately doomed petition at the White House website. The petition proposed a three-point national referendum, as follows:

1. Retire all government employees with full pensions.
2. Transfer administrative authority to the tech industry.
3. Appoint [Google executive chairman] Eric Schmidt CEO of America.

"It's time for the U.S. Regime to politely take its exit from history and do what's best for America," she wrote. "The tech industry can offer us good governance and prevent further American decline."

When Tunney posted her petition online, the press treated it as comic relief that came from nowhere—a flamboyant act of corporate kiss-assery. Some noted with bemused incuriosity that Tunney, an avowed anticapitalist "tranarchist" (transgender anarchist), was at one time a prominent and divisive fixture of the Occupy Wall Street movement. Yet few looked into exactly how she became a hard-right seditionist after being, in her own words, "redpilled." The red pill was a shorthand reference to a scene in *The Matrix* where Laurence Fishburne turns Keanu Reeves into a kung-fu Bodhisattva with a dose of . . . something. But in techie circles, this phrase had taken on another meaning. The red pill philosophy referred to a collection of blogs focused on misogynistic pickup artistry, neofascist agitprop, and other awful reactionary tropes. Like many others who posted online using the NRx hashtag—short for "neoreactionary"—Tunney left no mystery as to the catalyst for her fascist awakening. "Read Mencius Moldbug," she urged her Twitter followers.

Who is Mencius Moldbug?

The name sounds like some magickal incantation from the works of Aleister Crowley. Mencius is the Europeanized name of an ancient Chinese philosopher who advocated revolt and championed "true kings." "Moldbug" is apparently a coinage. Together they form the online pseudonym of Curtis Guy Yarvin, a San Francisco software engineer and antidemocracy agitator.

Through his prolific online writings and occasional speeches, Yarvin has inspired thousands of others to denounce democracy and pluralism as impediments to the new aristocracy of brains. Naturally, he found a receptive audience among Silicon Valley's futurist elite. In 2010, Yarvin spoke to an exclusive "senior associate reception" at the Foresight Institute's annual conference at the Palo Alto Sheraton Hotel. The Foresight Institute is a prestigious yet quirky nonprofit organization that researches and promotes "technologies of fundamental importance for the human future, focusing on molecular machine nanotechnology, cybersecurity, and artificial intelligence." The subject under discussion was the problem of future governance.

"The only solution is a single, strong leader," Yarvin said.

There's this search for algorithms that can solve the problem of decision making . . . Well, it's unquestioned in the private domain that what you need is an executive with personal authority. For me, that's just the obvious, glaring solution that's just sitting there.

Such talk is what led Yarvin's obscure clique of neoreactionary subversives to be derided as "geeks for monarchy." The label was apt. Before he became the intellectual lodestar of this nascent technofeudalism, Yarvin lived the obscure, comfortable life of a frustrated poet, failed academic, and typical tech dude. He was born in 1973 to two federal civil servants. His father—who was Jewish, as Yarvin, sensitive to accusations of anti-Semitism, took pains to point out—worked as a minor diplomat in the Foreign Service. As Yarvin later noted self-consciously, he was the only man in his immediate family without a PhD. He completed an undergraduate degree at Brown University—his father's alma mater—but dropped out of a graduate computer science program at UC Berkeley in the early 1990s. A programmer in the Bay Area during the dot-com bubble, Yarvin managed to make a small pile of money by joining an established startup a few months before it went public. "I only made out like a thief, not like a bandit," he wrote. In

2002, after the crash, he bought a half-million-dollar home in a well-to-do neighborhood in San Francisco. Thus ensconced, Yarvin set out to "retire as an independent scholar," occupying his time by reading fringy political blogs and scouring Amazon for old reactionary treatises. By his own account, he spent $500 a month on books.

In 2007, he launched a blog of his own, under the pen name Mencius Moldbug. Yarvin's project: to promote a "DIY ideology . . . designed by geeks for other geeks." As such, his treatises were heavily informed by the works of J.R.R. Tolkien and George Lucas, with a lesser debt owed to the dyspeptic Victorian Thomas Carlyle. Yarvin affected an anachronistic, grandiose tone, echoing the style of his favorite nineteenth-century reactionary polemicists.

As Moldbug, Yarvin railed against the "Brahmins" of "the Cathedral"—a term he used to refer to an oppressive, communistic nexus of newspaper editors, university professors, and federal bureaucrats such as his own parents. Yarvin's unorthodox thesis—although it might be more accurately described as a hyperorthodox thesis—was that modern Western civilization suffered from "chronic kinglessness." Although his prose was discordant and at times impenetrable, Yarvin gained a small but devoted following and confirmed the private prejudices of a certain subset of frustrated Silicon Valley techies, some of whom, like Yarvin's audience at the Foresight Institute, were searching for answers to the problems of governance in a world of rapid technological change.

In 2012, readers of the official Moldbug blog, Unqualified Reservations, were invited to attend a conference in Long Beach where Yarvin had been persuaded to speak "against my better

judgment." Before moving on to the substance of Yarvin's presentation, it's worth explaining a few things about the venue. The BIL
"unconference" was a lower-rent alternative to the upmarket TED
Conference and, in the spirit of the Edinburgh Fringe Festival,
chased TED wherever it went. The name was a really stupid joke—a
reference to "the most excellent" nineties B comedy, *Bill and Ted's
Excellent Adventure.* (There was no acronym or cryptic allusion:
BIL was just "Bill" capitalized and misspelled.) However, BIL was
not some disorderly open mic night. The organizers had rented
space on Long Beach's floating convention center, the RMS *Queen
Mary.* And the previous year's unconference had been written up
on the front page of the *Wall Street Journal.* BIL's programs were
characteristically packed with California oddities, and in 2012
there were so many "sex positive" talks—covering everything from
"orgasmic meditation" to polyamory and sex tips for "geeks, intro-
verts and self-identified Aspies"—that a dedicated "boiler room"
was set aside for them. BIL's bread and butter, however, was the
typical stuff of Silicon Valley pipe dreams: indefinite life extension, the Singularity, genetic engineering, and space travel. Amid
some evident kooks lurked a sizable contingent of aerospace engineers and executives, including Virgin Galactic CEO and former
NASA chief of staff George T. Whitesides. BIL was, in short, a
who's who of free-market techie futurism.

Yarvin knew he would have friends in the audience and among
the invited speakers—and a number of others attending surely knew
who he was. Yet given the provocative and seditious nature of his
talk, he did not reveal his real name onstage or in the conference
program. He spoke as Moldbug. At the time, Yarvin was making

an effort to disassociate his name from his political propagandizing. His chosen title was innocuous enough: "How to Reboot the U.S. Government." But the program hinted at mischief:

> Is your government infected with viruses, worms, malware and spyware? . . . Do you feel frustrated, confused, apathetic and annoyed? Does your stomach cramp up every time you hear the word "change"?
>
> Neighbor, we have just the red pill for you. Don't ask what's in it. You don't want to know. Here's a glass of water—don't think, just swallow.

Chinless in profile, with his hair parted down the middle, Yarvin took the stage wearing a brown shirt. It was a curious sartorial choice. He wasted no time answering the central question: How would one go about "rebooting" the government? "I like to simplify things, so I've reduced this very complicated problem to a simple four-letter acronym, which is RAGE," Yarvin said. "And RAGE stands for Retire. All. Government. Employees." A smattering of applause rose from the crowd. "Very, very, very simple," Yarvin said, clearly pleased with himself.

It got crazier from there, as Yarvin assailed the accepted "World War II mythology"—namely, who was to blame. Alluding to debunked revisionism popular among postwar neo-Nazis, he cast Hitler's unprovoked invasions as forgivable acts of self-defense. Such knowledge was suppressed, Yarvin claimed, by America's ruling communists, who devised an "extremely elaborate mechanism for persecuting racists and fascists"—political correctness.

Although he feigned ignorance of the Red Scares, Yarvin complained the anticommunist purges of the 1950s had not gone far enough. "McCarthyism failed for many reasons, but the most succinct is what Machiavelli said: If you strike at a king, you need to kill him," as Yarvin wrote on his blog. On camera before a live audience, however, he played coy with the same argument. "Should we stop persecuting racists and fascists or should we start persecuting communists and socialists? Very difficult question," he said.

He was, in the spirit of many a provocateur, just asking questions.

Probably everyone in this room grew up believing in democracy. So here's an interesting question for people who believe in democracy . . . Why do you believe in democracy, exactly? Why do people who grew up in the Soviet Union believe in communism?

If you believe it's a moral necessity, why? Why do people have a right to political power? Again, I would say, difficult questions.

Yarvin was ready with a suggestion. "If you actually want to change your political system, you have to resign from it. You have to quit, you have to stop voting, you have to say, 'I don't believe in any of this stuff,'" he said.

According to Yarvin, democracy was a myth that needed doing away with. "A government is just a corporation that owns a country," he said. "It so happens that our sovereign corporation is very poorly managed. There's a very simple way to replace that, which is the same way we deal with all corporations that have failed: we simply delete them." In other words: Retire. All. Government. Employees. Yarvin conceded that the police and the military would need to stick around—but nonprofit organizations and universities would definitely need to go.

And finally, he repeated his call for revolutionary despotism. "If Americans want to change their government, they're going to have to get over their dictator phobia," he said. Here at last was the core of Yarvin's argument. A faint murmur rose from the crowd.

After eighteen minutes, Yarvin's time was coming to an end. An organizer indicated that the program was running behind schedule and that Yarvin would have no time to answer questions. Yarvin relinquished the stage to audible, if not overwhelming, applause.

More important, no one booed.

Like other writers in the blossoming neoreactionary scene, Yarvin was a proponent of "human biodiversity," which is basically racism in a lab coat. Extrapolating from this concept, Yarvin's pseudointellectual contemporary, Nick Land, a British former academic living in Shanghai, has hailed the impending global reign of "autistic nerds, who alone are capable of participating effectively in the advanced technological processes that characterize the emerging economy." HBD, the acronym used to further obscure the racist reality of "human biodiversity," invariably refers to supposed differences in intelligence across races. It is so spurious that a Wikipedia article on the subject was deleted because, in the words of one editor, it is "purely an internet theory," rejected even by those genuine academic experts who are inclined toward genetic determinism as an explanation for human behavior.

Yarvin's faith in HBD informed his politics. He wrote that the U.S. Civil War hadn't freed the slaves but rather "nationalized" them as "dependent" wards of the state. Elsewhere, Yarvin called slavery "a natural human relationship" akin to "that of patron and client."

"I am not a white nationalist, but I do read white-nationalist blogs, and I'm not afraid to link to them," Yarvin insisted. "I am not exactly allergic to the stuff." Indeed. He praised a blogger who advocated the deportation of Muslims and the closure of mosques as "probably the most imaginative and interesting right-wing writer on the planet." Hectoring a Swarthmore history professor in the comments section of the academic's personal blog, Yarvin rhapsodized on the superiority of colonial rule in southern Africa. He expressed special fondness for the former colony of Rhodesia, where wealth and land ownership were prerequisite to political enfranchisement. Yarvin also declared that blacks in South Africa were better off under apartheid.

As more people came to know what the name Moldbug stood for, Yarvin began to have more trouble in mixed company.

In 2015, organizers of the Strange Loop programmers' conference in St. Louis, Missouri, canceled a scheduled talk by Yarvin lest his political views "become the focus" of the gathering. Soon Yarvin became a cause célèbre for a certain kind of free speech purist—those advocates who always pipe up loudest in defense of right-wing white men. At *Slate*, the programmer turned writer David Auerbach objected to the "cowardly and irresponsible" decision by conference organizers, calling it "censorship," and concluded that "plenty of repellent people have contributed to science" (never mind that Yarvin's contributions were next to nil). At the *National Review*, David French—an attorney and writer briefly promoted by Bill Kristol and Mitt Romney as a possible third-party candidate in the 2016 presidential election—defended Yarvin as a victim of "leftist intolerance" and lamented yet another example of political correctness run amok. (Neither Auerbach nor French endorsed Yarvin's political program.)

In 2016, the story seemed to repeat itself after Yarvin submitted a talk to another programmers' gathering, LambdaConf in Boulder, Colorado. After much hand-wringing, the organizers decided to place Yarvin on the program. Many sponsors and speakers backed out. With his professional reputation threatened, Yarvin backtracked and sought to muddy the waters around the abhorrent propaganda he published as Moldbug. "I am not an 'outspoken advocate for slavery,' a racist, a sexist or a fascist," he wrote in an open letter about the LambdaConf controversy.

I am also not plotting any sort of world domination. I am neither a leader or [*sic*] a member of any subversive reactionary organization.

I'm just a writer, and my values are mostly the same as yours. I oppose what you oppose. I just oppose it with different ideas.

Such obfuscations by Yarvin and his defenders worked, for the most part—conference organizers did eventually cave in and rescind

his invitation, but the ensuing press coverage of the controversy
was decidedly ambivalent. An *Inc.* magazine report on the controversy was typical in the way it hedged, noting that Yarvin's "writing has been interpreted as supportive of the institution of slavery"
when in fact his writing *was* supportive of slavery. Those who had
signed a petition against Yarvin's inclusion were added to "a list of
confirmed SJWs"—"social justice warriors," who support feminism, liberalism, racial equality, lower-class empowerment, and
other manifestations of supposed "cultural Marxism"—kept by an
alt-right blogger for the benefit of "those who wish to keep their
organizations free of the creatures."

For all the fuss it caused, Yarvin's disinvitation was no violation of his free speech rights. Though it should go without saying,
no private venue, virtual or physical, has an obligation to host
anyone else's views.

Yet successfully posing as victims of the liberal tyranny was a
great coup for the neoreactionaries. They didn't need to convince
everyone that white supremacist monarchy was the best system—
they never would—but they did need credible third-party defenders and, as Yarvin noted, recruits. In the six years after Yarvin
founded his blog, he had attracted, by his own count, half a million visits. But it was not the size of Yarvin's audience that mattered so much as the nature of it. And when it came to reaching
influential readers, Yarvin was punching above his weight. Because
he formally rejected anti-Semitism and wrapped his most toxic
arguments in a snug swaddling of purple prose and code words,
Yarvin's blog appealed beyond the fascist underground to a more
socially acceptable assortment of "men's rights" advocates, gun

nuts, disillusioned Occupiers, and well-credentialed Silicon Valley entrepreneurs.

Slowly, Moldbuggian concepts and coinages began trickling into the mainstream right-wing lexicon. Neoreactionary lingo in the raw first began to pop up in conservative media outlets including Breitbart News, the Daily Caller, the *American Conservative*, and *National Review*. In less than a decade, the loosely federated movement of neoreactionary writers had grown to the point where the project could survive the loss of any one voice, and in another few years, this strange and seemingly antisocial movement would even establish a beachhead in the White House.

An early sign of the mainstreaming of this esoteric school came from Patri Friedman, a grandson of the famed economist Milton Friedman. In early 2014, the young, libertine free market scion praised Moldbug for inspiring "an entire school of red pill political philosophy." Friedman wanted to improve the image of neoreaction by using TV-ready, buzzword-laden euphemisms like "competitive governance" rather than referring directly to the Moldbuggian ideal of corporate dictatorship. In a Facebook post, he called for "a more politically correct" neoreactionary movement, with room for women and nonwhites, in what appeared to be an effort to cover toxic ideas with the veneer of tolerance and the language of campus liberalism. This "sanewashing" campaign, to borrow a phrase from Dale Carrico—an academic rhetorician in San Francisco who was both a skeptic and a close observer of the techno-utopian futurists, whom he calls Robot Cultists—was successful. Neoreactionary ideas were buffed and polished for polite company, then spread via social media to mass audiences by the apologists for a new global order that places tech executives at the top. Some of those apologists do concede that Silicon Valley rule would mark a reversion to feudalism, but then, they say, there is no alternative. "Our tech titans could save us from global ruin. Alas we fear aristocracy more than apocalypse," the young conservative writer James Polous wrote on Twitter. Polous elaborated the point in an essay for *The Week*. It was a bracing cry for society to hand over all power to the "tech titans," who, he argued, are "plainly higher and better" than "we peons." The innate superiority of the techies made the establishment of a new technofeudalism inevitable, Polous argued, but the failure of democracies to address climate change made it urgently necessary.

> Why don't we turn Washington into the biggest venture capitalist in the world, and hand Silicon Valley a blank check marked "climate"? Because it makes them masters of the universe . . .
>
> Unless we get over that resentful queasiness about the new ruling techno-class we're winding up with anyway, we'll just keep choking on climate.

In other words, resistance is futile. Not that many would bother. As antiestablishment sentiment has deepened in recent decades, tech elites somehow lucked into an exemption. One public opinion poll, taken by Gallup in 2012, found that an overwhelming share of the American public placed "a great deal" of trust in only one institution: the military, with 75 percent approval. Congress was the least-trusted institution, at 13 percent approval. And a majority lacked trust in organized religion, the medical system, the presidency, the Supreme Court, public schools, and newspapers. Four in five distrusted the economic institutions of organized labor, banks, and big business. However, another poll, also taken in 2012, found that 82 percent of Americans had a favorable opinion of Google. Two-thirds felt favorably toward Apple. Nearly three in five approved of Facebook. Zuckerberg was bigger than Jesus. In 2015, Gallup reran its poll and found that confidence in government and most other institutions had fallen even lower, while another poll of consumer brands showed that Google, Apple, and Facebook had maintained the same high levels of public admiration. Americans hate the government, and they don't much like big corporations, either, but years of propaganda have convinced them that the tech companies are somehow different, that Silicon Valley nobility are uniquely enlightened, benevolent, and cool—not your average *jerk* billionaires!

It was both curious and striking how many of the technofeudalist cheerleaders shared a common patron. This neoreactionary hero was everything writers like Moldbug wanted in a king—wealthy, cunning, ruthless, conservative, white, and nerdy. He was the PayPal founder, Facebook board member, major shareholder in a CIA-funded company, Donald Trump delegate, distinguished Stanford alumnus, venture capitalist, and Silicon Valley billionaire Peter Thiel. Here was a rich, powerful man, regarded by many as a public intellectual, who, three years before White House adviser Steve Bannon declared war on "the administrative state," was willing to say, regarding the "monolithic monstrosity" of government, that "breaking it down is probably an improvement."

Tech's most dangerous billionaire was born in Germany to conservative Christian evangelicals. His father was a chemical engineer who worked for international mining companies. Young Thiel attended a series of schools in apartheid-era South Africa, where his father helped mine uranium, before his family finally settled in Foster City, California. Thiel enrolled in an American public school just in time for puberty. As an awkward J.R.R. Tolkien enthusiast, Thiel was not popular. However, he was very good at math. "My path was so tracked that in my 8th-grade yearbook, one of my friends predicted—accurately—that four years later I would enter Stanford as a sophomore," Thiel recalled.

At Stanford, Thiel cofounded a student chess club. In his second year, seething over his lack of peer validation, he ran for student senate on an insurgent platform. "As an outsider looking at the current student government, I am disgusted," Thiel declared in a candidate's statement printed in the student paper. "As a member of several student organizations that could not receive funding (supposedly because of a 'lack of funds'), I am furious." Thiel campaigned ferociously against the "multicultural overkill" of minority student associations; maneuvered to defund the Pro-Choice Alliance and the Women's Center Collective; and sought a politically opportunistic "investigation" into a faculty candidate of Chinese ancestry who had once written an article for a communist journal, likening the situation to "a Nazi teaching German studies," denying charges of McCarthyism.

Five years later, Thiel, then a graduate student in the law

school, was still serving on the Stanford student government. The senate Publications Board recommended that no funds be allocated to the *Stanford Review*, a conservative campus newspaper Thiel had founded with backing from the conservative Collegiate Network (which was in turn backed by the Koch and Scaife Foundations). However, in his capacity as Appropriations Committee chairman, Thiel reversed the recommendation and awarded $4,000 in student funds to the *Review*. This was Thiel's "first entrepreneurial venture" and, in its hypocritical reliance upon administrative subsidy as well as its reactionary tilt, indicative of a pattern.

After graduating law school, Thiel coauthored a book, *The Diversity Myth*, attacking Stanford's tolerant attitude toward affirmative action, feminism, and gay rights activism. Thiel himself was gay, although he said later that he hadn't realized it at the time. His eager culture warring paid off, and Thiel was selected to interview for clerkships with U.S. Supreme Court justices Antonin Scalia and Anthony Kennedy. Neither hired him, but he still landed on a golden pillow at the white-shoe law firm of Sullivan & Cromwell in New York. Thiel quit his first real job after seven months and three days. He lasted a little longer at his second job, as a derivatives trader at Credit Suisse, before quitting once more and moving back to California—"the best state in the U.S."—where he founded Thiel Capital with $1 million raised in large part from family members.

His first startup, the company that became PayPal, was a subversive political venture from the get-go. PayPal's express ambition was to privatize currency itself and, as Thiel said, make it "nearly impossible for corrupt governments to steal wealth from their people through their old means." It would also make it nearly impossible for legitimate governments to lawfully collect taxes from shady racketeers. Among the first big clients PayPal solicited: offshore casinos. "A great company is a conspiracy to change the world," Thiel later wrote. His startup even charted its growth with a "World Domination Index." The 1999 Neal Stephenson novel *Cryptonomicon* was, in Thiel's words, "required reading" for employees—the plot of the nine-hundred-page novel involves the creation of a digital currency beyond governmental control.

Thiel's loathing for government spending did not apply when the government spent money on him. His next big startup, Palantir—a name borrowed from Tolkien—depended for survival upon the least transparent, least accountable, and most profligate extension of the federal government, the CIA. The agency invested in Thiel through its Silicon Valley VC front, In-Q-Tel. With Palantir, this self-described "civil libertarian" became an important player in the growth of a secretive, invasive, and patently unconstitutional global surveillance apparatus. Asked in a 2014 online chat if Palantir was "a front for the CIA," Thiel replied, "No, the CIA is a front for Palantir." With 70 percent of the U.S. intelligence budget going to the private sector, this dismissive wisecrack was not so much an outright denial as it was a sly wink at the extent of corporate dominance over even the most powerful federal agencies.

In 2012, Palantir was competing with a consortium of more established contractors including General Dynamics, Northrop Grumman, Lockheed Martin, and SAIC for a piece of a $10.6 billion

Pentagon program to develop "battlefield intelligence" software that purported to help soldiers locate hidden bombs. One large customer, the U.S. Army, seemed to be leaning toward the competing product. In an effort to alter the outcome, Palantir hired a lobbyist named Terry Paul, a retired Marine Corps brigadier general, at an annual rate of $320,000. Paul was a "close family friend" and personal "mentor" to Duncan Hunter Jr., the Republican member of the House Armed Services Committee who soon took up Palantir's cause. Such was their bond that when Hunter was considering enlisting in the U.S. Marines, he turned to Paul for advice.

The congressman pulled out all the stops to bend the Army procurement process to Palantir's benefit, hectoring then Army chief of staff General Raymond Odierno about the Army's failure to give more money to Palantir. Odierno finally snapped, "I'm tired of somebody telling me I don't care about our soldiers." The general retired in 2015, and Palantir's bid advanced through the Army bureaucracy. After Trump's electoral victory in 2016, an early Palantir employee and partner at Thiel's Founders Fund, Trae Stephens, joined the transition team in a role that would see him "shape policy and vet Defense Department staff." When Trump announced his crackdown on immigrants, Palantir, which held intelligence analysis contracts with Immigration and Customs Enforcement, among other Homeland Security agencies, stood to directly benefit, as did another defense company incubated at Founders Fund—Palmer Luckey's Anduril, "the flame of the West" in Tolkien mythology.

Thiel's companies did not merely exert political influence through the hiring of well-connected lobbyists. He was also a leading financier of technofeudalist and neoreactionary thinkers, both in Silicon Valley and beyond.

Thiel donated to multiple organizations that invited Curtis Yarvin to promote his deranged political ideas, namely the Foresight Institute and an organization now known as the Machine Intelligence Research Institute, which is dedicated to the promotion of artificial intelligence and which supported the BIL Conference. And in 2013, Thiel became a direct patron of Yarvin himself. Thiel's Founder's Fund and the venture capital fund Andreessen-Horowitz were the key players in a $1.1 million seed investment round for Yarvin's strange startup, called Tlon. The name Tlon referenced a short story by Jorge Luis Borges in which "a secret society of astronomers, biologists, engineers, metaphysicians, poets, chemists, algebraists, moralists, painters, geometers . . . directed by an obscure man of genius" built a "brave new world" that forced old cultures and countries into extinction. Yarvin's title at Tlon was, appropriately enough, "benevolent dictator for life." His cofounder was a young man named John Burnham who, at age eighteen, accepted $100,000 from Thiel to skip college and go directly into business. Instead of mining asteroids as he originally intended, Burnham wound up working with Yarvin. Tlon had no product when Thiel invested, at least not in the conventional sense. Its efforts were directed at completing a sprawling piece of software called Urbit, which was essentially an attempt to rewrite some of the fundamental code allowing computers to operate and communicate with one another.

Although Yarvin claimed his software work was entirely distinct from Moldbug's pompous agitation, keen technical observers noted that the open-source code for Urbit was peppered with ideological allusions. For instance, as the symbolic basis for Urbit, Yarvin chose an alphabet composed not of Roman, Cyrillic, or Greek letters but of "runes" in the volkisch tradition.

It must be said that Thiel has never publicly endorsed Yarvin's blog or the neoreactionary program in general. Neither, given the opportunity, has he denounced it. In a 2014 question-and-answer session on the website Reddit, a user named ExistentialDread asked Thiel directly, "What is your view on Neoreaction?" Thiel replied with a virtual wink. "Sounds like a self-contradiction—if you're reactionary, why do you need the 'neo'?" he wrote. One former employee of the Singularity Institute, which Thiel funded, who had made the billionaire's acquaintance described Thiel as "a decent guy" who "stood up to multiculturalism" and has "the guts to support 'wacky' ideas." He added: "I wouldn't be surprised if he has read his Moldbug. I know he knows Moldbug."

I can confirm that Thiel is in communication with Yarvin on matters political. After Thiel learned from a mutual acquaintance that I was working on this book, he passed the word to Yarvin, who emailed me his congratulations. I had hoped to meet Yarvin for lunch—at his suggestion—but the invitation eventually vanished behind a tiresome smokescreen of reading assignments and insults.

After I explained some of Thiel's connections to neoreaction in the *Baffler*, Thiel was quoted in the *New York Times* calling my report "flattering" but a "full-on conspiracy theory." I thought that was rich, given his avowed penchant for "world domination," and all the more so after Thiel confessed to orchestrating an elaborate

conspiracy to destroy his enemies, namely Gawker. When I asked
Thiel for further comment, he didn't reply. Later, in 2017, BuzzFeed
reported that Yarvin claimed to have watched a recent election at
Thiel's house, and considered himself a political counselor to the
billionaire VC, whom Yarvin deemed "fully enlightened." (I have no
evidence that Thiel endorses Yarvin's views on Hitler or slavery.)

There is definitely a whiff of Moldbug in Thiel's own commentary. In addition to providing financial patronage, Thiel also provided intellectual inspiration to the neoreactionaries. Nick Land
called Thiel's antidemocratic critiques "a crucial catalyst for the
emergence of the Dark Enlightenment"—a term the neoreactionaries use to describe the ascent of their movement.

In 2012, Thiel delivered a lecture at Stanford that explained
his views regarding the divine rights of Silicon Valley CEOs. The
lecture nominally concerned some theories of historical "mimetics"
by Thiel's favorite old philosophy professor, René Girard. But Thiel's
lecture also contained a heavy dose of neomonarchism:

> A startup is basically structured as a monarchy. We don't call
> it that, of course. That would seem weirdly outdated, and
> anything that's not democracy makes people uncomfort-
> able. We are biased toward the democratic-republican side
> of the spectrum . . . But the truth is that startups and found-
> ers lean toward the dictatorial side because that structure
> works better for startups.

Might a dictatorial approach, in Thiel's opinion, also work better for society at large? He never said so in his Stanford lecture

(he said pure dictatorship is unideal in a company, although he did cast tech CEOs as the heirs to mythical "god-kings" such as Romulus). But Thiel, for all his petulance, was a sophisticated man. He knew where to draw the line in public. He knew that ordinary people got "uncomfortable" when powerful billionaires started talking about the obsolescence of participatory government and "the unthinking demos," as he put it in a 2009 essay for the libertarian journal *Cato Unbound*. This was the infamous essay in which Thiel condemned what he saw as the consequences of women's suffrage and declared, "I no longer believe that freedom and democracy are compatible." Thiel later minimized but did not repudiate his *Cato Unbound* article. "It was late at night. I quickly typed it off," he told the blogger Tyler Cowen in a 2015 interview. All the same, Thiel said, "You could never disown anything that you've written."

The rise of the neoreactionaries was not exclusively a coup orchestrated from above with the help of powerful, well-connected hyperlibertarians like Thiel, Patri Friedman, and Trump's campaign financier, the tech billionaire Robert Mercer. It was also a movement from below, embraced by thousands—and eventually perhaps by millions—of disaffected young people. While the neoreactionaries expounded at tiresome length about their aims, they revealed their individual motivations only in glimpses. Justine Tunney, the Google engineer–cum–Moldbug booster, provided one such peek inside the neoreactionary mind. In a 2014 blog post addressing "Silicon Valley and geeks in general," Tunney called for a new "Nerd Nationalism" motivated primarily by personal resentment. "We don't fit into this society and we never will," she wrote.

> We're placed in public schools that bore us—when we're not being assaulted and ridiculed by bullies. We have trouble procreating because society finds us sexually repulsive. We're ridiculed in the press. We're unwanted in our communities. Angry kids throw bricks at our buses when we go to work. We're denied a voice in our government.

But a new day had dawned. "We've grown powerful thanks to the tech industry," Tunney wrote. "In many ways, I feel that geeks already *rule* the world, we just haven't figured out how to *reign*. So we need to up our game, get smart, and start asking ourselves what we can do to *put the fear* in all these people."

Who were "these people" who needed to feel fear? It was not totally clear. Elsewhere in the essay, Tunney singled out "normal people"—or, as they were called elsewhere in the neoreactionary milieu, "normies" or "normalfags." As Tunney explained, normies were "bullies" who "disrespect" or mistreat "super-smart socially-awkward nerd[s]" such as herself. Elsewhere on her website, she offered a rundown of the innate cognitive "algorithm" whereby humans rank and classify others based on intelligence, wealth, physical strength, and—least usefully of all, in her view—"charisma" or "attractiveness." Those who got by based on good looks or charm were, in Tunney's view, "unskilled unintelligent parasites." In the parasites' defense, not everyone could be as smart as the reclusive masterminds who spent their days and nights plotting the real-life revenge of the nerds.

No single scapegoat united the neoreactionaries in hatred. Their loathing was a live wire of high-wattage rage flapping like a whip in a storm over anyone imagined to receive preferential treatment. Blacks and Latinos, Muslims and Jews, leftists and ladies—anyone who threatened the fragile ego of the vengeful nerd may feel the sting of punishment. But it should be clear that the neoreactionaries were, by and large, young white males embittered by "political correctness"—a term that represented the perceived loss of their social advantages to an undeserving mob of brainwashed social justice warriors. Significantly, these radicalized youth saw in the miraculous futuristic designs of men such as a Peter Thiel and Elon Musk a vision that was entirely compatible with their notions of racial supremacy, and they expected to personally benefit in the tech titans' new order. To certain devotees, Musk's dream of human settlements on Mars offered an escape from this benighted earth, where their wretched enemies would be left behind, in a final act of vengeance by the tech-savvy master race. "I say the last thing the shitskins would see of the white race is a gigantic chasm erupting, and a colony ship launching towards the stars," one anonymous young man wrote on a forum frequented by neoreactionaries. These young men saw themselves as possessing secret knowledge—hidden histories, scientific certainties, and political proofs—suppressed by the nefarious hand of the Cathedral. This was the powerful mystical significance of "the red pill." Through coded language and symbols of affinity, this ideology turned personal frustration into camaraderie and a sense of purpose.

Not all schemes of redemption and vengeance inspired by this online movement have been chimeras. Numerous American terrorists in recent years have been, by their own accounts, radicalized online and indoctrinated into extreme forms of misogyny, scientific racism, pro-Nazi historical revisionism, and other branches of "red pill" philosophy. Elliot Rodger, the misogynist mass shooter who killed six people near the University of California, Santa Barbara, in 2014, was a red-pilled "incel"—involuntary celibate—and a self-professed fascist, not to mention a YouTube vlogger who, after his crime, racked up millions of views. Dylann Roof, the racist, unemployed ninth-grade dropout who murdered nine black parishioners at a church in Charleston, South Carolina, in 2015, posted coded appeals to Heil Hitler on his website, The Last Rhodesian; by the killer's own account, his racist awakening began when he typed "black on White crime" into Google. "I have never been the same since that day," he said. Chris Harper-Mercer, who went on a shooting spree in Roseburg, Oregon, some months after Roof's rampage, had online accounts containing Nazi references, and police said he had written in support of white supremacist causes. News of Harper-Mercer's murder spree, which killed ten, prompted speculation on neoreactionary forums that the long-awaited "beta uprising" of virginal shut-ins had begun. Not quite. But in Charlottesville, Virginia, in August 2017, a large audience of Americans finally saw the real beta uprising in the violent Nazi rally that shut the city down, terrorized the population, and culminated in the vehicular homicide of a local leftist woman, Heather Heyer, in a crowd of antifascist protesters, dozens of whom were also injured. The terrorist was a twenty-year-old Nazi from Ohio, James Alex Fields Jr., whose Facebook page was filled with swastika memes, leering Pepes, and other by now familiar neofascist iconography. While no doubt mentally unbalanced, these young killers were, more importantly, targeted by a sprawling and sophisticated online propaganda campaign.

The prototype for these killers was Anders Breivik, whose 2011 massacre in Oslo, Norway, targeted young leftists and whose detailed manifesto circulated in online fascist forums where strategies were set and tactics debated. Curtis Yarvin wrote about Breivik. His objection to the Oslo massacre was that it was insufficient to "free Norway from Eurocommunism." Terrorist violence—or "folk activism," in his preferred framing—was not "inherently wrong." The problem with terrorism was, Yarvin argued, that it was ineffective when employed by right-wingers. "There are plenty of historical contexts in which right-wing terrorism did work—for instance, Germany in the 1920s. In these contexts, it was legitimate," Yarvin wrote. He had a better plan: "Rape is beta. Seduction is alpha. Don't slaughter the youth camp—recruit the youth camp."

The single most successful red pill recruitment push began in 2014, with the so-called "Gamergate" episode, which demonstrated how the combination of misogynistic pickup artistry, "men's rights" activism, pseudoscientific racism, neofascist historical revisionism, and the new "nerd nationalism" snowballed into a campaign of cruel, relentless, and violent intimidation. As the blogger Steve Alexander of Reaxxion, "a gaming site for men," admitted, "Before GamerGate, I didn't know what the red pill was."

This twisted episode revealed its full horror when a young woman's bitter ex-boyfriend egged on a campaign of stalking and harassment perpetrated by denizens of the website 4chan, the troll-riddled message board where "normies" fear to tread. This young woman, Zoe Quinn, happened to be an independent video game developer whose recent work was favorably received by critics but—being an introspective departure from the usual shoot-'em-up style of game—was abhorred by the misogynistic gamers of 4chan. The self-described Gamergaters spun a grand conspiratorial narrative concerning "ethics in video games journalism," claiming that Quinn had "bribed the media into liking her shitty non-game with her vagina." Using personal identifying details provided by Quinn's obsessive ex, the Gamergaters proceeded to stalk, slander, and threaten Quinn, as well as her friends and defenders— the social justice warriors. They also went after any other women imagined to have obtained advantages based on their gender— and anyone who criticized the sexist, racist, and otherwise bigoted culture of video games, which can be summarized in two words describing the content of the typical mass-market product in the medium: boobs and bullets. Some women even had SWAT teams raid their homes after Gamergate supporters made false emergency calls. Quinn and her family members were forced to relocate in an attempt to escape the constant electronic harassment that the police and courts were powerless to stop. Another hate mob target, Anita Sarkeesian, who had posted a feminist critique of video game culture to YouTube, was forced to cancel a university speaking appearance after an anonymous caller threatened to carry out "the deadliest school shooting in American history" if she showed up on campus. For its targets, Gamergate was a prolonged, intense, and terrifying experience. For the harassers, it was more like . . . a game. For pretty much everyone else, it was just another baffling oddity of internet culture. I, too, assumed it was frivolous—until I looked into the details.

The press made big mistakes in covering this story, but the biggest mistake had nothing to do with the Gamergaters' farcical hand-wringing over journalism ethics. Rather, the mistake was in adopting the misleading language of the harassers—specifically, in using their word, Gamergate, as a frame for its ongoing coverage. This word signaled to anyone who was not already immersed in the juvenile subculture of video games that the matter was a sideshow, not worthy of their attention. Many in the mainstream press also failed to recognize that one major component of the Gamergate campaign was an elaborate effort to mislead the media, intimidate critics, and recruit new allies by pushing red pill ideas—not only cartoon memes like Pepe and Kek but dubious graphics purporting to show the progress of "white genocide," pithy homilies to "Western culture," and disingenuous defenses of the free speech privileges of armed Nazis allegedly threatened by scrawny leftist college kids—into the wider culture. Having been radicalized by what amounted to a fascist propaganda network of online troll communities such as 4chan, the Gamergaters saw themselves as engaged in a political project that was simultaneously overt and covert. The overt side engaged in absurdly high-minded discussions about "ethics in game journalism." The covert element, led by the most dedicated partisans, was racist and neoreactionary in orientation. It saw video games as the product of "high-tier Aryan male engineering" under assault by social justice warriors in the thrall of Jewish conspirators. Gaming, after all, was the milieu that produced YouTube's most successful vlogger, PewDiePie, who made "joking" references to Hitler and the Holocaust amid sincere claims of white victimhood to millions of tween followers, unbeknownst to most of their parents, even as he showed them how to slaughter virtual monsters and win over buxom virtual heroines. What the press obligingly trivialized as Gamergate was, in fact, the first neoreactionary terror campaign. At its height, a federal judge, Katherine Bolan Forrest, received death threats after being targeted by Gamergate's most dreaded shock brigade, an online gang known as Baphomet that gathered on 8chan, a more militant cousin to the 4chan boards.

How closely all of this prefigured the rhetoric of the Trump campaign and presidency: fake news, fake judges, men's rights, white power, full frontal assault—and no apologies, ever! These bitter fruits shared a common root. Writing in the *Guardian*, the novelist Pankaj Mishra persuasively described a connection between the Charleston massacre, the atrocities of the Islamic State, and various secessionist movements, of which Trump must be considered a part along with Brexit. These insurgencies were, Mishra wrote, direct by-products of "the entrepreneurial age." The basic problem, as Mishra saw it, was that globalized capitalism created far too many "superfluous young people"—that is, losers. The gap between the promise and the reality of capitalism created "simmering reservoirs of cynicism and discontent." In this new order, "everyone was supposed to be an entrepreneur." The more typical experience, however, was one of "defeat and humiliation," and the contradiction fueled an "apocalyptic and nihilistic mood" that sometimes erupted in violent outbursts of rage. In a mirror image of their rising young socialist opponents in the United States, Britain, and Europe, the militant youth of the alt-right have rejected capitalism in favor of the fascist alternative. The press mostly missed this story as it was happening, but the young agents of change were clear about their goals, and about globalized capitalism's role in creating an opening for extremist movements.

There may be no better exemplar of the rightward drift of autodidactic reactionary internet natives than the precocious futurist and Thiel beneficiary Michael Anissimov. Born in 1984 in the Bay Area, Anissimov became obsessed with the pursuit of technological utopia at age eleven after reading a book about nanotechnology—atom-scaled robots that could either save the world or end it, per the stock mythology of sci-fi-flavored futurism. From a young age, Anissimov worked tirelessly to ingratiate himself with techie futurists like Thiel and Kurzweil, eagerly volunteering for their organizations and working his way up the ranks. His career prospects seemed bright until late 2012, when he lost his job at the Thiel-funded Singularity Institute. The newly unemployed Anissimov soured on his old mentors in the futurist scene, and his own views darkened. He soon publicly and "wholeheartedly" embraced the tenets of neoreaction—especially the racist bits. As he explained in a blog post, his ideological progression was only natural, a product of "long and hard thought . . . combined with gentle reactionary nudging by Mencius Moldbug."

Anissimov's political journey began by "studying the findings of modern cognitive science on the failings of human reasoning" and wound up at the writings of "serious 19th century gentlemen denouncing democracy," as he and his new neoreactionary pals wrote on a blog they founded, More Right. The name was intended to tweak an existing blog called Less Wrong. It also worked as an allusion to a book by one of Anissimov's new intellectual favorites, the late Italian totalitarian occultist writer Julius Evola. A favorite of postwar fascist terrorist groups throughout Europe, Evola had written a book called *Fascism Viewed from the Right*, in which he argued that Hitler and Mussolini failed because they were not extreme enough, and too populist. Evola favored a return to aristocracy. His name became more familiar in the American mainstream after then Breitbart chairman Steve Bannon (who would go on to become Trump's campaign strategist and White House adviser) mentioned the heretofore obscure writer's name in a BuzzFeed interview. As one scholar of right-wing traditionalism later told the *New York Times*, "The fact that Bannon even knows Evola is significant." It was more than significant—it was alarming.

Some who had been paying close attention to the techno-utopian scene were less than astonished to see Anissimov, long praised as a rising star, go the Nazi way. After reading one of Anissimov's neoreactionary rants in 2014, the academic blogger Dale Carrico published the following told-you-so:

> Now, for years and years before what you call Anissimov's "jolt to the right" I have accused him of advocating a reactionary politics of plutocratic corporatism, fetishistic

militarism, and anti-democratic eugenic and technocratic elitism . . . Of course, he whined and denied this as name calling but never responded to the substance of what I was saying. Now he lets his fascist freak flag fly, I can't say that I am at all surprised.

Anissimov took to posting paranoid white supremacist rants on Twitter. Why, he asked, do "blacks get your own continent"? "European whites are being replaced and destroyed by 'diversity,'" he cried. He denounced miscegenation and declared that women should be confined to the home. After having his Twitter account suspended for alleged harassment, Anissimov took to the social networking site Ask.fm and answered hundreds of detailed questions about himself and his views. He explained how he was paying the bills: "I get paid to write scientific articles. Most of my writing doesn't have my name attached to it. I don't spread around who my clients are, so it's impossible for my political enemies to get me fired or otherwise mess with my employment." He namechecked his favorite political party: Golden Dawn, in Greece. He listed his favorite "scholars," including Moldbug, Evola, Schopenhauer, and Adolf Hitler. "Jews," he wrote, "make up a bunch of stories to discredit Hitler."

Anissimov's ludicrous reading of history came from—where else?—online sources. He had taken a number of college-level computer science courses but never completed a degree. And somewhere along the way he had reconnected, at least in his imagination, with his "white Russian" ancestry. Anissimov wanted to reinstitute the aristocracy, which he believed had instilled "a sense of mutual respect, understanding, and camaraderie that today's politicians can only blink in confusion about." As he saw it, "traditional" social hierarchy, as opposed to the "ultra-egalitarian" status quo, was the best buffer against the "hyper-empowered masses." Only old-fashioned authoritarianism, he felt, could save the world from terrorists wielding futuristic weapons of mass destruction:

> Untraceable killer cybernetic mosquitoes for anonymous assassinations. Mobsters with fullerene muscles a hundred times stronger than steel. Nuclear enrichment centrifuges you can build in your basement. Combined with a largely unrestrained, laissez-faire anarcho-capitalist or simply neoliberal capitalist system, we have a recipe for disaster. Only through embracing Traditional structures and patterns did I see a way out of this conundrum.

He saw no contradiction whatsoever between his new hyper-traditionalist social views and the peppy futurism he had long endorsed. They were, as he saw it, intrinsically linked, and on that one thing, at least, he was correct.

VIII

Onward, Robot Soldiers

If anything comes close to encapsulating the dreams and desires of the rising elite, it is the Singularity, which is simultaneously a prediction, a program, and a set of doctrines. As a prediction, the Singularity refers to that rapturous moment when our technological capabilities exceed currently understood limits of physics and consciousness. Advances made within military laboratories, corporate research departments, and hacker houses will accelerate until the sheer energy of all that innovation ignites a great spark, at which time all will behold the physical and metaphysical merger of humanity and computers. Then, once there is no more distinction between man and machine, all matter will awaken, bringing about a new era in which the disembodied hive mind of what was once *Homo sapiens* unifies the cosmos in eternal ecstasy. That's the idea, anyway. The Singularity is the most popular subset of "transhumanist" thinking, an eclectic set of theories that posit that the human species, by converting its brain power into more and more advanced forms of technology, will one day wrest control of the evolutionary process from nature and simply *decide* how it will thereafter exist in and interact with the universe. Unlike some transhumanist factions that obsess over biology and genetics, the Singularity singles out computers—specifically, the development of advanced artificial intelligence—as the catalyst for an allegedly inevitable and willful transformation of the species.

The person most closely associated with this concept is the author, inventor, and tech executive Ray Kurzweil. Kurzweil is now known primarily as a purveyor of far-out ideas, of which the Singularity is only one, but his early pronouncements are remarkably restrained in comparison. In a 1984 conference speech, he lamented the overly optimistic predictions of AI researchers, who were forever claiming that the holy grail of the field, "artificial general intelligence"—a computerized mind equivalent to that of a human, in capabilities if not in design—was just a decade or two away, only to be proven wrong time and again. Such romanticism, he said, had created a "credibility problem" that plagued the field. In 1990, MIT Press published Kurzweil's first book, *The Age of Intelligent Machines*, which collected predictions from more than twenty authors. In keeping with his earlier restraint, Kurzweil limited himself to extrapolations based on technologies that were already under development, including portable wireless computers. But by 1999, with the new millennium looming, Kurzweil had decided to reinvent himself as a techno-fortuneteller. That was the year when he published his follow-up, *The Age of Spiritual Machines*, and with it became the leading purveyor of the technological romanticism he once tut-tutted. He predicted, correctly, that in 2009, people would "primarily use portable computers, which have become dramatically lighter and thinner"—a less impressive feat of precognition if you knew, as Kurzweil did, that such technology was well along in the research and development pipeline at the time of his writing. His more substantive predictions regarding life in 2019 fared worse: "Rapid economic expansion and prosperity has [*sic*] continued," he predicted. By 2099, he wrote, "software-based humans" would leave their noncybernetic ancestors behind and manifest multiple personas at will, like virtual gods. With the publication of *The Singularity Is Near* in 2005, Kurzweil finally blossomed into the top guru of technomystical woo-woo. There would be no more talk of dead ends in AI. Very soon, he said, computers would think as humans do. What's more,

> there will be no distinction, post-Singularity, between human and machine or between physical and virtual reality . . . Ultimately, the entire universe will become saturated with our intelligence. This is the destiny of the universe.

What happened to the old, cautious Kurzweil? Cynics assumed he resorted to hyperbole in order to grab headlines and sell books. And indeed, *The Singularity Is Near* became a *New York Times* bestseller, with a quarter of a million copies sold over ten years. The book received a particularly enthusiastic reception in Silicon Valley. *Wired* magazine founder Kevin Kelly called it "a seminal document" presaging "the beginning of utopia." Bill Gates offered a blurb for this "intriguing" book: "Kurzweil is the best person I know at predicting the future of artificial intelligence."

Others viewed Kurzweil's transformation in a different light. "Ray Kurzweil is a genius. One of the greatest hucksters of the age," biologist and blogger PZ Myers declared. Kurzweil maintained that if his critics in academia and elsewhere failed to see the truth of the impending Singularity, as he did, it was because they were simply behind the times. "Scientists are trained to be skeptical, to speak cautiously," he wrote. But the exponential pace of innovation, he argued, meant skepticism and caution now threatened "society's interests."

And to Kurzweil, "society's interests" boiled down to accelerating the Singularity, which, practically speaking, meant arranging for American tech companies to have every resource at their disposal and every law in their favor. It's no surprise, then, that Kurzweil and his Singularity theories found many fans inside the executive suites of major tech companies—Bill Gates was not an outlier. In terms of public relations, Kurzweil's boundless and ostensibly scientifically grounded optimism about the dazzling digital future was a tremendous asset to Silicon Valley. In December 2012, news broke that Kurzweil had taken a job at Google. At the time, I was curious.

I wanted to know, why did this predominant global corporation put such faith in an idiosyncratic technomystic? What were its plans for him? Kurzweil's recent patent applications—a "meal replacement beverage" sweetened with egg white powder, a sound-canceling "sleep-aid" helmet, and a "poetry screen saver"—suggested that his prime years as an inventor had passed. Yet Kurzweil's title was to be director of engineering, which sure sounded important. I read that Google's cofounders, Larry Page and Sergey Brin, had been fans of Kurzweil since their days as students at Stanford and that Page invited Kurzweil to join the company after hearing a summary of his most recent book, *How to Create a Mind*, about artificial intelligence. Such a prominent hire suggested not only a deep confidence in Kurzweil's competence, but an endorsement of his vision. Which led to further questions. What did it mean that the leaders of a corporation more powerful than most governments were willing to tacitly endorse what Kurzweil called Singularitarianism? Was it not extraordinary that these iconic and influential tech magnates would lend credence to the Kurzweilian prophecy that further human evolution meant an irreversible merger with machines and the sacrifice of our individual biological identities to an immortal hive mind? Was such a thing actually possible? If there was substance to Singularitarianism, then the ascension of Kurzweil at Google would one day be seen as a decisive moment in history, analagous to the Roman emperor Constantine's conversion to Christianity. And if the Singularity turned out to be nothing more than some lunatic reverie, a daydream for some lifelong science fiction fans who had lucked into tremendous wealth, I still had questions. Namely, where I could get whatever these guys were smoking?

The answers were in Amsterdam.

In 2009, with funding from Page and a number of other early Google employees, Kurzweil had lent his imprimatur to a new venture called Singularity University, which aimed to spread Singularitarian thinking among a globally diverse student body composed of current and future leaders in the public and private sectors. Back in Mountain View, I had spied the SU campus from the trail near Google's headquarters. Tuition for the intensive ten-week summer program there was far beyond my means—$30,000.

But SU also staged two-day traveling seminars called Singularity
Summits. The next summit was to be held in Amsterdam.

The promotional materials promised fantastical revelations to
all who attended. Sessions on the "revolution in robotics and artificial intelligence" would cover the latest in drones, "telepresence,"
and something called "deep learning." Other speakers would explore
the possibilities of bodily implants, exoskeletons, 3-D-printed
organs, and nanomedicine. There would be sessions on "organizing society for accelerating change," which was to tack government and the relationship of technology to "unemployment and
inequality." Finally, for those looking to cash in on this sneak peek
at the future, the summit would feature sessions on startups and
entrepreneurship in the era of "exponential technology"—a shorthand phrase describing, per Kurzweil's theories, how the pace of
invention has allegedly accelerated through history, bringing us
to this moment on the cusp of the Singularity. "Exponential technology will disrupt all industries," the online brochure announced.
"Learn how to understand the impacts these technologies will
have on your business and how to capitalize on the huge opportunities of the 21st century." The link to the registration form bore a
warning label: "Disrupt or be disrupted."

Tickets to the summit cost $2,500, and so naturally I applied
for a press ticket, hoping that the organizers would waive the fee in
exchange for the expectation of publicity. Miraculously, it worked.
I booked plane tickets and packed a bag for Holland.

I arrived one day before the Singularity Summit. My hostel was
a converted brothel across the street from the headquarters of a
major Dutch bank. In the common area, I met Bobby, an earnest

young visitor from San Francisco. "Gotta love Uber!" he said, hailing a ride. It seemed there was no escaping the global tyranny of the California imperium. A former federal law enforcement officer, Bobby said he had gone to work for a U.S. government contractor based, for tax reasons, in Europe. We bade *vaarwel*, for Bobby was on his way to meet some lady friends at a local "coffee shop." I struck up a conversation with another hostel guest, a shy Scandinavian who worked as a programmer for some pointless mobile app. However, as conversations with programmers often do, the discussion quickly petered out. Which was fine. I took a short stroll and procured a trio of handily prerolled spliffs containing a strain called Cheese. Tiring, I went back to my room.

Cheese, it turned out, was formidable stuff. I slept through my first alarm and had to rush to get to the summit on time. The morning was cool, the streets swarming with bicycles. I walked hastily along a canal to the Leidseplein, a large square in central Amsterdam, where, around the corner from the imposing Hotel Americain, I found the glass facade of the De La Mar theater. It hadn't always been so sleek. During wartime the theater was a prototypal Big Data archive, housing records for the "voluntary" Nazi labor program, Arbeitseinsatz, which sent Dutch citizens to toil in German fields and factories. In January 1945, an underground gang of saboteurs and assassins, backed by the Allies and known as the goon squad, fire-bombed the building. The Nazis avenged that crime against quantification by executing five suspect labor bureau employees against the wall where everyone could see. Or so I had read. This morning's lessons, I expected, would be less macabre, more upbeat.

A prim doorman waved me through the doors into the lobby of the De La Mar. Inside the theater was all polished stone, red velvet, and crystal chandeliers. The other arrivals, mostly middle-aged and business-suited, chatted cheerfully. I checked my jacket and the Cheese, then claimed my personalized lanyard at the reception table. It was marked PRESS, which would open up some conversations but foreclose many others. It also featured the logo of summit sponsor Deloitte and a slogan playing off the theme of the event: "Ignition—Building Tomorrow by Launching Today." The most important thing about my badge was that it granted access to an upstairs VIP area, where the line for coffee was shorter, and where everything on the menu was vegetarian and presumably Kurzweil-approved for longevity. At a nearby bistro table temporarily converted into a standing desk, I found the frazzled Dutch publicist who had arranged my credentials. I hovered awkwardly as he finished his phone call, then introduced myself. The publicist told me nine hundred people had registered for the summit, including seventy-five other journalists. No wonder he was busy. He said this summit was the largest event in SU history. I took care to write that down in my notebook so he could see: *largest . . . ever . . .* Having satisfied the implicit terms of our arrangement as publicist and journalist, I said goodbye and joined the crowd now shuffling upstairs into the grand auditorium.

I squeezed past an SU camera crew interviewing some eager conferencegoer and found a seat high in the upper gallery. Then the room went dark. I felt a surge of anticipation, but only for a second. Suddenly I felt a stinging pain. The pain was coming from inside my head. An orchestral surge blared through the auditorium. I cringed. We were watching a video.

The visuals on the tall screen lacked the visceral impact of their musical accompaniment. Headshots of the scheduled speakers appeared one after another, punctuated by a simulated lens flare. With a whoosh came a series of snapshots from Summits past: A man at a podium. People at desks. A whiteboard. The incongruous crescendo arrived with a thundering rumble and the glare of a supernova, which dissolved into the SU logo.

As I peered down into the lower rows of the theater, I saw seats filled with middle managers from insurance companies, electrical utilities, and other humdrum institutions representing the most conservative, risk-averse business traditions of Europe. Some, I would learn in chats between sessions, shared my fascination with Kurzweiliana, but many more were drawn by the promise of beating the market with fresh intelligence on new technologies. At least, that was what persuaded their employers to pick up the tab for a midweek conference in Europe's adult Disneyland.

The broad managerial interest in Singularitarian thinking was articulated at the outset of the Summit by John Hagel, an executive from Deloitte's "Center for the Edge," which helped "senior executives make sense of and profit from emerging opportunities"— that is, to catch up with Silicon Valley buzzwords. Deloitte was the Summit's prime sponsor and had sent the largest contingent. "Why is Deloitte doing this? It's a selfish reason," the executive said. "If we don't, our techs, our lawyers, our auditors, and our consultants will be out of business in a few years."

There was the answer. Deloitte had sponsored the Singularity
Summit because, in a tall glass tower somewhere, accounting
majors were debating the actuarial implications of the Singularitarian future, when millions of transhuman policyholders might
enjoy indefinite lifespans, and running cost-benefit analyses on
investments in supposedly imminent tech ventures such as extra-
planetary mining expeditions. I should have known: It was all
about money. And so it ever would be, apparently.

No one who graced the stage at the Summit spoke more directly
to this underlying money lust than SU cofounder Peter Diamandis. Although Ray Kurzweil was the university "chancellor," he
seemed to be more of a figurehead. It was Diamandis who had
pitched the idea for SU to Kurzweil, who in turn pitched it to the
Google guys, who supplied seed money. With his finely combed
hair, his wide smile, and his smartly tailored suit, Diamandis stood
out next to the comparatively unpolished SU faculty. He was a
dashing debate society president among chess club dorks, a born
closer whose optimism knew no bounds. A Harvard- and MIT-
educated medical doctor and aerospace engineer, Diamandis "gave
up on NASA" and resolved to become the Commodore Vanderbilt
of outer space. He founded the International Space University in
Strasbourg, France, to promote private-sector space exploration.
Later, he established the X Prize Foundation, which awarded
cash to teams competing to solve various technical challenges such
as prototyping "universally accessible" personal helicopters or
landing an entirely privately funded robot on the moon, as stipu-
lated by the $30 million Google Lunar X Prize.

Like a lot of lucky, wealthy people, Diamandis had developed some curious ideas about why some people are rich and others poor, and about the secrets to success in business. "You can become a billionaire by doing *anything*. Find what is in your heart and soul, and do that," he told the Summitgoers. Apparently, Diamandis had scoured his own soul and found a passion for the extractive industries. Where others looked to the stars and felt wonder, Diamandis saw spoils ripe for plunder. "The Earth is a crumb in a supermarket filled with resources," he said. His asteroid mining venture, Planetary Resources, was an effort to gain first-mover advantage on exploiting the mineral wealth of places beyond earth. "In the same way that we Europeans looked toward the New World to colonize for resources, we as humanity can look toward space as the ultimate supply of resources," he said.

The same ahistorical and romantic view of conquest pervaded the Summit, frequently punctuated by charts going up. SU chief executive Rob Nail, a gangly Stanford-educated robotics designer who wore a plaid blazer and a Google Glass that pinned back his shoulder-length hair, borrowed some of his slideshow from *The Singularity Is Near*—"the intellectual inspiration for the university." Beside a chart with a rising trendline, which depicted the "exponential" march of human invention, was a portrait of Chancellor Kurzweil, who smiled impishly down on the audience, as though amused by a private joke. "One of the advantages of being in the futurism business," Kurzweil once wrote, "is that by the time your readers are able to find fault with your forecasts, it is too late for them to ask for their money back."

As his charts indicated, Nail was bullish on the future. "We've had great wars, depressions, technological boom cycles and downturns, and yet technology has progressed beautifully on this exponential curve," he said. "I think it's probably the most exciting time that all of humanity has ever lived." He held up his smartphone. "This is not a phone," he said solemnly. "This is a teacher, this is a doctor, this is so many other things. And the fact that there's tens of millions of apps now means we're in a totally different realm altogether . . . Which creates a lot of opportunities for all of us." Was this the grand vision of the future? Smartphones? What a marvelous grift this was, charging $2,500 per head to rehash Apple advertising copy for two days. And while it was banal in many respects, SU offered more than an upscale version of the familiar Silicon Valley conference racket. It was a collective effort not just to forecast the future, as Nail put it, but to "steer" it. And given how much corporate power was represented inside the auditorium, the group gathered in that theater in Amsterdam actually was capable of changing policies and transforming economies. In this sense the Summit resembled the vision of the Factory I had heard from Google's Tom Chi. Both projects shared a mission to "influence the influencers"—and in this case, at least, it was working.

The Summit was as much a strategy session as it was a business seminar. Sometimes the political subtext became the text. The bold tech-empowered future would require an "update" to "our leadership structures," as one Summit speaker put it. "The Constitution needs to be updated," he said. "It's the software that runs our society."

The next social software update would certainly crush all sorts of workers, as Rob Nail made clear when he spoke once more about robots and the automation of all labor. "It's not going to be just blue-collar labor that's replaced—or enhanced," he said. Managers would also have robot replacements, he went on. This warning was echoed by SU past president and in-house ethicist Neil Jacobstein, a wry veteran of the revolving-door establishment who previously worked as a consultant for NASA, the Pentagon, and large contractors like Boeing. Jacobstein cited a recent study claiming that within the next twenty years, 47 percent of U.S. jobs would be subject to some kind of automation. Certain professions, he noted, have obstinately resisted the trend—notably lawyers, teachers, and doctors. "Assuming zero new technology breakthroughs, professional work—white-collar work—is ripe for disruption," Jacobstein said. "White-collar workers often have the reaction, 'Well, all jobs can be automated—except ours, of course.' But they're not immune either." Doctors, for instance, might be put out by the development of handheld medical devices that can diagnose diseases with a wave of the hand, he said. Such devices would no doubt first be deployed "in places with low guild protection, like Africa." But the whole world was their laboratory.

Beyond subverting "guild protections" for workers and human test subjects, there were other ways Jacobstein felt society must radically adapt to suit the technologists' desires. Antivirus-style surveillance programs could be deployed to monitor the world for "anomalies and misbehavior," preserving order and preventing sabotage. He was proposing law enforcement via algorithm. Many Americans were already familiar with the experience of running a

red traffic light, then getting a ticket in the mail along with a surveillance camera photo of their car crossing the intersection. What
Jacobstein proposed was something much more sophisticated and
intrusive.

Practically speaking, such a perfectly automated tyranny would
require nigh-infinite computational power. No worries! As the
Summit speakers told it, "exponential technologies" made such
advances all but inevitable. Jacobstein clicked forward in his slideshow to the most awesome spectacle yet to tower over the summit
stage. It was an illustration of a ginormous silicon brain floating
through a cloudy blue sky. Perplexingly, a bright red line crossed
the brain. There was no caption. The explanation was left to
Jacobstein. "One could imagine, without having the confines of
the human skull, that we could build an artificial neocortex with
the surface area of this auditorium. Or Amsterdam. Or Europe.
Or the planet," he said. "And you might think, 'Wow, that's a little
excessive.' But it turns out it's not excessive."

During a lunch break, I was able to sit down with Jacobstein. I
had so many questions. What, I asked, would be the fate of democracy in a society dominated by proprietary AI? Jacobstein regarded
me with a look of pity. "These are complicated issues that require
thoughtful, in-depth analysis, and they don't lend themselves well
to sound bites," he said. Jacobstein added that SU urged its students to think carefully "about the business, technical and ethical
implications of technology." This seemed like a good time to bring
up the sky brain. "One of your slides was a super-intelligent artificial neocortex the size of a planet," I said. "Maybe it's my feeble

human brain, but I just can't imagine what sort of governing structure could contain such a thing."

It wasn't so simple, he said. People fear what they don't understand. And "exponential technologies like AI" were, in his view, a way to resolve once and for all the "failures of our ability to implement our own moral code." Complicated details like whose moral code would be programmed into the giant floating sky brain, with its invincible legions of law enforcement drones, were best left to the most brilliant and morally upright. In short, the problem was indeed my feeble human brain.

"I have very little faith in politicians, but I have a lot of faith in technology," Jacobstein told me. This was a view widely shared by SU speakers, faculty, and leadership. A man in the audience had a question for Diamandis. "In the past we had revolutions," the man asked. "What are the new solutions?" The answer that came back, unsurprisingly: technology. Technology was the solution, and it could also constitute a kind of revolution. "Governments don't get disrupted gracefully," Diamandis said. He had some strong feelings about politics and the failures of "representative democracy" as distinct from "actual democracy," whatever he meant by that. But if there was one clear takeaway from his remarks, it was his contempt for any political action that might impede corporate profits, such as conservation and regulation. As he saw it, limits on the expansion of capital threatened technological innovation—and vice versa. And because only technology could save humankind from existential threats such as climate change, anything but unbridled technocapitalism was folly. "The world has truly become an extraordinary place. And it isn't better politicians that got us there," Diamandis said; "it's the impact of technology over the last hundred years." Existing political leadership, he went on, should, "at the least, step out of the way."

As impressed as they already were with themselves, the Summit speakers shared an obsession with human "enhancement" and the creation of new, superhuman races. These developments might come about through the creation and manipulation of some powerful artificial intelligence, as Jacobstein described, or through the creation of cyborgs—humans merged surgically with machines—or through other means.

But don't call it a master race! Such unsettling subjects were framed rather innocuously as conversations about AI and "governance." More than any of his SU contemporaries, Jacobstein had a matter-of-fact delivery that made his Frankenstein schemes sound pleasant and agreeable. "Let's talk about augmentation. Do we really need to augment our brains? The answer is *yes*," he said.

He made it sound like a trip to the Genius Bar. "The human brain hasn't had a major upgrade in over fifty thousand years. And if your cell phone or your laptop hadn't had an upgrade in, say, five years, you'd be appropriately concerned about that," he said. I knew that Google, among others, was working on cybernetic brain implants. The lead SU faculty booster of this brand of "enhancement" was a big Texas-born biotech scientist and engineer named Raymond McCauley, whose talk on self-guided evolution included a lengthy discussion of "bio-hacking." He flicked to a slide showing a tiny radio frequency identity chip of the kind used to track retail merchandise and cattle. "What kind of a crazy person would implant something like this?" he asked. McCauley then summoned some friends from backstage: Hannes Sjöblad, the SU ambassador to Sweden and chairman of the transhumanist association there, and Tom van Oudenaarden, who ran a piercing studio in Utrecht.

Clearly some mischief was afoot. McCauley said he had made a last-minute change to his SU-approved talk. "I'm a hacker," he said. "I learn by doing. So I'm going to go ahead and see what it's like to get an implant and be a cyborg today." The audience stirred. The SU camera crew scrambled onto the stage. While the piercer prepared his kit, the transhuman ambassador, Sjöblad, took over the mic. Sjöblad said his local "maker community" has been implanting one hundred volunteers with RFID chips "just to see what happens."

They hadn't found many uses for embedded identification chips beyond indulging their own laziness. Some replaced their door keys with electronic locks. "Or I take my phone in my hand and it's automatically unlocked and I can start using it instead of having to type a pincode or whatever," Sjöblad said. "There are some guys in the Netherlands, they store Bitcoin in these implants." Now that was impressive—they'd found a way to make virtual currencies even more impractical than they already were. Within two years' time, Sjöblad's cyborg evangelism would help persuade companies in Sweden and Wisconsin, USA, to "offer" microchips to their employees.

McCauley's sterilized arm lay flat on a table and was shown in close-up on the theater screen. A thick white needle cast its shadow over his skin. "If some of you folks are squeamish," McCauley said, "you might want to look away." The needle closed in. It was over in a second. We had witnessed the birth of a cyborg to a midwife with a mohawk. McCauley rose to applause. But there was some commotion. He was bleeding. Someone wiped drops from the floor around his feet. "I'm not in any kind of pain," he said. "In the future I think all of us are going to end up with something like this, and we will upgrade them about like we upgrade our iPhones. So think about that."

McCauley discussed another route to the transhuman future: genetic engineering. Before joining SU, he had cofounded Bio-Curious, a Sunnyvale, California, nonprofit with a mission to normalize technologies like genetic engineering by providing a low-cost biology lab for "anyone who wants to experiment with friends." McCauley predicted that childhood disease prevention would open the back door to human genetic modification. Already, he said, it was an open secret that wealthy American couples skirted regulations and taboos by traveling to places like Singapore, Hong Kong, Cairo—and Amsterdam—to have gene doctors assess and— feasibly or not—select the sex, height, eye color, personality, and musical ability of their fetal children. "I see requests all the time . . . 'I want a kid who's tall and good at soccer and gets along with everybody,'" McCauley said.

It was eerie how closely the transhuman vision promoted by Singularity University resembled the eugenicist vision that had emerged from Stanford a century before. The basic arguments had scarcely changed. In *The Singularity Is Near*, SU chancellor

Kurzweil decried the "fundamentalist humanism" that informs restriction on the genetic engineering of human fetuses.

In 2012, an interviewer prompted Kurzweil to account for the difference between his transhumanist Singularitarian vision and the old eugenics programs. "Eugenics was—first of all, the technology of it didn't work, and was antihuman," Kurzweil said. "It involved killing people as opposed to enhancing people." But eugenics *was* also all about "enhancement." Moreover, the problem with eugenics was not that the technology didn't work. The problem was that it was a racist, authoritarian, and violently nonconsensual program in pursuit of indefensible goals. There must be no mystery about this. The troubling legacy of the crackpot eugenicist racism that defined Gold Rush California lives on in the biotech startups sprouting up in and around Silicon Valley. These companies promise a better world through applied genetics. The most famous—familiar to anyone who has encountered its multimillion-dollar advertising campaign—is Google's 23andMe, which sells mail-order genetic sequencing services to the general public. The marketing ingeniously presents it as not only a potential health benefit, but as the fun indulgence of an innocent curiosity, like some super-sciencey high-tech yuppie version of heredity research websites like Ancestry.com. Medical ethicists have knocked 23andMe for pushing unnecessary screening to people without heritable risk, and for hoarding customer data that could later be sold to insurers or advertisers. But the company's ambitions appear to be much bigger. In 2013, Google obtained a patent for "gamete donor selection based on genetic calculations"—a tool for selecting "allowable permutations" in "hypothetical offspring."

The system assessed characteristics including "height, eye color, gender," disease risk, and "personality." In plain language, Google had patented a tool to create "designer babies." But plain language is anathema to Big Tech and its world-changing designs. "Biotech" sounds so much better than "selective breeding programs managed by corporations." Another hot startup in the eugenics space, Counsyl, received backing from top VCs by promising to make genetic screening so cheap as to be universally available. The company claims its mission is to provide "reproductive autonomy" and argues that its products will help the poor. Counsyl boasts that its low-cost genetic tests can sometimes be covered by health insurance, but it never mentions the likelihood that such tests could become a prerequisite for coverage. Like 23andMe, some ethicists have slammed Counsyl for exploiting the weakly regulated market in genetic data in ways that drove humanity "down the slippery slope toward attempts to control IQ, weight, height and other factors," as the science journalist and biotech consultant Steve Dickman put it.

The way Silicon Valley biotech companies marketed themselves did not inspire confidence. Their websites invariably showed smiling white people posing in spotless white apartments stocked with white furniture. But the politics of eugenics has changed with the times. Counsyl's cofounders are Asian American, and one of the smiling couples on its website includes an East Asian man. The hierarchy of race in Big Tech today makes room at the top for *certain* Asians—especially non-Muslim Indians, as well as Chinese, Koreans, and other East Asians. The definition of "white" has always changed with time and place. In today's tech industry, at least, it's clear that Asians are deemed "more white" and certainly more employable than their Black and Latino peers. There is even a swath of Silicon Valley–style prejudice that prized Asian techies for their presumed superior intelligence.

When I caught up with McCauley the day after his exhibitionistic surgery on the Singularity Summit stage, he claimed to be recovering quickly. He showed me the stout bandage on his hand and the smartphone app he used to control the chip now permanently embedded in his body. The app bore an all-caps warning:

DO NOT FORGET YOUR PASSWORD!

McCauley was still figuring out what to do with his new implant. He was thinking about using it as a kind of wireless keychain. But it was a bit humdrum to get himself chipped just to open the front door. He was thinking about adding a secret chamber, like a speakeasy or a panic room, to his house. "I can use this to unlock a hidden door or passage," he explained.

I asked McCauley about the vibe at the SU campus. "In some ways, it's exactly like being a sophomore in college with the three smartest guys and girls in the dorm, and it's four o'clock in the morning and no one wants to go to bed," he said. "It's eighty people who are the smartest people in their countries, and they're all riffing on each other, coming up with new ideas and trying to solve the world's problems—and make a buck while doing it.

"Man—it's so powerfully addictive, it's almost like a drug," he said. "It's almost like being in a cult. If we wore silvery jumpsuits, I would be really worried."

"Really?" I asked. "You don't go without food and then do a bunch of exercise, or do repetitive chanting—right?"

"We have plenty of protein," McCauley replied. "Groupthink tends to be very discouraged . . . But there is this real belief in technological positivism that sometimes approaches an almost religious fervor."

Ding ding ding! Maybe it was the meager buffet, or maybe it was the Cheese, but I'd noticed that after several hours in a dark room absorbing an overwhelming torrent of Singularitarian propaganda, I had lost all capacity to recognize the bizarre, the outlandish, or the abominable. It was a giddy feeling. I feared I might soon surrender body, mind, and soul to the euphoric glow of the divine exponential. I had a moment of panic when I tried to exit the auditorium to use the bathroom and found the door locked from the outside. But then someone came in from outside through an adjacent door. Whew! If there was any brainwashing going on, it was strictly consensual.

Technology was identified as the true official religion of the modern state more than seventy years ago by the late Christian anarchist philosopher Jacques Ellul. A remarkable man, and a leader of the French underground resistance who sheltered refugees from the Holocaust, Ellul survived a global catastrophe that was enabled by scientists and engineers only to find that these same technicians, these false priests, would rule the century. And how he loathed them. "Particularly disquieting is the gap between the enormous power they wield and their critical ability, which must be estimated as null," he wrote.

If, as Ellul has it, technology is the state religion, Singularitarianism must be seen as its most extreme and fanatical sect. It is the Opus Dei of the postwar church of gadget worship. Ray Kurzweil may be the best-known prophet of this order, but he was not the first. The true father of Singularitarianism is a sci-fi author and retired mathematics professor from Wisconsin named Vernor Vinge. His earliest written exposition of the idea appeared in the January 1983 issue of *Omni*, an oddball "science" magazine founded by Kathy Keeton, once among the "highest-paid strippers in Europe," according to her *New York Times* obituary, but better known for promoting quack cancer cures and for cofounding *Penthouse* with her husband, Bob Guccione. In this esteemed journal, amid articles on "sea monkeys, apemen and living dinosaurs," Vinge forecast a looming "technological singularity" in which computer intelligence would exceed the comprehension of its human creators. The remarkable exponential growth curve of technological advancement was not about to level off, Vinge proclaimed, but rather to accelerate beyond all imagining. "We will soon create intelligences greater than our own," Vinge wrote. Unlike later writers, he did not see this as necessarily a positive development for humanity. "Physical extinction may not be the scariest possibility," he wrote. "Think of the different ways we relate to animals." In other words, our new robot overlords might reduce humans to slaves, livestock, or, if we're lucky, pets.

Like many creative types, Vinge lacked the business savvy to fully exploit the market potential of his ideas. That task fell to Ray Kurzweil. A consummate brand builder, Kurzweil turned Vinge's frown upside-down and recast the Singularity as a great big cosmic party, to great commercial success. Douglas Hofstadter, the scientist and author, derided Kurzweil's theses as "a very bizarre mixture of ideas that are solid . . . with ideas that are crazy." Nevertheless, it was a winning formula. By 2011, *Time* magazine named Kurzweil one of the one hundred "most influential people in the world" and endorsed the Singularity sect in a cover story. While seemingly "preposterous," the magazine declared, the prospect of "super-intelligent immortal cyborgs" deserved "sober, careful evaluation."

> Even though it sounds like science fiction, it isn't, no more than a weather forecast is science fiction. It's not a fringe idea; it's a serious hypothesis about the future of life on Earth.

This is absurd. Science begins with doubt. Everything else is sales. And Kurzweil is more salesman than scientist. In his writing and speeches, he has recycled the same tired catchphrases and anecdotes again and again. His entire argument hangs on two magic words: Moore's Law, the theory that computer processing power grows exponentially each year. The theory, which was first conceived of by Intel cofounder Gordon Moore (and later named after him), doubles, incidentally, as a kind of advertisement for Intel microchips. Moore's Law also inspired Kurzweil's own Law of Accelerating Returns, which encapsulates his belief that the pace of *all* technological innovation is, over time, exponential. Within decades, Kurzweil figures, the unstoppable evolution of gadgetry will bring about the Singularity and all it entails: unlimited energy, superhuman AI, literal immortality, the resurrection of the dead, and the "destiny of the universe," namely, the awakening of all matter and energy.

Kurzweil may not be much of a scientist, but he is an entertaining guru. His fake-it-till-you-make-it approach seems in good fun, except when he uses it to bluff through life-or-death problems. What's worse, powerful people take him seriously, because he is forever telling them what they'd like to hear and zealously defending the excesses of consumer capitalism. Like techno-utopians such as Peter Thiel, Kurzweil has long argued that corporate interests should be calling the shots in the "new paradigms" of the future. Such views are unsurprising coming from a longtime corporate executive and salesman. Fossil fuels wrecking the planet? No worries, Kurzweil declares. We'll crack the problem of cold fusion soon, and nanobots—always with the nanobots!—will restore the ruined environment. As America's fortunes and prospects faded through the aughts, Kurzweil's sanguine reveries sold more copies than ever, and the author insisted that things were better than ever and soon to be even more amazing.

For every conceivable problem, there is a plan, and it's always the same plan: Someone in the future will invent something to solve it. Kurzweil has delivered the one true American faith the people were always waiting for, and it turns out to be an absurdly optimistic form of business-friendly millenarianism, which could pass for a satirical caricature of the tech worship Jacques Ellul identified.

The trick will be to survive a few more decades, until the inventions of atom-scaled medical nanobots and digital backups of human consciousness. "We have the means right now to live long enough to live forever," Kurzweil writes. "But most baby boomers won't make it." This led to his other scammy obsession—life extension. To help his own rapidly aging generation survive until the arrival of the technological tipping point when they might upload their memories and personalities to a Google cloud server—around 2045, he figures—he promotes a program of diet, exercise, and unproven life-extending supplements. If all else fails to ward off the Reaper, one can always have one's body or brain frozen for later resuscitation, a process known as cryonics, which Kurzweil endorses as a last resort.

Kurzweil's morbid obsession with disease and death led him into the depths of tech-abetted unconventional medicine, where many a Singularitarian followed. He received a diabetes diagnosis at age thirty-five. Displeased with insulin treatment, he set out to find a better way. The result was an idiosyncratic and ever-changing menu of herbal medicine, plus hundreds of daily nutritional supplements and a custom fitness regimen. The details are laid out in two books that Kurzweil co-wrote with his doctor, Terry Grossman: *Fantastic Voyage: Live Long Enough to Live Forever* and *Transcend: Nine Steps to Living Well Forever*. The latter includes sixty-nine pages of recipes, including one for carrot salad sweetened with stevia, yum yum. *Skeptic* magazine slammed *Fantastic Voyage* as "the triumph of hope over evidence and common sense" and suggested that some of its advice might actually be harmful.

Kurzweil and Grossman shamelessly cashed in on their presumed authority by selling loosely regulated supplements to credulous consumers under the label of "Ray and Terry's Longevity Products—where science and nutrition meet." The authors' website shills dubious formulations including an $86 "Anti-Aging MultiPack" that promises a one-month supply of "smart nutrients." As proof of efficacy, Kurzweil offers himself. Although he is seventy at this writing, he has long claimed that his true "biological age" was twenty years younger. The lens suggests otherwise. In 2014, Kurzweil began sporting a new hairdo—longer, straighter, and several shades darker than before. The sudden change worried some commenters on his website, kurzweilai.net. Was it a hairpiece? An unfortunate dye job? Or maybe Kurzweil had finally stumbled across a real miracle pill?

I am by no means the first to label Singularitarianism a new religion or a cult. Kurzweil himself has said the comparison was "understandable," given the preoccupation with mortality. However, he rejects the argument that his sect is religious in nature, because he did not come to it as a spiritual seeker. Rather, Kurzweil writes, he became a Singularitarian as a result of "practical" efforts to make "optimal tactical decisions in launching technology enterprises." Startups showed him the way!

Being a Singularitarian, Kurzweil claims, "is not a matter of faith but one of understanding." This is a refrain Singularitarians share with Scientologists, for L. Ron Hubbard always marketed his doctrines as "technology." This tic makes Singularitarians impossible to argue with. Because they believe that they have arrived at their beliefs scientifically, anyone who disputes their ludicrous conclusions must be irrational. If this sect did not have the ears of so many powerful men in business, politics, and military affairs, its leaders might seem clownish. But they are serious, dangerously so.

There was always something fundamentally misanthropic about the Singularitarian vision, with its drive for the elimination of the body and its echoes of Christian millenarianism. A Scottish science fiction writer, Ken MacLeod, has been credited with having first mocked the Singularity as "the Rapture for nerds" in a 1999 novel, *The Cassini Division*. MacLeod tells me he merely borrowed the phrase from an online forum of futurists who embraced the Singularity, especially its apocalyptic overtones. In subsequent years, MacLeod found himself increasingly horrified by the deranged utilitarianism he found among the online Singularitarians. Perhaps the most extreme example came in a post by a programmer named Robert J. Bradbury, five days after the September 11, 2001, terrorist attacks. Bradbury's missive began with the subject line "TERRORISM: Is genocide the logical solution?" His concern was not vengeance, he claimed, but science. As he saw it, the people of "Afganistan" [*sic*] were unlikely to contribute to the hastening of the Singularity—and indeed, by harboring terrorists, might delay its arrival. If their existence slowed down the onset of the Singularity by six months or more, he reasoned, "the value of their lives is negative" and "a plan of genocide to bury the country in rubble seems justified." Bradbury proposed an aerial bombardment sufficient to "knock the population back to the sub-cave-person level."

The author of this bloodthirsty screed was no illiterate barstool general. Bradbury was a Harvard-educated programmer who had been an early employee at Oracle—the world's second-largest software company after Microsoft. He went on to found Aeiveos, a private corporation devoted to quixotic life extension research, bankrolled by Oracle CEO Larry Ellison, who had a well-documented obsession with finding the real-life fountain of youth. Bradbury's friends and business associates included luminaries of the transhumanism scene such as Kurzweil. When Bradbury died in 2011 at age fifty-four, the chairman of the transhumanist Institute for Ethics and Emerging Technologies, George Dvorsky, remembered the would-be nuclear genocidaire as a "generous, driven and often outspoken individual" who "railed against the needless deaths of people the world over."

Being eccentrics, longtime inhabitants of the Singularitarian subculture were willing to overlook clear expressions of lunacy among their own. Consider young Mike Anissimov, who, before coming out as a Hitler fanboy, ingratiated himself with Ray Kurzweil, whose parents fled Austria shortly before Kristallnacht. (I have no evidence that either Kurzweil or Thiel knew about Anissimov's anti-Semitism while they were associated with him.) In high school, Anissimov founded a life extension organization of his own called the Immortality Institute. And over time he became involved, one way or another, in basically every one of the leading futurist organizations in the United States, from the World Transhumanists Association, now called Humanity+, who believed in self-directed human evolution through cybernetic implants and genetic engineering, to the Lifeboat Foundation, a Nevada-based nonprofit dedicated to "helping humanity survive existential risks." Kurzweil eventually hired Anissimov as a consultant for his own company, Kurzweil Technologies, and when *The Singularity Is Near* was published in 2005, he used multiple quotations from the then twenty-one-year-old blogger as epigraphs. Anissimov at the time was employed as the advocacy director at the Singularity Institute for Artificial Intelligence, funded by Peter Thiel, whose own ideas, buoyed by money, were gaining prominence.

Thiel's support for technophilic extremists did not stop with Anissimov. The billionaire was, for example, among the most important clients of an outfit called the Alcor Life Extension Foundation, which promised to freeze the dead for later resuscitation. Max More, an Alcor employee and self-proclaimed guru of "extropian" futurism, had given a presentation on "cryonics as a bridge to an indefinitely extended life" at the same BIL conference where Thiel donee Curtis Yarvin appeared. The bearded British life extension researcher Aubrey de Grey spoke at BIL that year about his work in "anti-aging bioscience." De Grey whiled away most of his days at the Thiel-funded, Mountain View–based SENS Research Foundation, a nonprofit organization also dedicated to the quixotic cause of achieving human immortality. Yarvin booster Patri Friedman led an organization called the Seasteading Institute, which was also funded by Thiel, with the outlandish goal of building privately owned countries on large offshore platforms.

Fortune magazine in 2014 described Thiel, the aggrieved chess club president and Tolkien obsessive, as "perhaps America's leading public intellectual." His admirers were willing to overlook certain quirks, such as his claim that American democracy deteriorated as a result of women's suffrage and his reported interest in a procedure called parabiosis that involved receiving transfusions of young people's blood for the purpose of hopefully extending his own lifespan. What great questions consumed the feted mind of this aspiring vampire lord?

Not catastrophic global warming. He considered the problem "banal" and, with all the expertise and authority conferred by his undergraduate degree in philosophy, declared all of climatology a "pseudoscience."

Not good government. "A well-functioning government" was, in his mind, "not really that realistic."

Not the plight of the oppressed. Not war, not sin. Not love or the secret of happiness.

No, Thiel's preoccupation was why the futuristic fantasies of 1950s science fiction had failed to arrive on schedule. Where was the Mars colony? he wondered. Where was his flying car? Thiel channeled his sundry frustrations into a pessimistic "stagnation thesis" that marked him as a contrarian among his VC cohort. At every opportunity, Thiel argued that the products of the most recent tech booms didn't amount to much in the way of meaningful innovation or civilizational progress. This was merely stating the obvious, yet he refused to accept the equally obvious corollary: Technology does not equate to progress. The fundamental confusion around this fairly obvious point reflects the entitled view of a wealthy lifelong consumer and pedigreed capitalist. Technology, from this perspective, produces countless entertaining diversions and useful, time-saving tools; even when those tools are deadly weapons, they serve humanity by advancing the dominance of the self-evidently superior society that produces them. Any technology that reduces the need for human labor and increases economic productivity, moreover, must be good; even if it means that more

workers starve for want of employment, the superior technological society benefits from this "advance" because the productivity
gains that are captured and hoarded as profits may be reinvested
in still more new technologies that reduce the social need for human
labor while increasing profits. Does the perpetuation of unjust
class structures by technological means count as "progress" in any
meaningful sense? Clearly not. But Thiel, like so many techno-
utopian plutocrats, assumes that since gadgets had made him rich,
gadgets must save the world. "The only way forward for the developed countries is rapid innovation and progress in the advanced
technologies," he said at the 2009 Singularity Summit, held at the
92nd Street Y in New York and organized by Mike Anissimov.
Otherwise, he warned, the economy would collapse completely. In
his mind, as in Bradbury's, accelerating the arrival of the Singularity was "the single most important political, cultural, economic,
technological question that we have."

Whatever genuine concerns Thiel might harbor for the fate of
America and the planet, he has never lost sight of the interests of
the most important person—Peter Thiel. He has reportedly used
his fortune to obtain citizenship in New Zealand, along with a
remote lakeside retreat where he might weather the apocalypse.

While Thiel was preparing his escape routes, his younger
admirer Mike Anissimov was doing the same, albeit in his own low-
rent way. Like Thiel, he didn't intend to endure the unraveling of
the present system while waiting around for the Singularity to
bring salvation. In 2014, Anissimov let slip plans for an "inten-
tional community"—don't call it a neoreactionary cult!—in the
Idaho wilderness. (Anissimov took down his website with a draft

of the scheme from the internet after I asked him about it, but he later self-published a $5.99 "Idaho Project" e-book.) His half-baked proposal included an appeal for recruits and funds. He estimated a hardy group of settlers would need only $170,000 in the first year to set up camp. The pooled investment would purchase, in Anissimov's reckoning, "20 acres, on a hillside"; a trailer home buttressed by "posts and particle board"; and a year's worth of frozen and dehydrated food. "No farming needed! You can live your entire life, until age 100, on delicious Costco freeze-dried food for just $1,000 a year, how about that!" Anissimov wrote. "I've done it for long periods of time."

"The plan," he went on, was "not to go in with a bunch of computer programmers," but rugged folk who don't mind the cold. Although he claimed "there are many, *many* women who would love to live in a community such as this," they wouldn't be allowed. Women, Anissimov wrote, "complain about anything that isn't perfect" and would pose a "distraction" to the settlers as they built a world apart.

"The key idea here," Anissimov wrote, "is freedom."

By freedom, he meant escape. Or, as it was more commonly known among Silicon Valley elite, *exit*. The religious-apocalyptic mentality of the techie Singularitarians found synthesis with their intrinsic social frustration in the political act of secession.

Thiel eventually abandoned Seasteading as too impractical, reckoning that there were other ways to achieve his dream of escape. Yarvin, who was never fully on board with the seafaring secessionists—he'd been uninvited from a Seasteading conference after directing a homophobic slur at another slated speaker—had his own alternate proposal for a future global order free of small-minded normie meddlers. He called it the Patchwork—a "global spiderweb" of hundreds of thousands of "mini-countries, each governed by its own joint stock corporation without regard to the residents' opinions." The scheme, Yarvin explained, was designed to emulate "the most interesting, detailed and elegant European forms" of feudalism, and would finally cure the "cancer" of leftism, since the only way to dissent in such a system would be to leave and become a refugee. Journalistic "swine" would also fare poorly, as would the "well-armed thugs" of "the ruling underclass"—that is, black people. Asians, though, would be welcome, particularly Chinese people, who are, in Yarvin's assessment, "congenitally smarter than white people."

Using California as an example, Yarvin sketched out on his blog a plan to achieve this ideal civilization. The first step, naturally, would be appointing a dictator. "We could say that California needs a 'CEO,' or that it should be 'run like a startup,'" he suggested.

Once in power, Yarvin wrote, the dictator's first move might be to throw the former governor of California and various municipal leaders in Alcatraz prison. Lock him up! "A new civil service, of top startup quality, must certainly be hired," he went on. "Perhaps some Googlers could be drafted. Once peace is achieved, the Dictator's goal is order."

If Yarvin's plan seems dangerous and unhinged, that's because it was. Foreigners would be deported, the poor evicted. "Sell their slums out from under them," he wrote. "Demo everything, spray for roaches, rodents and pit bulls, smooth the rubble out with a bulldozer or two, and possibly a little aerial bombing; erect new residential districts suitable for Russian oligarchs."

Yarvin at least admitted that such brutality would be necessary to realize his vision of a corporate Patchwork world. Others who shared a vision on devolved government tended to gloss over what might be the messy parts. Andreessen-Horowitz partner and Counsyl cofounder Balaji Srinivasan has proposed "cloud cities" and "cloud countries" of like-minded renunciates to be organized online. With $2.5 million in backing from his own VC fund—a conflict of interest not unheard of in Silicon Valley but egregious even by the tech industry's incestuous standards—he cofounded a startup called Teleport to hasten such efforts by helping "digital nomads" find places abroad to live and work, with the ultimate aim of making citizenship a competition rather than a birthright.

Srinivasan laid out the grand design in an essay for *Wired*. He predicted that "the internet will spur a wave of internal migrations as online communities begin gathering in person." The latest buzzword for networked computers—"the cloud"—served as Srinivasan's metaphor for the future of all human social organization. His essay began with a lament for the bygone spirit of Manifest Destiny. "Every square foot of earth is already spoken for by one (or more) nation states, every physical frontier long since closed," Srinivasan wrote. But there was hope: "With our bodies hemmed in, our minds have only the cloud—and it is the cloud that has become the destination for an extraordinary mental exodus." Inevitably, in Srinivasan's view, online social networks would coalesce as "cloud formations" of people in the physical world. "We may begin to see cloud towns, then cloud cities, and ultimately cloud countries materialize out of thin air," he wrote.

Srinivasan's vision of exit differed slightly from Anissimov's and Yarvin's. It was equally ridiculous but in novel ways. "Unlike so-called secessionists," he wrote, "the specific site of physical concentration would be a matter of convenience, not passion; the geography incidental and not worth fighting over." The perpetual struggle of civilization had long seemed to be who occupied what land, on what terms. Here at last was a permanent solution. The intractable Israeli-Palestinian conflict would simply vanish into the cloud, along with those tiresome Pacific Heights squabbles about so-and-so's new sun deck blocking their neighbors' views of the Bay.

Srinivasan did acknowledge some limits to his precognition. He wasn't sure where or how the first cloud cities would appear:

> They could be countries formed by internationally recognized processes similar to the ones that created 26 new countries over the past 25 years, a pattern noted by Marc Andreessen. They could be regions of the world set aside by global agreement for experimentation, as discussed by Larry Page. They could be floating cities in international waters as put forth by Peter Thiel, or one of the more ambitious 80,000 person colonies on Mars desired by Elon Musk.

Srinivasan set what was then a new record in techie temerity with a provocative speech at Y Combinator's "startup school" in 2013. The speech laid out a plan for what Srinivasan called "Silicon Valley's ultimate exit," a way to "reduce the importance of decisions made in D.C."—in short, to undermine the government for the benefit of tech companies. "It basically means: build an opt-in society—ultimately outside the United States—run by technology," he said. "And this is actually where the Valley is going."

The government was not Srinivasan's only target. He called upon the audience of startup founders to sabotage every civic institution that might act as a counterbalance on tech company power. Like a wartime commander briefing troops on the plan of attack, Srinivasan identified the enemy's most valuable targets:

> There's four cities that used to run the United States in the postwar era:
> - Boston with higher ed;
> - New York City with Madison Avenue, books, Wall Street, newspapers;
> - Los Angeles with movies, music, Hollywood; and, of course,
> - D.C. with laws and regulations, formally running the country.
>
> I call them the Paper Belt after the Rust Belt of yore. In the last twenty years, a new competitor to the Paper Belt arose out of nowhere: Silicon Valley. And, by accident, we're putting a horse head in all of their beds. We are becoming stronger than all of them combined.

It was hard to believe that the proverbial severed cephala appeared "by accident," when Srinivasan so clearly reveled in the attendant disruption—praising Bitcoin, for instance, for making it impossible for the government "to seize money," otherwise known as collecting taxes. And it was remarkable how closely his conception of establishment power, the Paper Belt, mirrored Moldbug's Cathedral. Srinivasan proceeded to reel off a list of start-ups that had disrupted the economic engines of the Paper Belt. Los Angeles, he said, "was really the first on the hit list, starting in '99 with Napster" and followed by the rise of Apple iTunes, BitTorrent, Netflix, Spotify, and YouTube. "We're going after newspapers, we're going after Madison Avenue, we're going after book publishing, we're going after television," Srinivasan said with undisguised glee, recalling the battering taken by New York media from online competitors such as Google AdWords, Twitter, Blogger, Facebook, and Amazon's Kindle "e-reading" device. "Boston was next in the gunsights," he said, with the country's oldest, most elite educational institutions challenged—albeit less successfully, so far—by startups like Khan Academy, Coursera, and Udacity. "And, most interestingly, D.C.," Srinivasan continued. By which he meant "government regulation in general—because it's not just D.C., it includes local and state governments. Uber, Airbnb, Stripe, Square, and the big one, Bitcoin, are all things that threaten D.C.'s power."

Srinivasan stopped short of endorsing armed revolt—but only because it would fail. "They have aircraft carriers, we don't. We don't actually want to fight them. It wouldn't be smart," he said. All the same, he went on, "it is not necessarily clear that the U.S. government can ban something that it wants to ban anymore."

As tempting as it would be to laugh off Srinivasan's scheme as a digitized confederacy of dunces, it's important to remember that he is a former Stanford professor and partner in a $4 billion venture capital firm, not some basement-dwelling 4chan troll with no life prospects. His comrade in resentment, Peter Thiel, even offered Srinivasan's name to the Trump White House in January 2017 as a possible appointee to lead the Food and Drug Administration (although he wasn't picked). This brand of techie secessionism appeals to a growing number of wealthy, powerful people who seek—as wealthy, powerful people have sought throughout history—to remove any and all restrictions on their behavior, to fix their exalted status in perpetuity, and to abandon the lower classes to their fate.

Echoes of the kind of secessionism espoused by Srinivasan may be heard from the highest levels of the industry. Recall the startling remarks by Google cofounder Larry Page at the company's developer conference in 2013. An audience member gingerly asked how Page would address the incipient backlash against techie disruption "and focus on changing the world." Page replied with platitudes, at first. Then he suggested that new "mechanisms" might be needed to deal with change. What sort of mechanisms?

> Maybe some of our old institutions, like the law and so on, aren't keeping up with the rate of change that we've caused through technology . . . I mean, the laws when we went public were fifty years old. The law can't be right if it's fifty years old—like, it's before the internet.

"We also haven't built mechanisms to allow experimentation," Page continued. "There's many, many exciting and important things you could do that you just can't do because they're illegal or they're not allowed by regulation." Perhaps the world needed to set aside "some safe spaces" for techies "where we can try out some new things and figure out what is the effect on society, what's the effect on people, without having to deploy it kind of into the normal world." Page may have meant something more benign, but it seems to me and many others that he was advocating another form of secessionism.

An anonymous tech reporter with the *Verge* who covered Page's speech was struck by the humdrum audience response. "What's weird is the absolute lack of reaction to any of this in the room," the reporter wrote. "Page is saying he wants a separate country to try out new laws and no one is even murmuring about it."

Perhaps the blasé reaction reflected the perception, particularly widespread among techies, that corporate brands are already operating on a higher level than governments. In a testament to the growing power of the emerging corporate sovereigns, Denmark in 2017 became the first country to appoint a "digital ambassador," whose job was not to conduct diplomacy with foreign states but to "establish and prioritize comprehensive relations with tech actors, such as Google, Facebook, Apple and so on." After Trump's election, could anyone be blamed for preferring to deal with a group of Americans, the tech tycoons, who, while unelected, still held great power, and whose apparent intelligence, aptitude, and stability stood in contrast to the result of our democratic process? The public sphere's loss is the private sphere's gain. To the extent that these companies accelerate American decline, they accumulate more power for themselves—and, per the dominant Singularitarian ideology, they expect that power to last in perpetuity.

• • • • •

The future looks rosy indeed for the kings of Big Tech, grim though it may appear for the rest of us. But the biggest winners of technocapitalism—men such as Larry Page and Peter Thiel and their flunkies—are increasingly aware that the system that has ennobled them creates enemies faster than allies. And they are afraid. In 2015, the *New York Times* reported growing demand for secure "panic rooms" among wealthy urbanites fearing civil unrest. According to *Forbes*, some wealthy landowners have taken additional exclusionary measures, like securing the perimeter of their estates with infrared cameras and booby-trapping the interiors with smoke screens and pepper-spray grenades. When fortification fails, there is retreat. At the 2015 Davos World Economic Forum, Robert Johnson, an economist close to the liberal financier George Soros, said he knew "hedge fund managers all over the world who are buying airstrips and farms in places like New Zealand because they think they need a getaway." Thiel, it seemed, would have company. Another Davos participant, the former World Bank economist Stewart Wallis, linked elite fears of wealth confiscation to the Singularitarian dream of space colonization. "If they can get off to another planet, some of them would," Wallis said. "The rich are worried and they should be worried."

Indeed they should be, for many reasons. Existing institutions are glaringly inadequate to address the problems of the moment, from ecological destruction to untenable levels of economic inequality. And the rich aren't the only ones who have cause for concern. Who, after all, is in a better position to benefit from this instability and disruption? The new tech kings, or we the peons?

Yet even if American institutions endure in the near term, the general drift is toward increasing corporate control over all aspects of life. By virtue of their relative public popularity, their massive cash reserves, and their proven capability to disrupt and consume other industries, the top tech companies are poised to assume a disproportionate share of that control. With no threat from a unified opposition, the forces of concentrated private power will be free to establish their eternal aristocracy of brains, their world run by software, with law enforcement by algorithm and music by machines, sexless, airless, treeless, gray, sterile, and bug-free. There will be robot butlers and fresh young blood aplenty for the rich, and for the rest of us, just work, work, work, work, work, work . . . until death. Now is no time for retreat. There is no redoubt, no exit, no escape. Not for us. What, do you think Elon Musk plans to save a seat for you on the last rocket to Mars?

EPILOGUE

Bonfires in the Valley

My foolhardy ordeal in Silicon Valley ended some time after I realized that if I was going to live in a tent like a homeless person, I didn't need to pay Airbnb for the privilege. I had gained neither character nor status nor money by enduring the humiliation of pitch competitions. It seemed that the only winning move in the startup game was to not play, as the eminently sensible computer that ran the U.S. nuclear weapons complex in the movie *WarGames* might have put it. On the long flight home from California to rejoin my very patient wife, I felt an immediate and overwhelming sense of relief.

But had I truly escaped? Could anyone? Earning a living increasingly meant toiling under the tech industry's terms, and the process of self-commodification that it encouraged was becoming mandatory. It's no secret that Silicon Valley's electronic minions follow you everywhere in your pocket. They see everything, and they report everything they see. They know more about you, by the numbers, than you know about yourself. What you forget, they remember. What you seek, they store. We are tagged and tracked like calf and cow, profiled de minimis, and poked with thousands upon thousands of urgent yet pointless instructions from the ether. Create your account. Log in to continue. Click yes to agree. *Ding!* You have notifications. Could that be your boss? Shouldn't you be working? Why are you reading this? Click. Swipe. Share. We insist. Anxious? Have some dopamine. *Ding!* Have some more. Boredom was once possible. Idle hands made tremendous things. Today, no one is idle. Everybody's working, even when they tell themselves they're taking a break. It is said that "data is the new oil." But we are the data; the new oil is us. And unlike oil, we are a renewable resource.

The startup bubble that began around 2005 ended approximately twelve years later without fanfare. Easy money for half-baked startups dried up, as did the initial public stock offerings of overhyped companies. Wannabe entrepreneurs, a demographic that once declared, "San Francisco or bust," are now increasingly amenable to gentrifying more affordable cities such as Pittsburgh or Detroit instead. The causes are complex but the result is evident: Silicon Valley simply isn't making unicorns like it did a few years ago. Crucially, though, this most recent bubble didn't collapse suddenly and with a loud bang, as with the 2000 dot-com fiasco. Rather, the surface of the bubble solidified like a cocoon. What looked like another absurd example of American excess, a high-tech tulip mania, was actually a glimpse at something much more remarkable: a fundamental economic transformation, much like the one brought about by the 2008 financial crisis. The Wall Street bailouts elicited by that crisis rendered the U.S. government subservient to capital in ways not seen since the Great Depression, but the Web 2.0 unicorns pulled off a subtler, and potentially more consequential exploit by turning their ostensible customers into a source of invaluable data as well as free labor.

Wall Street no doubt rivals Silicon Valley for its sheer gaudy greed, but when it comes to madly grandiose ambition to dominate the universe, the techies have no peer. They are betting that future generations will look to them, the gadget peddlers—not governments—for bread, justice, and security. This is not so far-fetched. Tens of millions of Americans already are effectively citizens of Apple, citizens of Uber, citizens of Amazon; the policies of these corporations mean as much to their daily lives as all the laws on the books, and their brand identities certainly inspire more loyalty than the national government does these days. The tech tycoons' carefully cultivated image as clear-eyed, hard-working problem-solvers in the frontier tradition supplies two things Americans are desperate for: validation and hope. As a people, Americans are reared to be optimists. But this means that they are also, as one noted entrepreneur of frontier times observed, suckers. And they fail to understand something that seems obvious to people from other parts of the world: as bad as things are, they can always get worse.

I knew the tech companies' visions could be ugly. I'd seen as much up close. But once again I failed to imagine the full scale of the miseries and cruelties that this new elite class—disarmingly eccentric and infantile at times, infuriatingly smug at others—was prepared to inflict upon the people of the world for the sake of some faux utopia. Whole countries would be broken in the mad scramble for a profitable Singularitarian future. And not just the little countries.

After leaving the Bay Area, while I was writing this book in September 2016, I joined my wife in rural East India, where she'd taken a teaching post at an upstart university bankrolled by Davos types from around Asia. The state of Bihar was about as far as a person could get from Silicon Valley. We lived in an old hotel that had been requisitioned by the university and renovated to serve as housing for students and a few faculty. Just outside the gates, families tended scrawny goats and lived under tarps in the dirt. They shared a single, hand-pumped well, and oftentimes a cell phone, too. But that's not to say they weren't sophisticated users of technology. A short walk up the muddy road, peddlers in tin-roofed huts sold SIM cards with unlimited high-speed data plans at discount rates. And all the kids were on WhatsApp. A credulous tech optimist such as Thomas Friedman would have marveled to see such beacons of modernity. Surely, development and prosperity were just around the corner!

Not quite. When the disrupters came for India, they came with all the force of the overflowing Ganges. In the name of progress and on the advice of some so-called experts and self-interested tech companies, prime minister Narendra Modi in 2016 undertook a grand and eminently disruptive economic project called "demonetization." With no advance warning or public discussion, Modi's government announced that two denominations of the national currency—the five-hundred- and one-thousand-rupee notes— would no longer be considered legal tender. These notes, which comprised nearly 90 percent of all cash in circulation, would need to be deposited and exchanged for new bills in larger denominations. But this hassle was all for the best, the government explained—pulling the cash from circulation would "encourage" the widespread adoption of smartphone apps for digital payments.

In reality, the demonetization announcement created an instant, panicked nationwide bank run, and prompted all manner of hoarding. Commerce slowed almost to a standstill, except for the lines at ATMs, which stretched on forever for months on end. Responding to criticism of the policy, the government offered up various, often contradictory rationales: rebalancing the cash supply, boosting the economy, and fighting corruption (it's much harder to bribe someone or avoid taxes with an app that records every transaction than it is with cash). But there was one justification the government never backed away from: demonetization, it said, was modernization. India was leapfrogging toward a "digital and cashless economy," with a big assist from some well-connected tech startups.

The sudden announcement was accompanied by a tremendous marketing campaign for government-approved mobile payment apps. These included full-page ads that took over the front pages of all the major newspapers showing Modi's smiling face along with his endorsement for a new smartphone payments app called Paytm, which had arrived just in time to capitalize on the government-mandated disruption of the national currency. Modi's political rivals alleged his party had entanglements with this formerly obscure startup. Indead, Paytm seemed to have come out of nowhere, was majority owned by Chinese investors, and was fronted by a fresh-faced, party-hopping Indian techie who might as well have come from Bollywood central casting for a musical remake of *The Social Network*. (Both Modi's party and the company denied any such allegations of impropriety.)

In true Silicon Valley fashion, Paytm's app was confusingly designed, riddled with bugs, and simply not up to the job of processing every little daily transaction for a customer base of one billion people who now relied on it, because paper currency had been effectively declared obsolete. The government made no provisions for the hundreds of millions of Indians who could not easily access the app, which, again, was broken anyway. The shopkeepers and vegetable vendors in our small town didn't have shoes, much less a smartphone; in such places, Paytm was a nonfactor, and crops rotted by the ton after the winter harvest because no one had paper currency to buy them. The result of Modi's decision to force a proprietary mobile payment system on his country can glibly and accurately be described as chaos. In the cities, many sick and elderly people died in the long ATM lines—in at least one case, a doctor refused treatment after demanding cash, which was, of course, what everyone was waiting in line for. It was easy to spend an entire day traipsing from one machine to another, only to find them all out of cash. But these problems were largely invisible to India's wealthy and middle class, who hired servants to do their shopping and thus escaped the battle of will and endurance that suddenly characterized routine commerce. For these people, Modi's anticorruption rhetoric resonated deeply, and Paytm, for all its flaws, was a lifestyle enhancement as well as a point of pride— another sign of India's rise. International journalists also missed the disastrous consequences of demonetization, at least at first.

They by and large dutifully repeated the government line that demonetization and the attendant mobile payments revolution were strong signals to foreign capital that India was "open for business." Indeed it was. Modi had turned the country into a laboratory for one of the most ill-considered and damaging experiments ever inflicted by a tech startup upon an unwilling group of people. And Paytm had shown that Peter Thiel's original dream for PayPal's "World Domination" (his words)—digital, privatized currency—could be made real by fiat, should other methods fail. "India's Demonetization Could Be the First Cash Domino to Fall," one *Forbes* commentator enthused.

There is every reason to think that India's experiment with demonetization could be replicated elsewhere. That's in part because, as I said, the reporting mostly failed to accurately convey the consequences. Rather, in the style of the tech press, it repeated official propaganda about how mobile payments would "unleash" India's economic potential and praised Modi's "high-risk, high-stakes" gamble on the future. What had actually happened, though? The state had countenanced what amounted to a monopoly to a select group of nobles in the form of a corporation to mint the new coin of the realm. As I stood in line one day at a machine guarded by a man with a gun, waiting for cash that never came, and cursing in frustration at a smartphone app that was useless for the task at hand—buying food—I thought, this is it: this is what happens when the techies are given the free rein they seek.

We live in a world that's getting stranger by the day—and certainly more volatile. I'm not inclined to play prophet like Ray Kurzweil, but I'm sure we will endure further "disruptions" at the hands of the Silicon Valley tech companies. Which is why, as much as I'd like to laugh off each and every wild prediction made by the Singularitarians I met in Amsterdam, I'm obliged instead to concede that seemingly impossible new technologies will no doubt emerge—either despite the urgent political and environmental crises facing the world, or in response to them. The scary thing is that some inventions, once unleashed, cannot realistically be controlled. This is why decisions regarding the distribution and development of world-changing technologies cannot be left to the exclusive discretion of a few overconfident rich guys with Stanford pedigrees and a shocking disregard for history, politics, language, and culture, to say nothing of the struggles of the poor.

It is no wonder the Singularitarian fantasies have captured the imaginations of the world's most zealously self-interested businesspeople: these visions promise ultimate, permanent power. The stated ambitions of America's tech oligarchs are almost comically solipsistic—endless lifespans, superhuman powers, personal hyperspeed transport. They truly imagine themselves as a superior race. And while it is unlikely that they will attain everything they imagine, it is unfortunately true that this hyper-elite class will reap the benefits of any new technologies society develops, while the costs will fall, as ever, on the rest of us. This will not be a situation without precedent. It's exactly how things were with the rotten kings of yore. But if history teaches us one thing, it's that complex problems often have simple solutions. Off with their heads.

Acknowledgments

If it's true that suffering builds character, I owe many thanks to Airbnb. In the same spirit, I must thank those who declined to be interviewed, especially Ray Kurzweil, Peter Thiel, and Curtis Yarvin—my three muses. I'm genuinely grateful to everyone who *was* interviewed, as well as all those pseudonymous people—roommates, conferencegoers, barflies—whose stories were included in this book. Thanks to my shrink, to my wife, Patricia Sauthoff, and to the voters of Oregon, whose wise passage of Measure 91 ensured the timely and relatively painless completion of this book. Thanks to my agent, William Callahan at Inkwell; to my editor at Metropolitan, Connor Guy; and to publisher Sara Bershtel, who read the six-hundred-page first draft. I owe everyone at the *Baffler* a bottle of champagne; good thing for me it's such a small staff. Salud to Dave Denison, Lauren Kirchner, Chris Lehmann, Noah McCormack, and John Summers. Cheers to *Willamette Week* and its diaspora, especially Aaron Mesh, Mark Zusman, James Pitkin, Beth Slovic, and Nick Budnick, who all saved my ass again in 2017. A number of couches were dented in the production of this book. Thanks to P. J. Tobia and Heather Courtney; Dave Maass and Megan O'Connor; and

Dan and Ploy Ten Kate. Dianne Conrad, Mark Higginson, Young Misions, Erica Nelson, Chloe Peacock, Daniel Simpson, Hank Stern, and Adam Weinstein provided moral support and security consultation. Thanks, finally, to Ziggy, and to David Solomon: rest in peace, friend.

Notes

Introduction: Billionaire or Bust

1   *It was a niche news website*   War Is Business, warisbusiness.com.

6   Silicon Valley Index   jointventure.org.

Chapter I: Poor Winners

12   *Simone*   is a pseudonym. As is Racy Laydeez.

19   *Yelp makes money*   Kathleen Richards, "Yelp and the Business of Extortion 2.0," February 18, 2009, eastbayexpress.com; David Lazarus, "Yelp's Practices Sound to Some Like Extortion," March 31, 2014, latimes .com; "The New Establishment," October 2011, *Vanity Fair*.

19   *Nancy Pelosi*   "Yelp HQ Ribbon Cutting and Yelp Foundation Grants Announcement," November 11, 2013, youtube.com.

24   *Adrian*   is a pseudonym.

25   *But within a year, Groupon was in the gutter*   See my report, "Cheat Local!" August 16, 2011, wweek.com.

26   *Toby*   is a pseudonym.

29   *Toxic Sludge Is Good for You*   John Stauber and Sheldon Rampton (Monroe, ME: Common Courage Press, 1995).

30   *Obamaphone*   Cord Jefferson, "The 'Obama Phone' Program Has Nothing to Do with Obama," September 28, 2012, gawker.com.

31   *Lawrence*   is a pseudonym.

31   *Angry Birds*   Andy Robertson, "'Angry Birds 2' Arrives 6 Years and 3 Billion Downloads after First Game," July 16, 2015, forbes.com; Douglas MacMillan, "Zynga Flashes $1.8 Billion Searching for the New FarmVille," April 17, 2012, bloomberg.com; Tarmo Virki, "Chirpy Angry Birds Maker Eyes IPO Golden Egg," May 7, 2012, reuters.com.

33   *Zynga's basement data center*   John Rath, "Zynga to Boost Investment in Data Centers," July 8, 2011, datacenterknowledge.com; Robert

McMillan, "For Zynga, a Journey from the Cloud to Home—and Back Again," May 8, 2015, wsj.com.

34   *it had just secured "an outsized sum"*   Sarah McBride, "Startup Nerd-Wallet Raises $64 Million in First Round of Funding," May 11, 2015, reuters.com.

35   *Large valuations were clearly critical*   Alex Wilhelm, "Startups, Late-Stage Valuations, and Bull," February 15, 2015, techcrunch.com; Ellen Huet, "Benchmark's Bill Gurley: 'Stop Cramming Money into Private Companies,'" February 12, 2015, forbes.com; Sarah Lacy, "Stewart Butterfield on His Unicorn Status: 'It's Arbitrary as Fuck. There's No Logic to What You Get Valued At,'" February 10, 2015, pando.com.

35   *"Despite the perception"*   "How to Determine the Value of Your Pre-Revenue Startup," January 2015, entrepreneur.com.

36   *a seven-year lease*   Blanca Torres, "NerdWallet Signs Lease for New Market Street Headquarters in San Francisco," June 13, 2014, bizjournals.com.

36   *"Fail Wall"*   Julie Balise, "At NerdWallet, Nerds and Finance Rule," June 17, 2015, sfgate.com.

36   *"room to grow"*   Joe Gose, "Office REITs Counting on Record Rent Levels in San Francisco," September 3, 2014, theregistrysf.com; Dan Levy, "San Francisco's Blighted Market Street Reborn as Tech Hub," September 18, 2013, bloomberg.com.

37   *Tim Chen*   Jonathan Shieber, "Scorching FinTech Market Keeps Attracting New Players as NerdWallet Raises $64 Million," May 11, 2015, techcrunch.com.

39   *The robot's owner*   Evgenia Peretz, "Bluebloods and Billionaires," October 2013, vanityfair.com.

39   *"a trail of robot pieces"*   Philip Matier and Andrew Ross, "Goliath the Robot Attacked in Pacific Heights," January 8, 2006, sfgate.com.

39   *Not far from Ellison's* place   Ashlee Vance, "The Startups on San Francisco's Billionaires' Row," September 7, 2012, bloomberg.com.

40   *"Its interiors are filled"*   Tracy Elsen, "San Francisco's Most Expensive Home Makes It Official, Lists for $39M on the MLS," January 28, 2015, sf.curbed.com.

40   *Zuckerberg purchased four properties*   Joel Rosenblatt, "Inside the Strange Fight over Mark Zuckerberg's Bedroom," February 9, 2015, bloomberg.com.

41   *Palo Alto passed an ordinance*   Katharine Mieszkowski and Lance Williams, "To Shield Tech Executives, California's Biggest Water Users Are Secret," April 16, 2015, revealnews.org.

Chapter II: Slums as a Service

44 *Magdalena* is a pseudonym.

44 *Beau* is a pseudonym.

49 *riots had broken out* Rachel Swan, "Which Does San Francisco Hate More: Muni, Techies, or Cops?" October 30, 2014, sfweekly.com; Kevin Montgomery, Twitter post, October 30, 2014; Zoë Corbyn, "Silicon Valley: The Truth about Living with the IT Crowd," August 17, 2014, theguardian.com.

59 *Luna* is a pseudonym.

60 *Mike* is a pseudonym.

Chapter III: Gigs Make Us Free

77 *"entrepreneurialism-in-a-box"* Katie Benner, "A Secret of Uber's Success: Struggling Workers," October 2, 2014, bloomberg.com.

78 *Academic surveys found* Panagiotis G. Ipeirotis, "Demographics of Mechanical Turk," March 2010, New York University; Lilly C. Irani and M. Six Silberman, "Turkopticon: Interrupting Worker Invisibility in Amazon Mechanical Turk," 2013, UC Irvine.

85 *"incredible vision"* "Fiverr Secures $15 Million in Second Round Funding from Accel and Bessemer, Grows 600% since 2011," May 3, 2012, yahoo.com.

85 *"making people slaves"* Ayala Tsoref, "Brains Behind 'Micro Jobs' Sensation Fiverr Have Amazon, eBay in Their Sights," March 5, 2015, haaretz.com.

88 *Rhoda Lee* is positively not her real name.

94 *He got the idea from a book* Mark Anastasi, *The Laptop Millionaire* (Hoboken: Wiley, 2012).

Chapter IV: Selling Crack to Children

97 *Aron Cohen* is a pseudonym.

117 *Child abuse videos* Charlie Warzel, "YouTube is Addressing its Massive Child Exploitations Problem," November 22, 2017, buzzfeed.com.

Chapter V: It's Called Capitalism

123 *Vinton G. Cerf* Cerf's graduate thesis built upon his adviser's work on what they called a "snuper computer," the purpose of which was, for the first time, to monitor the behavior of users on a remote device. "It was a very unfortunately named project," Cerf said later. Much later in life, as "chief Internet evangelist" at Google, the world's largest (albeit usually censored) corporate surveillance operation, Cerf opined that "privacy may actually be an anomaly" in historical terms.

124 *"a backroom deal"* Jay P. Kesan and Rajiv C. Shah, "Fool Us Once Shame on You—Fool Us Twice Shame on Us: What We Can Learn from the Privatizations of the Internet Backbone Network and the Domain Name System," *Washington University Law Review* 79, number 1, 2001.

124 *plunder of public assets* "Review of NSFNET," Office of Inspector General, National Science Foundation, March 23, 1993; Janet Abbate, "Privatizing the Internet: Competing Visions and Chaotic Events, 1987–1995," *IEEE Annals of the History of Computing* 32, number 1, January–March 2010.

126 *Google issued* David A. Vise, "Google, SEC Settle over Stock Options," January 14, 2005, washingtonpost.com; Kevin J. Delaney, "Google, Its Lawyer Are Unscathed in SEC Investigation of Offering," January 14, 2005, wsj.com; Matt Southern, "Google Cracking Down on Bad Advertising Practices, Over 350 Million Ads Removed," January 17, 2014, searchenginejournal.com; Chris Strohm and David McLaughlin, "Google Targeted in State Crackdown on Illicit Drug Ads," July 24, 2014, bloomberg.com; Stanislas Jourdan and Guillaume Dasquié, "Les îles Bermudes, la planque à billets de Google," April 19, 2011, owni.fr; Jesse Drucker, "Google Revenues Sheltered in No-Tax Bermuda Soar to $10 Billion," December 10, 2012, bloomberg.com.

127 *FTC investigators* Andrew Orlowski, "Policy Tsarina Rachel 'Baby GIF' Whetstone Dumps Google for Uber," May 14, 2015, theregister.co.uk.

127 *"It's called capitalism"* Brian Womack, "Google Chairman Says Android Winning Mobile War with Apple: Tech," December 12, 2012, bloomberg.com.

128 *secret behavioral experiments* Susie Cagle, "Facebook Wants to Redline Your Friends List," August 24, 2015, psmag.com; James Grimmelmann, "As Flies to Wanton Boys," June 28, 2014, laboratorium.net; Charles Arthur, "Facebook Emotion Study Breached Ethical Guidelines, Researchers Say," June 30, 2014, theguardian.com.

128 *abuse of employment laws* Brad Stone, *The Everything Store: Jeff Bezos and the Age of Amazon* (New York: Little, Brown, 2013); Nathaniel Mott, "Amazon Faces Lawsuit Alleging Unfair Labor Policies," April 9, 2015, pando.com; Spencer Soper, "Inside Amazon's Warehouse," September 18, 2011, articles.mcall.com.

128 *starving state and local governments* Chris Isidore, "Amazon to Start Collecting State Sales Taxes Everywhere," March 29, 2017, money.cnn.com.

128 *Craigslist* "Lawsuit Accuses Craigslist of Promoting Prostitution," March 5, 2009, cnn.com; "Craigslist Sued Over Discriminatory Ads," February 9, 2006, Associated Press.

128 *PayPal* "Earth to Palo Alto," October 31, 2001, therecorder.com; Eric M. Jackson, *The PayPal Wars: Battles with eBay, the Media, the Mafia, and the Rest of Planet Earth* (Washington, DC: WND Books, 2004).

129 *Netflix* Tori Smith Ekstrand, "Should Netflix Be Accessible to the Deaf?," April 16, 2015, theatlantic.com; Eriq Gardner, "Netflix Beats Antitrust Class Action at Appeals Court," February 27, 2015, hollywoodreporter.com.

129 *LinkedIn* John Brownlee, "After Lawsuit Settlement, LinkedIn's Dishonest Design Is Now a $13 Million Problem," October 5, 2015, fastcodesign.com.

129 *TripAdvisor* Will Coldwell, "TripAdvisor: A History of Complaints," November 19, 2014, theguardian.com.

130 *In Portland, Oregon* Aaron Mesh and Beth Slovic, *Willamette Week*, 2014–2016.

130 *While that was going on* Mike Isaac, "How Uber Deceives the Authorities Worldwide," March 3, 2017, nytimes.com.

131 *Teaming up with the lobbying industry* Ben Smith, "Uber Executive Suggests Digging Up Dirt on Journalists," November 18, 2014, buzzfeed.com; "Uber Protests and Legal Actions," Wikipedia page created on February 12, 2015.

141 *Harvard Business School study* Deborah Gage, "The Venture Capital Secret: 3 out of 4 Start-Ups Fail," September 20, 2012, wsj.com.

142 *This company, called Clinkle* Amir Efrati, "Startup's Deep Roots: Stanford," April 3, 2013, wsj.com; Sam Biddle, 2013–2014, valleywag.com.

143 *Theranos* John Carreyrou, 2015–2016, wsj.com.

Chapter VI: Failing Up

148 *"I have hives"* Jon Christian, "Tumblr Has a Hardcore Meth Scene," May 11, 2015, vice.com.

148 *"a horribly mismanaged company"* Matthew J. Belvedere, "'Probably a Lot of Pot Smoking' at Twitter: Thiel," September 17, 2014, cnbc.com.

148 *"Before the Startup"* October 2014, paulgraham.com.

149 *"not having an idea"* "New: Apply to Y Combinator without an Idea," March 13, 2012, ycombinator.com.

151 *"permanent revolution"* Nevil Gibson, "In the Trenches of Silicon Valley," April 29, 2014, Stuff.co.nz.

151 *"A revolution is not a dinner party"* Weatherhead East Asian Institute, Columbia University.

151 *The spurious notion* Jill Lepore, "The Disruption Machine," *New Yorker*, June 23, 2014; Samantha Murphy, "Facebook Changes Its 'Move Fast and Break Things' Motto," April 30, 2014, mashable.com; Katy Waldman, "Let's Break Shit: A Short History of Silicon Valley's Favorite Phrase," December 5, 2014, slate.com.

153 *No More Woof* Marc Lallanilla, "Speak, Fido: Device Promises Dog Translations," January 3, 2014, livescience.com.

154 *Here again Uber pointed the way* Erica Fink, "Uber's Dirty Tricks Quantified: Rival Counts 5,560 Canceled Rides," August 12, 2014, cnn .com.

155 *Operation SLOG* Casey Newton, "This Is Uber's Playbook for Sabotaging Lyft," August 26, 2014, theverge.com.

164 *launched with $50 million in cash* Amy Schatz, "Pressing Fwd.us: How Silicon Valley's $50 Million Bet on Immigration Stalled," October 15, 2014, recode.net.

164 *spent nearly $2 million on lobbying* Senate Office of Public Records via opensecrets.org.

165 *The Zuckerberg-backed group* Joshio Meronek, "Mark Zuckerberg's Immigration Hustle," March 12, 2015, fusion.net; Matt Smith, Jennifer Gollan, and Adithya Sambamurthy, "Job Brokers Steal Wages, Entrap Indian Tech Workers in US," October 27, 2014, revealnews.org.

169 *Ross Ulbricht* Benjamin Weiser, "Ross Ulbricht, Creator of Silk Road Website, Is Sentenced to Life in Prison," May 29, 2015, nytimes.com; Joe Mullin, "Sunk: How Ross Ulbricht Ended Up in Prison for Life," May 29, 2015, arstechnica.com; *US v. Carl Mark Force IV et al.*, March 25, 2015, US District Court, Northern California Circuit, Case No. 3-15-70370.

169 *Blake Benthall* Evan Sernoffsky, Henry K. Lee, and Bob Egelko, "San Francisco Techie Is 'Silk Road 2.0' Mastermind, Feds Say," November 6, 2014, sfgate.com.

170 *OpenBazaar* Patrick Howell O'Neill, "OpenBazaar, a 'Censorship-Resistent' Online Marketplace, Gets $1 Million in Funding," June 11, 2015, dailydot.com.

182 *"the tech union"* "Google Wants In on On-Demand; Workers Want Rights," August 5, 2015, sfweekly.com.

183 *"#SF tech buses"* Joe Fitz Rodriguez, Twitter post, August 11, 2015.

186 *charged Rome with various* Proposed Charge Against International Vice President, Joint Council 7 President and Local 853 Principal Officer Rome Aloise, February 10, 2016, Independent Review Board; Brian

Mahoney, "Teamsters Investigated for Uber Expenses," January 27, 2016, politico.com.

Chapter VII: The Aristocracy of Brains

192 *a recent scientific paper* Stefania Vitali et al., "The Network of Global Corporate Control," October 2011, Swiss Federal Institute of Technology.

193 *The Factory* I found the place using public records. Unfortunately—or not!—I never made it inside. I knocked on the door of the mansion, but no one answered. A single candle flickered in the darkened vestibule. Later, observing the mansion from a hill in the park across the street, I saw an unremarkable white yuppie family exit through a side door. A black Chevrolet Suburban appeared and whisked them away before I could approach.

195 *Jeannie* is a pseudonym.

197 *Francis* is a pseudonym.

199 *Google's vast network infrastructure* google.com.

202 *Leland Stanford* Eric Rauchway, "A Great Story, but Not a Good One," *California History* 89, number 1, 2011.

202 *how many of his Chinese workers died* William F. Chew, "Transportation: Iron Rail to Golden Spike—The Blood and Sweat of the Nameless Railroad Builders," in *Portraits of Pride II: Chinese-American Legacies—First 160 Years in America*, Chinese Historical Society of Southern California, 2011.

203 *Robert Swain* George Wilson, "Swain Studies Industries on European Trip," May 22, 1934, stanforddailyarchive.com.

203 *Otto von Bolschwing* "Silicon Valley Felt Touch of ex-Nazi Masquerader," November 20, 1981, *San Jose Mercury*; Eric Lichtblau, *The Nazis Next Door: How America Became a Safe Haven for Hitler's Men* (Boston: Houghton Mifflin Harcourt, 2014).

205 *"We are all the victims of Islamization"* geertwilders.nl.

206 *his opponents in the Dutch Labor Party* "PvdA-Kamerlid Jan Vos: 'Geert Wilders Is Een Fascist'," September 17, 2015, dagelijksestandaard.nl.

207 *"I am fed up with the Koran"* Geert Wilders, "Enough Is Enough: Ban the Koran," August 10, 2007, geertwilders.nl.

212 *"geeks for monarchy"* was coined by Klint Finley, November 22, 2013, techcrunch.com.

214 *on the front page of the* Wall Street Journal Erica Orden, "For BIL,

Tagging Along with TED Proves to Be an Excellent Adventure," March 1, 2011, wsj.com.

222 *"Our tech titans could save us"* James Polous, "Silicon Valley Could Save the World from Climate Change. But We Don't Want Them To," May 26, 2015, theweek.com.

223 *Gallup reran its poll* "Confidence in Institutions," gallup.com; harrisinteractive.com.

224 *"monolithic monstrosity"* Peter Thiel interview with Glenn Beck, October 21, 2014.

224 *"My path was so tracked"* Peter Thiel and Blake Masters, *Zero to One: Notes on Startups, or How to Build the Future* (New York: Crown, 2014).

225 *PayPal* Jackson, *Paypal Wars.*

226 *In-Q-Tel* Robert Scheer, "How the Government Outsourced Intelligence to Silicon Valley," February 18, 2015, truthdig.com.

227 *a lobbyist named Terry Paul* Dave Maass, "Hunter Pushes for IED Software Connected to His Mentor," August 7, 2012, sdcitybeat.com; Proceedings Before the Committee on Armed Services, U.S. House of Representatives, September 15, 2009, gpo.gov.

227 *Odierno finally snapped* Jen Judson, "US Army Chief Lukewarm on Tactical DCGS-A Capability," April 12, 2016, defensenews.com.

227 *After Trump's electoral victory* Lizette Chapman, "Trump's Transition Team Adds VC from Thiel's Founders Fund," November 23, 2016, bloomberg.com.

227 *When President Trump announced* Spencer Woodman, "Palantir Provides the Engine for Donald Trump's Deportation Machine," March 2, 2017, theintercept.com.

228 *a short story* Jorge Luis Borges, "Tlön, Uqbar, Orbis Tertius," in *Labyrinths: Selected Stories and Other Writings* (New York: New Directions, 1962).

229 *One former employee* Michael Anissimov, writing on a blog subsequently removed from the Internet.

230 *Nick Land* "Premises of Neoreaction," February 3, 2014, xenosystems .net.

230 *Yarvin claimed to have watched* Joseph Bernstein, "Alt-White," October 5, 2017, buzzfeed.com.

237 *For its targets, Gamergate* My interviews with Zoe Quinn and Randi Lee Harper; "Game of Fear," May 2015, *Boston Magazine.*

238 *Katherine Bolan Forrest* Yannick Losbar, "Ross Ulbricht Silk Road Trial Judge Facing Death Threats on Dark Net," October 20, 2014,

cryptocoinsnews.com; Rich Calder, "Judge in Silk Road Case Gets Death Threats," October 24, 2014, nypost.com.

240 *His name became more familiar* J. Lester Feder, "This Is How Steve Bannon Sees the Entire World," November 15, 2016, buzzfeed.com; Jason Horowitz, "Steve Bannon Cited Italian Thinker Who Inspired Fascists," February 10, 2017, nytimes.com.

240 *Dale Carrico* Amor Mundi, "Anissimov's Jolt to the Far Right," March 5, 2014, amormundi.blogspot.com.

Chapter VIII: Onward, Robot Soldiers

246 *Page invited Kurzweil to join the company* David J. Hill, "Exclusive Interview: Ray Kurzweil Discusses His First Two Months at Google," March 19, 2013, singularityhub.com.

248 *I applied for a press ticket* See my report, "Cyborg Soothsayers of the High-Tech Hogwash Emporia," 2015, *Baffler* (no. 28).

259 *Sjöblad's cyborg evangelism* Bryan Menegus, "Company Offers Free, Totally Not Creepy Microchip Implants to Employees," July 24, 2017, gizmodo.com; James Brooks, "Cyborgs at Work: Employees Getting Implanted with Microchips," April 23, 2017, apnews.com.

261 *"gamete donor selection based on genetic calculations"* Anne Wojcicki et al., U.S. Patent 8543339 B2, December 5, 2008; Karen Kaplan, "23andMe's Designer Baby Patent Is 'a Serious Mistake,' Critics Charge," October 3, 2013, latimes.com.

266 *endorsed the Singularity sect* Lev Grossman, "2045: The Year Man Becomes Immortal," February 10, 2011, time.com.

270 *an online forum of futurists* who called themselves extropians.

272 *Max More* For more on cryonics and the extropians, see my report, "Everybody Freeze!," 2016, *Baffler* (no. 30).

272 *a procedure called parabiosis* Jeff Bercovici broke the news of Thiel's quasivampirisim in an August 1, 2016, *Inc.* magazine story titled "Peter Thiel Is Very, Very Interested in Young People's Blood." Breitbart News would months later dismiss Bercovici's report as "fake news" after his key source clammed up, though he and the magazine stood by the story.

273 *Not good government* "A Conversation with Peter Thiel," April 6, 2015, medium.com.

274 *Whatever genuine concerns Thiel might harbor* David Streitfeld and Jacqueline Williams, "Peter Thiel, Trump Adviser, Has a Backup Country: New Zealand," January 25, 2017, nytimes.com.

277 *Srinivasan laid out the grand design* Balaji Srinivasan, "Software Is Reorganizing the World," November 22, 2013, wired.com.

281   *His comrade in resentment*   Michelle Cortez and Anna Edney, "Trump Is Considering Another Thiel Associate to Lead FDA," January 13, 2017, bloomberg.com.

282   *An anonymous tech reporter*   "Live from the Google I/O 2013 Keynote," May 14, 2013, theverge.com.

282   *In a testament to the growing power*   Adam Taylor, "Denmark Is Naming an Ambassador Who Will Just Deal with Increasingly Powerful Tech Companies," February 4, 2017, washingtonpost.com.

283   *"panic rooms"*   Matt A. V. Chaban, "Still Secret and Secure, Safe Rooms Now Hide in Plain Sight," May 25, 2015, nytimes.com; Morgan Brennan, "Billionaire Bunkers: Beyond the Panic Room, Home Security Goes Sci-Fi," November 27, 2013, forbes.com; interview with Stewart Wallis, January 23, 2015, cnbcafrica.com.

Epilogue

289   *Paytm*   Madhav Chanchani, "Alibaba to hike stake in Paytm's marketplace for $177 million," March 3, 2017, economictimes.indiatimes.com; Sunny Sen, "Dance of the Damned: Is the Paytm Founder Celebrating Too Soon?," January 23, 2017, hindustantimes.com.

290   *The result of Modi's decision*   "The Cost of India's Man-Made Currency Crisis," January 9, 2017, nytimes.com; Nishant Saxena, "Demonetisation Death Toll: 90 people and Counting as Note Ban Takes Tragic Turn," December 9, 2016, catchnews.com.

Index

About the Author

Corey Pein is a longtime investigative reporter and a regular contributor to *The Baffler*. A former staff writer for *Willamette Week*, he has also written for *Slate*, *Salon*, *Foreign Policy*, *The American Prospect*, and the *Columbia Journalism Review*, among other publications. He lives in Portland, Oregon.